AQA History

AS Unit 1

Totalitarian Ideology in Theory and Practice, c1848–1941

James Staniforth

Series editor
Sally Waller

Nelson Thornes

Published in 2008 by:
Nelson Thornes Ltd
Delta Place
27 Bath Road
CHELTENHAM
GL53 7TH
United Kingdom

13 14 15 16 / 10 9 8 7 6 5 4

A catalogue record for this book is available from the British Library

978-0-7487-8269-7

Illustrations by: Roger Penwill, Gary Rees (c/o Linda Rogers Associates), David Russell Illustration

Page make-up by Thomson Digital

Printed in India by Multivista Global Ltd

Contents

Introduction

Nelson Thornes

Nelson Thornes has worked hard to ensure that this book offers you excellent support for your AS or A level course. You can be confident that the learning, teaching and assessment practice materials have been checked and are matched to the requirements of your specification.

How to use this book

The features in this book include:

Timeline

Key events are outlined at the beginning of the book. The events are colour-coded so you can clearly see the categories of change.

Learning objectives

At the beginning of each section you will find a list of learning objectives that contain targets linked to the requirements of the specification.

Key chronology

A short list of dates usually with a focus on a specific event or legislation.

Key profile

The profile of a key person you should be aware of to fully understand the period in question.

Key term

A term that you will need to be able to define and understand.

Did you know?

Interesting information to bring the subject under discussion to life.

Exploring the detail

Information to put further context around the subject under discussion.

A closer look

An in-depth look at a theme, person or event to deepen your understanding. Activities around the extra information may be included.

Sources

Sources to reinforce topics or themes and may provide fact or opinion. They may be quotations from historical works, contemporaries of the period or photographs.

Cross-reference

Links to related content which may offer more detail on the subject in question.

Activity

Various activity types to provide you with different challenges and opportunities to demonstrate both the content and skills you are learning. Some can be worked on individually, some as part of group work and some are designed to specifically "stretch and challenge".

Question

Questions to prompt further discussion on the topic under consideration and are an aid to revision.

Summary questions

Summary questions at the end of each chapter to test your knowledge and allow you to demonstrate your understanding.

Study tip

Hints to help you with your study and to prepare for your exam.

Practice questions

Questions at the end of each section in the style that you may encounter in your exam.

Learning outcomes

Learning outcomes at the end of each section remind you what you should know having completed the chapters in that section.

Web links in the book

Because Nelson Thornes is not responsible for third party content online, there may be some changes to this material that are beyond our control. In order for us to ensure that the links referred to in the book are as up-to-date and stable as possible, the web sites provided are usually homepages with supporting instructions on how to reach the relevant pages if necessary.

Please let us know at **webadmin@nelsonthornes.com** if you find a link that doesn't work and we will do our best to correct this at reprint, or to list an alternative site.

Introduction to the History series

When Bruce Bogtrotter in Roald Dahl's *Matilda* was challenged to eat a huge chocolate cake, he just opened his mouth and ploughed in, taking bite after bite and lump after lump until the cake was gone and he was feeling decidedly sick. The picture is not dissimilar to that of some A level history students. They are attracted to history because of its inherent appeal but, when faced with a bulging file and a forthcoming examination, their enjoyment evaporates. They try desperately to cram their brains with an assortment of random facts and subsequently prove unable to control the outpouring of their ill-digested material in the examination.

The books in this series are designed to help students and teachers avoid this feeling of overload and examination panic by breaking down the AQA history specification in such a way that it is easily absorbed. Above all, they are designed to retain and promote students' enthusiasm for history by avoiding a dreary rehash of dates and events. Each book is divided into sections, closely matched to those given in the specification, and the content is further broken down into chapters that present the historical material in a lively and attractive form, offering guidance on the key terms, events and issues, and blending thought-provoking activities and questions in a way designed to advance students' understanding. By encouraging students to think for themselves and to share their ideas with others, as well as helping them to develop the knowledge and skills they need this book should ensure that students' learning remains a pleasure rather than an endurance test.

To make the most of what this book provides, students will need to develop efficient study skills from the start and it is worth spending some time considering what these involve:

- Good organisation of material in a subject-specific file. Organised notes help develop an organised brain and sensible filing ensures time is not wasted hunting for misplaced material. This book uses cross-references to indicate where material in one chapter has relevance to material in another. Students are advised to use the same technique.

- A sensible approach to note-making. Students are often too ready to copy large chunks of material from printed books or to download sheaves of printouts from the internet. This series is designed to encourage students to think about the notes they collect and to undertake research with a particular purpose in mind. The activities encourage students to pick out that information that is relevant to the issue being addressed and to avoid making notes on material that is not properly understood.

- Taking time to think, which is by far the most important component of study. By encouraging students to think before they write or speak, be it for a written answer, presentation or class debate, students should learn to form opinions and make judgements based on the accumulation of evidence. The beauty of history is that there is rarely a right or wrong answer so, with sufficient evidence, one student's view will count for as much as the next.

Unit 1

The topics offered for study in Unit 1 are all based on 'change and consolidation'. They invite consideration of what changed and why, as well as posing the question of what remained the same. Through a study of a period of about 50 to 60 years, students are encouraged to analyse the interplay of long-term and short-term reasons for change and not only to consider how governments have responded to the need for change but also to evaluate the ensuing consequences. Such historical analyses are, of course, relevant to an understanding of the present and, through such historical study, students will be guided towards a greater appreciation of the world around them today as well as developing their understanding of the past.

Unit 1 is tested by a 1 hour 15 minute paper containing three questions, from which students need to choose two. Details relating to the style of questions, are given in Table 1 and links to the examination requirements are provided throughout this book. Students should familiarise themselves with these and the marking criteria before attempting any of the practice questions at the end of each section.

Answers will be marked according to a scheme based on 'levels of response'. This means that the answer will be assessed according to which level best matches the historical skills displayed, taking both knowledge and understanding into account. Take some time to study these criteria and use them wisely.

Marking criteria

Question 1(a), 2(a) and 3(a)

Level 1 Answers contain either some descriptive material that is only loosely linked to the focus of the question or some explicit comment with little, if any, appropriate support. Answers are likely to be

Table 1 *Unit 1: style of questions and marks available*

Unit 1	Question	Marks	Question type	Question stem	Hints for students
Question 1, 2 and 3	(a)	12	This question is focused on a narrow issue within the period studied and requires an explanation	Why did... Explain why... In what ways... (was X important)	Make sure you explain 'why', not 'how', and try to order your answer in a way that shows you understand the inter-link of factors and which were the more important. You should try to reach an overall judgement/conclusion
Question 1, 2 and 3	(b)	24	This question links the narrow issue to a wider context and requires an awareness that issues and events can have different interpretations	How far... How important was... How successful...	This answer needs to be planned as you will need to develop an argument in your answer and show balanced judgement. Try to set out your argument in the introduction and, as you develop your ideas through your paragraphs, support your opinions with detailed evidence. Your conclusion should flow naturally and provide supported judgement

generalised and assertive. The response is limited in development and skills of written communication are weak. *(0–2 marks)*

Level 2 Answers demonstrate some knowledge and understanding of the demands of the question. Either they are almost entirely descriptive with few explicit links to the question or they provide some explanations backed by evidence that is limited in range and/or depth. Answers are coherent but weakly expressed and/or poorly structured. *(3–6 marks)*

Level 3 Answers demonstrate good understanding of the demands of the question providing relevant explanations backed by appropriately selected information, although this may not be full or comprehensive. For the most part, answers are clearly expressed and show some organisation in the presentation of material. *(7–9 marks)*

Level 4 Answers are well focused, identifying a range of specific explanations backed by precise evidence and demonstrating good understanding of the connections and links between events/issues. For the most part, answers are well written and organised. *(10–12 marks)*

Question 1(b), 2(b) and 3(b)

Level 1 Answers either contain some descriptive material that is only loosely linked to the focus of the question or address only a limited part of the period of the question. Alternatively, there may be some explicit comment with little, if any, appropriate support. Answers are likely to be generalised and assertive. There is little, if any, awareness of different historical interpretations. The response is limited in development and skills of written communication are weak. *(0–6 marks)*

Level 2 Answers show some understanding of the demands of the question. Either they will be almost entirely descriptive with few explicit links to the question or they contain some explicit comment with relevant but limited support. They display limited understanding of different historical interpretations. Answers are coherent but weakly expressed and/or poorly structured. *(7–11 marks)*

Level 3 Answers show a developed understanding of the demands of the question. They provide some assessment, backed by relevant and appropriately selected evidence, but they lack depth and/or balance. There is some understanding of varying historical interpretations. For the most part, answers are clearly expressed and show some organisation in the presentation of material. *(12–16 marks)*

Level 4 Answers show explicit understanding of the demands of the question. They develop a balanced argument backed by a good range of appropriately selected evidence and a good understanding of historical interpretations. For the most part, answers show organisation and good skills of written communication. *(17–21 marks)*

Level 5 Answers are well focused and closely argued. The arguments are supported by precisely selected evidence leading to a relevant conclusion/judgement, incorporating well-developed understanding of historical interpretations and debate. For the most part, answers are carefully organised and fluently written, using appropriate vocabulary. *(22–24 marks)*

Introduction to this book

Totalitarian regimes

Fig. 1 *Parade of the SS guard at a party rally in Nuremberg in the late-1930s. The uniformity of the crowd is something totalitarian regimes try to create*

Exploring the detail

The words 'totalitarian' and 'totalitarianism'

Totalitario (toh-ta-li-tair-ee-oh) is the Italian word for 'totalitarian'. Try saying the word out loud to hear and feel the sense of the word. You could also try saying *totalitarismo* (toh-ta-li-tair-iz-moh), the Italian for 'totalitarianism'.

In 1925, Benito Mussolini invented a new term to describe the system of government that had been created in Fascist Italy. The word 'totalitarian' was not based on existing words. Instead it was created, chosen because of its sound. Saying the word out loud with an Italian accent helps convey what he meant.

If you listen to the sound and think of the impression it gives, what you hear is a strong, long word. The hard consonant sounds give an impression of strength. The length of the word gives an impression of grandeur. The word was meant to convey to the Italian people a system of government that was strong, powerful, lasting and all-encompassing. Accompanying the word was the definition of what 'totalitarian' meant, a definition that was daubed as a slogan on walls around Rome and other Italian cities: 'Everything within the state, nothing outside the state, nothing against the state.' It was the total rejection of the dominant ideology of liberalism and the political, social and economic freedom that had become the norm in the Western world. People did not have the right to be free to make decisions that were not in the interests of the state. In short, it meant total control of all aspects of people's lives.

Mussolini believed he was describing his government in Italy between 1922 and 1943. Joseph Goebbels, however, found the term useful for the new Nazi regime in Germany, arguing in November 1933 that Nazi rule must be 'a totalitarian state pervading all spheres of life'. George Orwell's novel *1984* describes a totalitarian state, Oceania, in which the people are taught to think exactly what the State prescribed, to the extent of believing that $2 + 2 = 5$. Orwell wrote the book in 1948, based on the totalitarian Soviet Union, the only totalitarian state to survive the Second World War. The term has therefore become useful to social scientists and historians in describing similar regimes that existed from the second decade of the 20th century to the current day. It is a term that is politicised and used today by politicians to label regimes that should be challenged by the free and democratic countries of the world. In part, 'totalitarian' is synonymous with evil and giving regimes this label has allowed them to be grouped together as evil. Therefore, historians use the term to describe Mussolini's Fascist Italy, Hitler's Nazi Germany and Stalin's communist Soviet Union, allowing all three countries classified and considered the same.

■ The roots of totalitarianism

There have always been governments that have been described using words that have indicated to people at the time, and to historians, that the regimes were in one way or another considered 'evil'. In the 17th century, the British spoke of the 'arbitrary government' of the French and Spanish, where the individual had no rights and the King was able to treat subjects as he wished. Louis XIV (1643–1715) epitomised European 'absolutism'; whether he really made the famous statement, *'L'État, c'est moi'* ('I am the State'), he certainly believed that he was appointed by God and that he was all-powerful and could rule the French people as he saw fit. French kings could arrest anyone they chose simply by signing a royal order, known as the *Lettres de Cachet*, and the Bastille was the prison that symbolised this use of the King's great and unrestrained power. The tsars of Russia enjoyed 'autocratic' power that granted the power of life and death over the subjects of the Russian Empire. The American Declaration of Independence of 1776 makes reference to the 'tyranny' of George III as the reason for the colonies' decision to break free. George III may not have enjoyed the power of life and death over his American subjects, but calling him a 'tyrant' left no one in doubt that the Americans considered he was abusing his power and the colonists. At the same time, European monarchs were described as 'despots'. All terms indicated that the ruler had uncontrolled power over their country and the people.

Each term was pejorative: it was used to indicate that the ruler was abusing the people. Each term indicated that monarchs could do as they wanted to their people. What none of the terms indicated was that there was a systematic attempt by the state to control all aspects of people's lives. The French feudal system granted rights and privileges, the tsars allowed literary criticism of the autocracy and the British courts protected the people from real 'tyranny'; George III's 'tyranny' was based on his refusal to allow American taxpayers to vote for the British parliament. The rulers did have great powers if they chose to exercise them, but the fact remains that in these societies the monarch did not, and could not, hope to control all aspects of people's lives. They lacked the ability to control their subjects totally, not least because they lacked the modern technology necessary to control communications.

Fig. 2 *The growth of dictatorship: Europe in 1939*

The 20th century saw a new term coined to describe countries where the all-powerful ruler was not necessarily a hereditary monarch. The age of the 'dictator' had arrived. By 1939, all of central and eastern Europe was governed by a dictatorship of one form or another.

Some of these dictatorships existed in countries where the military had stepped in and seized power, suppressing opposition and restricting individual freedom. The main aim of the dictatorships established in these countries was to provide order and stability and to prevent a (communist) revolution. Greece under Metaxas and Portugal under Salazar both followed this route. The dictatorships established in Russia (in 1917), Italy (1922) and Germany (1933) were different. In these countries one party seized power, suppressed opposition and restricted personal freedom. However, the regime went beyond seizing and consolidating power. It was not enough for the regime to be obeyed, as was the case in 20th century Portugal, 19th century Russia or 18th century France. The governments established by Lenin, Mussolini and Hitler wanted their people to believe, not just obey. It is this feature that distinguishes totalitarian dictatorships from other dictatorships.

■ Totalitarian regimes and Utopia

The reasons for seeking political power are many. Cynically, many of us suspect that the reason politicians seek power are self-serving: to make money, to ensure their place in history, to serve small sections of society that they 'owe'. Many politicians believe that they can make the world better. Essentially, therefore, there are two reasons why totalitarian dictatorships want total power:

■ To prevent others taking power, for fear of losing power and influence. This is the negative reason that is easiest for many of us to immediately understand.

■ To use power to create the perfect world, or **Utopia**. Totalitarian states believe they have discovered how to create the perfect world and therefore they want to have total control to ensure Utopia can be created. Sometimes the state may have to do things that the people do not like; this will be because the people do not understand the long-term benefit and the decision will bring Utopia closer. This is a more positive reason for seeking total control.

■ Key term

Utopia: literally means 'the place that does not exist', although it is taken to mean the perfect place. The term was used by Thomas More in his novel *Utopia* written in 1516, which describes an island with a perfect political and legal system that ensures the ideal society.

Fig. 3 *What do you believe in?*

■ Political ideas and totalitarianism

Traditionally, political ideas can be represented at different points on a straight line representing left, right and centre.

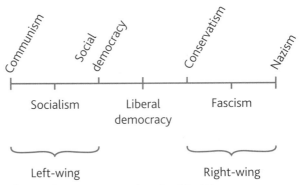

Fig. 4 *A linear representation of political ideas*

Representing political ideas in this linear manner has many advantages, but it is not necessarily appropriate when analysing totalitarian states. Stalin's communist Soviet Union and Hitler's Nazi Germany are as far apart as is possible on the chart, suggesting that the two regimes could not be more different. Certainly both Hitler and Stalin viewed each other as the ultimate evil and the ultimate enemy. The murderous Nazi–Soviet War in the East was the most brutal part of the Second World War, partly because it was a battle for survival between two ideologies that sought to destroy the other regime completely. However, in the years immediately after the Second World War historians started to describe extreme right-wing and left-wing systems of government as totalitarian. Initially the term 'totalitarian' had been proudly used by Mussolini to describe the new state he was creating. The Nazis had only rarely used the term to describe their system of government. Ironically, the Soviet Union had used the term to abuse fascist regimes! As the **Cold War** intensified, it became politically useful for the Western liberal democracies, especially the USA but also Britain, to link the undisputed evil of Nazism to the communist Soviet Union by calling both countries 'totalitarian'.

The Cold War was a war fought partly by propaganda and the totalitarian argument became valuable as part of the Western propaganda attacking the Soviet Union. In 1951, Hannah Arendt wrote about both the USSR and the right-wing governments in her book *The Origins of Totalitarianism*, drawing parallels between the Soviet Union and Nazi Germany. Five years later, two political scientists, Carl Friedrich and Zbigniew Brzezinski, suggested that totalitarian states share common features. These common features have been debated by historians and political scientists, but there is a reasonable level of agreement over the following key features:

■ An **official ideology** (set of ideas) that all citizens had not only to accept but also believe. These ideas could be adopted from a great work of political philosophy, as in the case of the Soviet Union where the Bolshevik Party considered themselves to be Marxists. Alternatively, the ideas could have been developed by the party or leader before they gained power, as in the case of Nazi Germany, where the Nazi Party's 25-point programme of 1920 and Hitler's biography *Mein Kampf* both set out Nazi ideas. They could even be the retrospective justification of policies that had already been put into practice, which was partly the case in Mussolini's Italy.

■ A **one-party state**, with the party becoming the organisation through which the country was increasingly run.

■ A monopoly over all the means of **mass communication**, including newspapers, radio, film and less obvious forms like art, music, literature and social rituals.

■ A monopoly over the means of **terror**, including the police, the secret police and the army.

■ A monopoly of **control over the economy**, meaning that the State owns all industry and all the country's land and, therefore, agricultural production.

■ Worship of the leader, to the extent that he or she is considered to be almost a god. This is referred to as the **cult of personality**.

An analysis of the Soviet Union, Fascist Italy and Nazi Germany suggests that all three states shared the six key features to a greater or lesser extent. Therefore, there is some sense in describing the three regimes as totalitarian. There is also value in considering whether other dictatorships that have been established around the world since 1945

■ **Did you know?**
Left wing and right wing
The term 'left wing' is traditionally used to describe those political ideas and parties who seek to transform the existing society in the interests of the working class. Ideas in the centre of the line are often referred to as 'centrist'. The term 'conservative' is traditionally used to describe those political ideas and parties that seek to conserve the existing society. They are considered to be to 'right of centre' and 'reactionary' – they are reacting against the proposed changes to a world they wish to conserve. 'Right wing revolutionary' is used to describe parties that seek to transform society and build a new state. The transformation they seek involves the creation of a strongly Nationalist State. All right-wing groups, whether Conservative or revolutionary, share a common hatred of the revolutionary left wing.

■ **Key term**
Cold War: this was a clash of ideologies. The nuclear strength of the USA and the Soviet Union meant that any conflict would bring mass destruction, so the war was fought by proxy and propaganda. The propaganda war meant the development of the 'totalitarian' analysis in the West as this meant that the Soviet Union could be linked to Nazi Germany. Many on the left in the USA and Britain were sympathetic to the Soviet Union, but no one denied the evil of Nazi Germany.

deserve to be called totalitarian. The communist States of China and North Korea certainly share many of these features. Saddam Hussein's Iraq has also been referred to as totalitarian, as has Libya under Colonel Gaddafi and even Spain under General Franco, although there is debate as to how far the States were fully totalitarian; for example, Franco's Spain lacked an official ideology.

If we return to our diagram of political ideas and parties, it makes more sense to draw this in a way that reflects the similarities of the totalitarian regimes and emphasises that the real opposite of both Nazism and Communism is not each other but liberal democracy.

If we represent political ideas and parties as a horseshoe, it is clear that totalitarian regimes from the left and right wings are closer to each other than they are to liberal democracy. The common features they share means they have more similarities than differences.

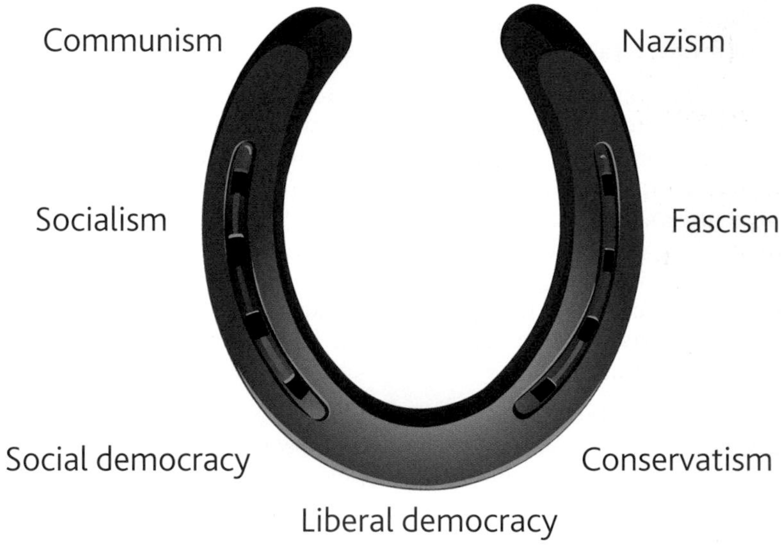

Cross-reference

Details of the features shared by these **ideologies** can be found on page 5.

Fig. 5 *A horseshoe representation of political ideas*

It is useful to remind ourselves about the differences between the regimes. Essentially, the three regimes were mainly different in their ideologies.

The differences between the right-wing totalitarian ideologies and Communism relate to the different approaches to social class and the nation. The views of each totalitarian dictator are expressed on the opposite page.

Fig. 6 *Key themes of totalitarian ideology*

When you have worked your way through this book, look back at this chapter to compare Stalin's Russia, Mussolini's Italy and Hitler's Germany with the key features of a totalitarian State to reach a judgement on the extent to which they were totalitarian.

■ Did you know?

Fascism and Nazism were similar, to the extent that it can be effective to think of the formula:

Fascism + racism = Nazism

This helps to explain why Nazism was more right wing than Fascism. Although Mussolini came to adopt anti-Semitic policies as he fell under the influence of Hitler (see page 78), anti-Semitism was not central to Fascism. In contrast, it was one of the defining features of Nazism.

Timeline

The colours represent the geographical locations of the events in the timeline as follows: Green: Totalitarianism in general, Red: The USSR, Blue: Italy, **Black**: Nazi Germany

1848	1861	1871	1887	1914	1917	1917
Karl Marx and Friedrich Engels write *The Communist Manifesto*	Unification of Italy	Unification of Germany culminates in the creation of the Second Reich	Execution of Lenin's brother turns Lenin into a revolutionary	Outbreak of the First World War. The war will destroy the German and Russian Empires and lead to the growth of Nationalism in Italy	**February** First Russian Revolution: Tsar Nicholas II abdicates	Bolshevik Revolution (Oct). Lenin establishes the Cheka, the Soviet secret police (Dec)

1923	1923	1924	1924	1925	1925
Mussolini passes a new electoral law and then wins a majority in the election, giving him the power to rule without the constraint of other parties	Inspired by Mussolini, Hitler attempts to seize power in the Munich Putsch. The putsch fails and Hitler is imprisoned where he writes his autobiography, *Mein Kampf*	Death of Lenin. A power struggle to replace him begins. Trotsky is the clear favourite, so Zinoviev and Kamenev unite with Stalin to stop Trotsky	The Italian socialist deputy Giacomo Matteotti is murdered by Fascists	Mussolini refers to the new 'totalitarian' government of Italy. Other political parties are banned and the Vidoni Pact bans strikes	Stalin and Bukharin defeat the United Opposition of Trotsky, Zinoviev and Kamenev. Bukharin supports the NEP, telling the peasants to enrich themselves

1932	1933	1934	1934	1935
Unemployment reaches 6 million in Germany. The Nazi Party becomes the largest party in Germany, but President Hindenburg refuses to make Hitler chancellor	Hitler becomes chancellor of Germany. The Enabling Act gives him the power to rule by decree for four years. Other political parties are banned. Hitler copies Mussolini and signs a Concordat with the Pope. The first concentration camp opens at Dachau	Sergei Kirov, Stalin's number two, is assassinated. Stalin introduces the Emergency Decree Against Terrorism, giving the NKVD greater powers	The Night of the Long Knives sees Hitler purge the SA and remove opponents of the regimes from within and outside the Nazi Party. Hindenburg dies and Hitler combines the positions of chancellor and president in the new office of Führer	The Nuremburg Laws marginalise Jews in German society

1939	1940	1940	1941	1941	1945
Outbreak of the Second World War. Nazi Germany and Soviet Russia have a non-aggression pact. Italy is too weak to join the war	Assassination of Trotsky by a Stalinist agent in Mexico. Stalin is now the only survivor from Lenin's original government of 1917	Italy enters the Second World War	Hitler invades the Soviet Union in pursuit of living space and his desire to destroy Communism. Italian troops fight with the Germans in the Soviet Union	Hitler begins the mass extermination of European Jews	Final defeat of totalitarian Italy and Germany. The Soviet Union emerges victorious from the Second World War

1918	1919	1919	1921	1922	1922
Lenin abolishes the Constituent Assembly. Beginning of the Russian Civil War, which the Bolsheviks had to fight until 1921 to consolidate their control of the Soviet Union. Lenin introduces War Communism	Germany signs the Treaty of Versailles, accepting responsibility for causing the First World War and therefore agreeing to pay reparations	Italy fails to gain territory expected following the Paris Peace Conference. Gabrielle d'Annunzio captures Fiume and establishes a State that inspires Fascist Italy	Lenin abandons War Communism and introduces the capitalist NEP. Party objections are ended by the Decree Against Factionalism, which prevents party dissent	Stalin becomes General Secretary of the Communist Party, a position that gives him unrivalled power	The King appoints Mussolini prime minister of Italy. This is followed by the symbolic March on Rome, which fascist propaganda presents as the seizure of power

1927	1928	1929	1929	1929	1930	1932
The NEP starts to fail. Stalin turns against Bukharin	Bukharin is defeated. First Five Year Plan for agriculture begins in the Soviet Union, ending the NEP	The Lateran Treaty between the Italian State and the Pope wins Mussolini the support of Italian Catholics	The Wall Street Crash leads to economic crisis in the USA and the economic collapse of Germany	Stalin celebrates his 50th birthday as undisputed leader of the Soviet Union. Seizure of grain from the peasants becomes the official policy in the countryside. Stalin decrees the elimination of the kulaks as a class	The Nazi Party becomes the second largest party in Germany	Ryutin attacks Stalin's policies. Stalin is unable to have him executed

1936	1936	1938	1938	1939
Italian victory in Abyssinia leads Mussolini to announce that Rome is once more the heart of a great empire	The beginning of the Show Trials and the Great Purge in the Soviet Union. During the next three years, 50 leading Bolsheviks are put on public trial and found guilty of crimes against the State. Millions of citizens are arrested and sentenced to imprisonment or death. The 1936 Constitution is introduced	Hitler expands Germany, uniting the Reich with Austria and annexing the Sudetenland from Czechoslovakia. Kristallnacht takes place, a pogrom against German Jews that marks the beginning of the exclusion of Jews from German society	Italy introduces anti-Semitic legislation as a result of the growing influence of Nazi Germany	The Italian parliament is replaced by the Chamber of Fasces and Corporations

1945	1948	1949	1949	1951	1953	1991
Start of the Cold War. Over the next four years, the Soviet Union establishes communist and totalitarian puppet States in Poland, Rumania, Hungary, Bulgaria and Czechoslovakia	George Orwell writes *1984*. The book describes a totalitarian State based on the Soviet Union	Germany is divided into capitalist, democratic West Germany and communist, totalitarian East Germany	Chinese Communist Party takes power	Hannah Arendt publishes *The Origins of Totalitarianism*	Death of Stalin. The worst excesses of Soviet totalitarianism end but dictatorship continues	Collapse of Communism in the Soviet Union

1 Marxist ideology, Lenin and Stalin

Fig. 1 *The founders of Communism: Marx, Engels, Lenin and Stalin*

In this chapter you will learn about:

- how the Bolshevik Revolution led to the establishment of the first totalitarian state

- Marxist stage theory, including the dictatorship of the proletariat

- how Marxist theory was adapted by Lenin and Stalin

- the power struggle to replace Lenin from 1924 to 1928: the strengths and weaknesses of Stalin, Trotsky, Zinoviev, Kamenev and Bukharin

- the role of ideology as it relates to the future of the revolution and the Soviet economy.

The Bolshevik Revolution and the first totalitarian state

The Bolshevik Revolution of October 1917 overthrew the Russian provisional government that had, in turn, forced Tsar Nicholas II to abdicate in February 1917. The Bolsheviks differed from other political parties in Russia primarily because they alone wanted to leave the First World War, and this policy was popular with peasants and workers as well as the armed forces. However, they also had a set of political ideas they were committed to because the Bolshevik Party was a Marxist party. As such, they had sought power to create a Marxist (or communist) state. They did not seize power to create a totalitarian state. The Bolsheviks freed political prisoners, ended press censorship and advanced personal freedom, particularly for Russian women whose lives were transformed by birth control and divorce. However, the changes were not universally popular and in 1917 the Bolsheviks only really had control over Petrograd and Moscow, the two main cities. Those citizens of the new Soviet Union who rejected the Bolsheviks' ideas and government resisted in the Russian Civil War, which lasted from 1918 to 1921. The war was brutal and it transformed the Bolsheviks and their leaders, V. I. Lenin and Leon Trotsky.

Fig. 2 *Lenin addresses the crowd in Red Square, Moscow, October 1917*

Key profiles

Lenin

Vladimir Ilyich Ulyanov (1870–1924), or Lenin, was the first leader of the Bolsheviks. Middle class, he studied law at Kazan university until his brother's execution by the tsarist government turned him into a revolutionary. Lenin studied the works of Marx but adapted them to fit the Russian context. He organised the Bolshevik Party into a revolutionary elite and plotted the October Revolution, even though Marx believed all revolutions would occur naturally. He was ruthless in power, creating the basis for the totalitarianism of Stalin. He did, however, object to the cult of Lenin that developed, considering it to be un-Marxist.

Leon Trotsky

Leon Trotsky (1879–1940) was born Lev Bronstein. He was a middle-class Ukrainian Jew, with a great intellect and an arrogance to match. He became a revolutionary in the late-1890s and was arrested in 1898 and sent into exile. Bronstein escaped and on his forged passport he first used the name Leon Trotsky, the name of his jailor. Trotsky planned the Bolshevik Revolution with Lenin and led the storming of the Winter Palace in Petrograd on his 38th birthday in 1917. His finest hour was the Civil War. He led the defence of Petrograd when it appeared it would fall in 1919 and created the Red Army which was 5 million strong by 1920.

Cross-reference

Marxist ideology is discussed on page 13.

The **cult of Lenin** is discussed on page 13.

Fig. 3 *Leon Trotsky. The leader of the Red Army addresses the troops*

■ Key term

Cheka: the All-Russian Extraordinary Commission for Combating Counter-revolution and Sabotage was led by a Polish aristocrat called Felix Dzerzhinsky. It had the power to investigate, arrest, interrogate, try and execute any opponents of the regime. The Cheka created the first Soviet labour camps and is estimated to have been responsible for around 140,000 deaths. It was replaced by the GPU in 1922.

Study tip

You need a clear understanding of the concept of totalitarianism as the basis for the rest of your studies. You could be asked about the success of one of the regimes in creating a totalitarian state, which means you would need to link your knowledge of the key features on pages 4–5 to what Stalin, Mussolini and Hitler actually did, which is covered in the rest of the book.

The communist Red Army was created with a brutal military discipline. If soldiers deserted, Lenin approved shooting every tenth man in the unit; this decimation was deemed necessary to install the discipline required to win the war. Some 48,000 former tsarist officers were recruited into the Red Army, with their families held hostage to ensure their loyalty. In December 1917, Lenin created the first secret police, the **Cheka**.

These measures were necessary to ensure the Bolsheviks won the war and therefore could impose their official ideology and pursue Utopia. No measure was too extreme in the pursuit of the communist ideal. In January 1918, elections were held for the new Russian parliament, the Constituent Assembly. The Bolsheviks failed to win a majority, so Lenin sent in the Red Army and dissolved the assembly. In March 1918, the last non-Bolsheviks left the government. In 1921, Lenin was facing opposition to the New Economic Policy (NEP). He forced the policy through and then introduced the Decree Against Factionalism on the last day of the 10th Party Congress in 1921. The decree meant it was no longer acceptable to argue with a party decision once the decision had been reached; instead it had to be accepted and defended. Those who criticised official policies would be guilty of factionalism (forming rival groups) and could be expelled from the party. Stalin later accused anyone who criticised his policies of 'factionalism'.

The pressure for an ideologically pure economy that would also ensure that the Bolsheviks had the weapons and food to fight led to the introduction of the economic policy known as War Communism. The policy involved the Bolshevik State taking control of all industry as well as seizing the peasants' surplus grain and, where there was no surplus, the grain the peasants needed to feed themselves. This caused a famine in which an estimated 5 million people died. Lenin ended War Communism in February 1921 when he introduced the NEP. It allowed private ownership of industry if fewer than 10 workers were employed, and State requisitioning of only a percentage of the surplus grain a peasant farmer produced. Lenin saw it as a temporary expedient: it restored economic stability but at the expense of Communism.

A crucial part of the fight was the propaganda employed by the Bolsheviks. Trotsky led the war effort from a command train that travelled the front line, with a printing press and loud speakers to get across the Bolshevik message of 'peace, land, bread and freedom'.

The Bolshevik victory in the Civil War was due in no small part to the ever-increasing control that the party and the State exercised over the Soviet people. These measures, however brutal, were justified because they ensured a Bolshevik victory and the establishment of Utopia. That millions died was of no consequence. It is a classic feature of totalitarian dictatorship that the end justifies the means. Lenin had laid the foundations for the totalitarian rule of Stalin and indeed the totalitarianism of both Mussolini and Hitler. Mussolini may have invented the word but Lenin was the real creator.

 Activity

Study the key features of a totalitarian state on page 5. How far had Lenin created a totalitarian state?

■ Marxist stage theory

The first key feature of a totalitarian state is an official ideology. The official ideology of the Soviet Union was Marxism, or Communism, the name that Karl Marx had given to his Utopia. Marx set out his ideas in two main works, *The Communist Manifesto* (1848) and *Das Kapital*

Fig. 4 *Karl Marx*

(1867). Although Marx was born in Germany, he lived most of his life in Britain. His political theory was based on his study of the history of Britain and his observation of life during the 19th century. Marx believed that there were six stages, or epochs, in human history and he had studied the first four in Britain. He considered his theories to be scientific rather than political, in that what he had observed had happened inevitably because of the conditions. He believed that his theory was scientific because whenever there were certain conditions, certain events would occur. These events he believed were struggles between different classes to gain the food, goods and services that were necessary to survive. These struggles would lead to the advance of human history from one stage to the next. Marx believed in **economic determinism**: in his view, the key to understanding human history was to understand that economics was the most powerful force. The class that had control of food, goods and services would also have real political power.

Primitive Communism
In this epoch men worked together in communities to survive. There were no private properties and no class differences. All men performed the same economic function, essentially hunter-gatherer. This stage would give way to one in which the most successful hunter-gatherer-warrior gained power and control over others.

Imperialism
In this epoch the emperor rules, his rule is initially based on his superiority at gaining resources. The emperor would own all land. However, as this stage develops, the emperor would become threatened by outsiders and therefore grant land to others, who in return would provide soldiers to defend the country. A new land-owning aristocracy was therefore created.

Feudalism
At the stage of feudalism, land was owned by the aristocracy. They would exploit the peasantry, who worked on the land but did not own it. The key resource was the food produced which the aristocracy could sell. The surplus of food led to the development of trade and industry and a new class of merchants who would want access to political power.

Fig. 5 *Marxist ideas: the different stages of human history*

Cross-reference

The importance of an official ideology in a **totalitarian state** is covered on page 5.

Key term

Economic determinism: Marx's belief that all history is shaped by scientific laws that are fixed and therefore are obeyed. The economic position of a country would determine the system of government and, when two different economic groups inevitably clashed, the next stage of human history would occur.

Capitalism

This was the stage Marx observed in Britain in the mid-19th century. There were two classes: the middle class of factory owners and merchants, or the bourgeoisie, and the working class or the proletariat. The bourgeoisie owned the means of production (the factories) and became increasingly wealthy, selling goods for a profit. They exploited the proletariat, paying them low wages which ensured that the proletariat lived in terrible conditions. Marx argued the proletariat accepted their position in society because of three great deceptions:

- **The Church** taught that suffering was all part of God's plan and that it brought a greater reward in the afterlife. It was for this reason that Marx famously called religion 'the opium of the masses'. Marx was also a materialist, which meant that he looked for rational explanations of events based on what could be seen, heard and touched, rather than accepting any supernatural force could be responsible. This meant he rejected any role for religion in society.
- **Trades Unions** served the bourgeois factory owners more than they served the working class. By seeking to improve workers' pay and conditions marginally they prevented the proletariat becoming revolutionary and overthrowing the bourgeois system of government.
- **Parliamentary democracy** deceived the working class into believing that they had control over government decisions. Although the working class had been given the vote in Britain in 1867, their lives did not improve because MPs were still middle-class factory owners who would not pass laws that were against their own interests. For example, Public Health Acts to provide clean water for the working classes in cities were permissive (they allowed local councils to raise taxes to pay for sewers, rather than forcing them to do so).

Therefore, for the proletariat to rise up and overthrow the bourgeoisie and end the stage of capitalism, it was crucial that the workers achieved a level of political awareness. This meant awareness that they were being exploited, and awareness that they made up the vast majority of the country and therefore they had the power. It was this need that led Marx to end the Communist Manifesto with the battle-cry:

'The proletarians have nothing to lose but their chains. They have a world to win. Proletarians of all countries, unite!'

Socialism

Marx believed that it was inevitable that the proletariat would become politically aware and that they would then rise up and overthrow the bourgeois government. During this stage, the dictatorship of the proletariat would develop in which workers' organisations would ensure that food, goods and services were distributed fairly according to people's needs. The State would achieve this through taxation of the middle class and the provision of benefits to the working class, as well as through State ownership of industry which would ensure profits were shared by all. Marx believed that the stage of socialism would be transitional. It would last long enough for the middle class to be re-educated to understand that equality was superior to private ownership. If necessary, elements of the middle class who refused to accept socialism would be eliminated.

Communism

This stage was Marx's Utopia. As everyone worked together for the common good and therefore had enough resources for their needs, there would no longer be any need for money and government could whither away. Society would be class-less. Furthermore, as this was the ultimate stage in human history, this stage would be reached in all countries. This would mean that the world would also become State-less as there would no longer be competition between different States.

Fig. 5 *(continued)*

Activity

Revision exercise

Study Figure 5 summarising Marxist stage theory.

1 Complete the table below.

Stage	Dominant class	Exploited class	Key resource
Primitive Communism			
Imperialism			
Feudalism			
Capitalism			
Socialism			
Communism			

2 Which stage(s) do not have an exploited class?

3 What does this mean in terms of Marx's view of human history?

£1.2bn pay day for the toga tycoon

By Sarah Butler and Rajeev Syal

Owner of Britain's biggest fashion chains says his record bonus is conservative.

EVEN by his own standards, it is a handsome pay day. Philip Green, the retail tycoon, has given his family Britain's biggest bonus of £1.2 billion.

The payout from Arcadia, his family giant that controls eight chains, including Topshop and Miss Selfridge, tops the £1.1 billion dividend received by the steel magnate Lakshmi Mittal last year. The self-made man, who left school at 16, has increased his family's wealth to about £6.1 billion.

Mr Green, 53, played down the size of the award. He told *The Times* that the bonus was relatively small, and could have been a lot bigger. 'I'm not unhappy,' he said. 'But in relation to the cash generated by Arcadia, the payment is actually quite conservative.'

Based on figures from the World Bank, his dividend is double the gross domestic product of Belize, and the same as Togo.

Mr Green has a reputation for working and playing hard. He owns a 12-seater Gulfstream G550 jet and a 200ft yacht, each worth about £20 million, and enjoys gambling at Les Ambassadeurs casino in central London.

He reportedly avoids tax on payouts from his companies by ensuring that transactions are in the name of his wife.

From Times Online, 21 October 2005

Activity

Source analysis

Study Source 1. Identify the reasons why Marx would argue that the bonus Philip Green awarded his family was unfair. Relate your answer back to what you have read about Marxist ideology on pages 13–15.

■ Lenin's adaptation of Marxist theory to Russia

Marx based his theories on his study of Britain. During the 19th century, Britain had a large working class whose labour was exploited. They worked long hours, in appalling conditions, for low pay, which ensured that their living conditions were equally grim. Marx therefore believed that it was inevitable that the British proletariat would rise up against the bourgeois factory owners and seize economic control and political power. Marx also believed that the socialist revolution was possible in his native Germany or the USA, both modern industrial nations with large urban proletariats. He would never have believed that the world's first socialist revolution would take place in Russia. Around 80 per cent of the Russian population were peasants, a defining feature of the stage of feudalism. Without considerable industrial development and a capitalist revolution to wrest power from the tsar and the aristocracy, a workers' revolution was a fantasy. Even after a capitalist revolution, there would need to be a growth in the proletariat, combined with their exploitation, their awareness of this exploitation and the power their numbers gave them. Russia was the most unlikely setting for a Marxist revolution.

Fig. 6 *Women and children harvesting in the field in Russia*

The Russian Marxist political party was the Social Democrats. Lenin had become one of their leaders, but he was increasingly concerned about how the party was organised and how the communist revolution could come about. In 1902, he addressed the problem of Russia's backwardness in his work *What is to be Done?* In it, he argued that a small, professional revolutionary elite should form the 'vanguard of the proletariat'. These revolutionaries would carry out the revolution for the working class.

The lack of highly skilled revolutionary forces is becoming increasingly marked and, without a doubt, cannot but affect the depth and the general character of the movement. Many strikes take place without the revolutionary organisations exercising any strong and direct influence upon them ... A shortage of agitational leaflets and illegal literature is felt ... The workers' circles are left without agitators ... In addition, there is a constant shortage of funds.

Our primary and most important practical task is to establish an organisation of revolutionaries capable of maintaining the energy, stability and continuity of the political struggle.

2

*V. I. Lenin, **What is to be Done?**, 1902*

A year later, the Social Democrat Party conference held first in Brussels and later in London saw the party split. Lenin's desire for a revolutionary elite was rejected by his old friend Yuri Martov as undemocratic and the two went their separate ways. Lenin's party took the name Bolshevik, meaning 'majority men', after Lenin had won a majority in the vote to determine who would control the party newspaper *Iskra* ('the Spark'). Martov's group became known as the Mensheviks, or 'minority men'. Trotsky sided with Martov; he would only rejoin Lenin and the Bolsheviks in the summer of 1917 after Lenin had approached him. This perceived lack of loyalty to the Bolsheviks and Lenin would be a crucial factor in the struggle for power after Lenin's death.

Table 1 *A summary of the differences between Bolsheviks and Mensheviks*

	Bolshevik	Menshevik
Revolution	The stage of Capitalism could be skipped and the bourgeois and proletarian stages could be telescoped into one	Russia was not ready for a proletarian revolution; a capitalist revolution had to occur first
The party	An elite party of professional revolutionaries	A mass organisation with membership open to trades unionists
Discipline	Authority to be exercised by the Central Committee of the party; this was described as 'democratic centralism'	Open, democratic discussion within the party; decisions to be arrived at by votes of members
Strategy	Rejection of co-operation with other parties and trades unionists; instead aimed to turn workers into revolutionaries	Alliances with all other revolutionary and bourgeois liberal parties and to work with trades unions in pursuing better wages and conditions for workers

Activity

Study Table 1, which summarises the differences between the Bolshevik and Menshevik parties.

1 Which party was more consistent with the ideas of Marx?

2 What were the strengths and weaknesses of the different approaches?

Lenin was a practical politician and the Bolshevik Revolution of October 1917 showed how he had successfully adapted Marxism. Power was more important than following Marxist theory, which might involve waiting decades for the time to be right for a workers' revolution. Therefore, Lenin:

1 skipped the stage of Capitalism and moved Russia directly from the stage of feudalism to the stage of Socialism

■ Key term

Political Testament: Lenin's final message to the Bolshevik Party, first written in September 1922. In it, he failed to name a successor, criticising all the leading Bolsheviks. He believed that the Central Committee should be increased in size and that all the leading Bolsheviks should rule collectively. In a postscript added in January 1923, Lenin proposed the removal of Stalin from his position as General Secretary of the Bolshevik Party.

■ Cross-reference

To recap on **War Communism**, see page 12.

2 ignored the need for a spontaneous revolution of the exploited workers who formed the majority in society and instead used a small revolutionary elite

3 abandoned the dictatorship of the proletariat in favour of the dictatorship of the party who represented the proletariat

4 accepted that the party relied on two classes: the proletariat and the poorer peasants

5 allowed the political system to determine the economic system, the exact opposite of Marxism where the political system was the inevitable consequence of the economic system. This meant imposing War Communism and its replacement the NEP when War Communism failed.

All the problems that the Bolsheviks faced after 1917 can be directly attributed to the decision to force the revolution. The Civil War, the problems of War Communism, the need to resort to the NEP and the problems with the peasantry were all because the Soviet Union did not have a proletarian majority. Lenin himself acknowledged the problem in his **Political Testament**, writing on 25 December 1922: 'Our party relies on two classes and therefore its instability would be possible and its fall inevitable if these two classes were not able to come to an agreement.' His adaptation of Marxist theory was so significant that the official ideology of the Soviet Union was Marxist–Leninism rather than Marxism.

■ The power struggle to replace Lenin, 1924–9

Fig. 7 *The leading Bolsheviks mourn Lenin. Carrying Lenin's coffin are (left to right): Stalin, Kamenev, Tomsky, Molotov, Zinoviev (partially hidden), Kalinin and Bukharin. Note the absence of Trotsky*

■ Cross-reference

Information on how **Marxist theory** was adapted by Stalin in the 1920s can be found on page 28.

Stalin's further adaptation of Marxist ideas is discussed in Chapter 2.

On 21 January 1924, Lenin suffered a third and fatal stroke. His death was critical for the Soviet Union's future because the struggle to succeed him meant a battle of personalities and political ideas. Both would have a fundamental impact on the future of the Soviet Union, on Marxism in the Soviet Union and on the development of totalitarianism. The struggle that took place between 1924 and 1928 would see Stalin emerge as victorious and adapt the existing Marxist–Leninist ideology into a more personal set of ideas that have become known as Stalinism – a truly totalitarian system.

The leadership candidates

The five principal candidates to replace Lenin as leader were Stalin, Trotsky, Zinoviev, Kamenev and Bukharin.

■ **Key profiles**

Joseph Stalin

Joseph Stalin (1879–1953) was born in Georgia as Joseph Vissarionovich Djugashvili, taking the name 'Stalin' or 'Man of Steel' from 1911 rather than his earlier alias 'Koba'. He trained as a priest in a seminary in Gori but read illegal works by Marx and Lenin, becoming a committed Marxist and a follower of Lenin. He raised money for the Bolshevik Party by robbing banks, for which he was arrested and sent into exile. Stalin returned to Petrograd in March 1917 and was made a member of the Central Committee in April, but he played little part in the October Revolution. He was a member of the Bolshevik government as Commissar for Nationalities, but his key position was General Secretary, a post Lenin gave him in 1922. By the start of 1923, Lenin was regretting this move and, on his death, Stalin was rank outsider in the race to succeed Lenin.

Fig. 8 *Joseph Stalin*

■ Cross-reference

Trotsky is introduced on page 11.

Leon Trotsky

By 1924, Trotsky had established himself as the obvious successor to Lenin. He had plotted the October Revolution, saved the new Soviet State in the Civil War and created the Red Army. However, both his success and his leadership of the army meant that other leading Bolsheviks thought he needed to be stopped. Trotsky was, at times, too arrogant, believing that power would simply pass to himself. This led one Bolshevik to recall that he had few deeply committed followers and he also reportedly told friends that he thought he would never be made leader because he was Jewish.

Fig. 9 *Leon Trotsky*

Grigori Zinoviev

Grigori Zinoviev (1883–1936) was a lower middle-class Ukrainian Jew. A close associate of Lenin, he returned to Russia after a period of exile with Lenin in April 1917. Along with his close friend Lev Kamenev, he opposed the October Revolution, favouring a period of co-operation with other left-wing parties rather than a one-party State. Lenin persuaded him to rejoin the leadership, making him leader of the Leningrad Party. He was also the first Chairman of the Comintern (the organisation responsible for spreading Communism abroad) and a member of the Politburo when it was reformed in 1919. He was charged with the defence of Petrograd during the Civil War, but the city had to be saved by Trotsky after Zinoviev panicked. His reputation was further undermined by his womanising; he had a particular taste for chorus girls.

Fig. 10 *Grigori Zinoviev*

Lev Kamenev

Lev Kamenev (1883–1936) was a university educated working-class Jew. He was an intellectual and a particularly talented journalist who ran the party newspaper before his arrest and exile in 1914. He returned to Petrograd with Stalin and the two of them ran the party before Lenin's return in April 1917. Like Zinoviev, he opposed the October Revolution. However, Lenin had great respect for him; he was not only made a member of the Politburo when it reformed in 1919, he also usually chaired the meetings. In addition, he was Head

Fig. 11 *Lev Kamenev*

of the Moscow Party. Kamenev was well liked but his reputation was damaged by three associations: he was married to Trotsky's sister, his son Lutik was well known in Moscow as a drunk and playboy (a thinly disguised Kamenev junior was the feature of a play in Moscow in the 1920s) and he worked closely with Zinoviev.

Nikolai Bukharin

Nikolai Bukharin (1888–1938) was an intellectual, but he was also a charming and an eloquent speaker and the most popular of the leadership candidates with the party and the peasantry. He returned to Russia after the February 1917 revolution, having met and worked with Lenin in Europe and Trotsky in New York. He was made editor of the party newspaper *Pravda* in 1918 and was a member of the Politburo from the early 1920s. He was also the leading party theoretician. He argued for economic policies based on co-operation with the peasantry and was the leading supporter of the NEP, seeing it as a long-term measure rather than a temporary compromise with the peasants. His policies were therefore regarded with suspicion by many Bolsheviks.

Fig. 12 *Nikolai Bukharin*

The successor to Lenin was, however, unclear. Lenin himself did not believe that any of the leading Bolsheviks should replace him, as he had made clear in his Political Testament.

> Since he became General Secretary, Comrade Stalin has concentrated in his hands immeasurable power, and I am not sure that he will always know how to use that power with sufficient caution. On the other hand Comrade Trotsky is distinguished not only by his outstanding qualities (personally he is the most capable man in the present Central Committee), but also by his excess of self-confidence and a readiness to be carried away by the purely administrative side of affairs.
>
> The qualities of these two outstanding leaders of the present Central Committee might lead quite accidentally to a split, and if our Party does not take steps to prevent it the split might arise unexpectedly. I shall not try to describe other members of the Central Committee according to their personal qualities. I will simply remind you that the October episode involving Zinoviev and Kamenev was not, of course, accidental but that it ought not to be used seriously against them, any more than the non-Bolshevism of Trotsky.
>
> Of the younger members of the Central Committee I would like to say a few words about Bukharin. Bukharin is without doubt the most able theorist in the Party and may legitimately be considered to be the favourite of the whole Party. But his theoretical views can only with greatest hesitation be regarded as fully Marxist.
>
> *Postscript, 4 January 1923:*
> Stalin is too rude, and this fault, entirely supportable in relations amongst us Communists, becomes insupportable in the office of General Secretary. Therefore, I propose to the comrades to find a way of removing Stalin from that position and to appoint another man who in all respects differs from Stalin only in superiority; namely, more patient, more loyal, more polite, less capricious and more attentive to comrades.

3   *Lenin's Political Testament, 25 December 1922*

Fig. 13 *Stalin with the men who were his colleagues in the 1920s and his victims in the 1930s. From left: Stalin, Rykov, Kamenev and Zinoviev*

Lenin's criticism of all the leading Bolsheviks was deliberate. He did not want any of them to rule alone, preferring a **collective leadership** to be established. Lenin probably felt that a collective leadership was more in keeping with Marxism and his own view of 'dictatorship of the party' to create a truly socialist State.

Lenin also had concerns about the personalities of the leading Bolsheviks. He recognised the arrogance of Trotsky who, because of his great intellect, often appeared to be talking down to normal party members. They were suspicious of Trotsky anyway because he was both Jewish and an ex-Menshevik, which is what Lenin was referring to in his Political Testament when he wrote of Trotsky's 'non-Bolshevism'. Lenin also believed Stalin was becoming too powerful as General Secretary, using the power to create a party loyal to him rather than Bolshevism. Lenin had also been disturbed by Stalin's actions in Georgia in 1922. After the Bolshevik Revolution, Georgia had declared independence from the Soviet Union. Lenin did not want the break-up of the Soviet Union and sent Stalin and his fellow Georgian Sergo Ordzhonikidze to negotiate the return of the State to the Soviet Union. Stalin instead forced Georgia to rejoin the Soviet Union, using the Red Army and the Cheka and directly ignoring Lenin's instructions. Stalin had also been rude and abusive to Lenin's wife in a phone conversation and, although he later was forced to send her a written apology, Lenin noted Stalin's rudeness in the postscript to the Political Testament. Stalin's abrasiveness and Trotsky's arrogance terrified Lenin, as he thought the two would clash and split the party.

Key term

Collective leadership: rule by several leading figures rather than by an individual. Lenin hoped a collective leadership would replace him and rule the Soviet Union after his death.

Stalin gave the speech at Lenin's funeral, in which he personally swore to continue the work of Lenin.

Stalin gave a series of lectures later published as 'Foundations of Lenin-ism', a basic guide to Lenin's ideas for the uneducated. Stalin made clear his commitment to Lenin and his ideas on how Trotsky and other Bolsheviks were not as faithful.

Stalin as General Secretary supervised the Lenin Enrolment – the expansion of the party in tribute to Lenin.

Stalin used the Decree against Factionalism to accuse opponents of factionalism and disloyalty to the memory of Lenin.

Fig. 14 *The Lenin legacy – how Stalin linked himself to Lenin and used this association to his advantage*

■ **Cross-reference**

Stalin's speech at **Lenin's funeral** is explored on page 44.

Stalin's supervision of the **Lenin Enrolment** is discussed on page 24.

The **Decree against Factionalism** is explained on page 12.

Lenin reached the conclusion that Trotsky needed to be controlled and he therefore argued that the size of the Central Committee should be increased to 50–100 members. However, the dynamite in the testament was that Stalin should be removed.

It was essential to Stalin that Lenin's loss of faith in him remained a secret. Lenin had become a god-like figure to the Russian people and the Bolshevik Party as the founder of the Soviet Union and the country's leader, through the Civil War and the challenges faced as a result of being the world's only communist country. All the leading Bolsheviks were desperate to associate themselves with Lenin and to appear to be his natural successor. Stalin was the most successful and this 'Lenin legacy' was a crucial strength of Stalin in the power struggle.

Stalin's survival

Despite Lenin's attempts to remove him, Stalin survived because of a combination of good fortune and political cunning:

■ Lenin was unable to act himself because of the strokes he had suffered. Stalin controlled access to Lenin.

■ Lenin had urged Trotsky to attack Stalin over his ill treatment of the Georgians at the 12th Party Congress in 1923, but Trotsky, in an example of the type of arrogant miscalculation that destroyed his chances of becoming leader, had done a deal with Stalin. In return for keeping quiet about Georgia, Trotsky was allowed to present his economic policies without criticism from Stalin or his supporters.

■ Before it was published, Stalin was informed of the comments of the Political Testament by Lenin's two secretaries, whom Stalin had appointed. He therefore ensured the testament was read to the Central Committee first. Kamenev and Zinoviev saw Trotsky as a much greater threat and so backed Stalin, arguing he had changed his ways. The Central Committee voted not to publish Lenin's final wishes.

The sources of Stalin's power

The Soviet system of government by 1924 was based on a parliament and a cabinet. However, these were not the sources of political power because

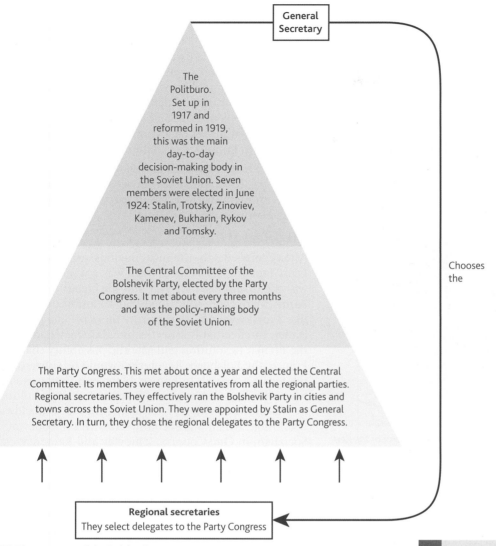

Fig. 15 *The structure of the Bolshevik Party*

all members of the government had to be members of the Bolshevik Party. The party was therefore the key to political power and the government was no more than the formal expression of the party's power.

Stalin as General Secretary

Stalin was made General Secretary in 1922, essentially because the job was considered to be a boring administrative role and just right for a man who had been described by a Menshevik as the 'grey blur'. As General Secretary he was dismissed as 'Comrade Card Index'. No one anticipated the power the post would give him.

■ Stalin had the power to appoint the Regional Secretaries. During the Civil War, Bolshevik officials who were captured were usually shot, meaning that Stalin was able to rebuild the party organisation. He was able to select his supporters to fill these posts.

■ Stalin could appoint, promote and demote the top 5,500 officials in the Soviet Union. As well as working in an office rather than in a mine or on a railway, these officials received privileges. They had holidays and lived in party housing, could use party *dacha* (holiday homes) and had access to party shops where luxuries like oranges were available.

■ **Activity**

Thinking point

Study Figure 15 showing the power structure within the Bolshevik Party. Why do you think Stalin's position as General Secretary was so important?

■ **Key chronology**

The three stages of Stalin's victory in the power struggle

1924 Stalin, Zinoviev and Kamenev v. Trotsky.

1926 Stalin and Bukharin v. Trotsky, Zinoviev and Kamenev.

1928 Stalin, Molotov, Kirov and Kaganovic v. Bukharin, Rykov and Tomsky.

Fig. 16 *Trotsky inspects the Red Army. His control of the Red Army led Zinoviev and Kamenev to side with Stalin*

Cross-reference

The concepts of **Worldwide Revolution** and **Socialism in One Country** are described on page 26.

Factionalism is discussed on page 12.

■ Stalin supervised the expansion of the party. In tribute to Lenin, the decision was taken to expand the Bolshevik Party. The Lenin Enrolment was therefore announced in 1924 and increased the party from 500,000 to over 1 million members in two years. These new members were young, inexperienced and lacking education; only 8 per cent had received any secondary education and less than 1 per cent had completed higher education, making them easy for Stalin to impress and manipulate.

■ Stalin had unrivalled knowledge of party members. He was the middleman between the Politburo and the government, with access to party files, and recording and conveying information.

The defeat of Trotsky

After Lenin's death, the most obvious successor was Leon Trotsky. This fact in itself was a weakness. Trotsky was the Commissar for War and the creator of the Red Army. Many were concerned that an ambitious man like Trotsky would use the army to secure his place as leader. Intellectual Bolsheviks like Kamenev had studied the French Revolution and saw the possibility that, as in France, the Bolshevik Revolution would be subverted by the leading general. In France, Napoleon Bonaparte had been a leading General and 15 years after the revolution he was crowned emperor. Trotsky believed in worldwide revolution, which Stalin countered with the policy of Socialism in One Country. Zinoviev and Kamenev therefore turned to Stalin and formed the Triumvirate to stop Trotsky, the 'Red Napoleon'. Furthermore, Trotsky had attacked Zinoviev and Kamenev in his essay 'Lessons of October' drawing attention to their lack of support for the revolution. This led to a counter-attack from Kamenev, Lenin or Trotsky, in which he made clear that Trotsky was an ex-Menshevik who frequently disagreed with Lenin. He was accused of inventing 'Trotskyism', a rival ideology to Leninism. Ironically, in 1924 Trotsky had argued:

> None of us desires or is able to dispute the will of the party. Clearly the party is always right. And if the party takes a decision which one or other of us thinks unjust, he will say, just or unjust, it is my party, and I shall support the consequences of the decision to the end.

Trotsky found he was unable to live up to these noble sentiments and was accused of factionalism. At the meeting of the Central Committee in January 1925 he was condemned. He resigned as Commissar for War, the position that had given him continuing control of the army.

Stalin also damaged Trotsky's leadership bid. Trotsky was recovering from malaria in the Crimea when Lenin died and Stalin told Trotsky the wrong date for the funeral; by the time Trotsky realised, it was too late for him to travel back in time. This disrespect for Lenin damaged Trotsky's public image further.

The defeat of Zinoviev, Kamenev and the United Opposition

After Trotsky's defeat, Zinoviev and Kamenev became concerned that Stalin was now the most powerful figure in the party. They were right. Stalin turned on them and Kamenev lost control of the Moscow Party. Zinoviev held on in Leningrad and launched an attack on the party policy of the NEP, arguing that it was capitalist and that the time had come to introduce rapid industrialisation. They also started to question Socialism in One Country, arguing that without an international revolution the economic backwardness of the country would destroy the Soviet Union. This was an attack on Bukharin as well as Stalin and so the two united. Stalin was able to brand their opponents as factionalists and Bukharin's popularity, combined with Stalin's control of the delegates, won the day. At the 14th Party Congress in December 1925, Kamenev's warnings against Stalin were shouted down by angry delegates who then defeated the programme of Zinoviev and Kamenev by 559 votes to 65. In 1926, Zinoviev lost control of Leningrad and was replaced as Chair of the Comintern by Bukharin.

The policy of ending the NEP and beginning rapid industrialisation was not new: it had been Trotsky's policy in 1924. Zinoviev and Kamenev therefore decided to make a tactical alliance with Trotsky, but this lacked credibility given their attacks on each other a year earlier. As their support lay outside the Central Committee, they held protest meetings which only confirmed that they were factionalists. In October 1926, they supplied copies of Lenin's Political Testament to the world's press, but it was too late. The Central Committee removed them from all positions of power and used the secret police against their supporters, seizing their printing presses. Trotsky was placed in internal exile in 1928 and deported from the Soviet Union in 1929. Kamenev was sent to Rome as Ambassador in January 1927 and expelled from the party at the end of the year. He was sent into exile in 1928 but was allowed to return to the party after denouncing Trotsky. Zinoviev was also expelled and re-admitted to the party in 1928.

The defeat of the Right Deviation

By 1926, the Soviet Union was effectively ruled by Stalin and Bukharin. Stalin, however, did not instinctively like the NEP, seeing it as a compromise with the peasantry and therefore with Socialism. The NEP was restoring economic stability but it was also a slow recovery. Now that the United Opposition had been defeated, he was keen to adopt their policies and to introduce rapid industrialisation.

Stalin no longer needed to support an alternative policy for fear of aiding the United Opposition, so he turned on Bukharin and his allies Aleksei Rykov and Mikhail Tomsky. Bukharin had no power base within the party to resist Stalin, but he was wary of making the same mistakes as the United Opposition and being accused of factionalism. Although in the summer of 1928 he pleaded with Kamenev 'If we don't unite, Koba will cut our throats', he never managed to organise an effective opposition group. Instead he argued for the NEP in the Politburo. This was futile and Stalin's supporters crushed what Stalin called the Right Deviation. Control of the party was all-important; as a disillusioned Stalinist remarked, 'We have defeated Bukharin not with argument but with party cards.' Bukharin was duly removed from the Comintern and lost his position as editor of *Pravda*. In November 1929, he lost his place on the Politburo. Rykov was head of the government as Chairman of the Council of People's Commissars, but he lost the post and was expelled from the Politburo. Stalin used his powers as General Secretary to purge the trades unions' leadership and Tomsky lost his post on the Central Council of Trades Unions and his place in the Politburo in 1930. On 21 December 1929, Stalin's 50th birthday, *Pravda* dedicated the edition to the 'Lenin of today'. His victory in the power struggle was complete. His more perceptive opponents recognised he was more a 'Red Tsar'.

Cross-reference

The policy of NEP is found on page 12 and on page 27.

Rapid **industrialisation** is discussed on page 27.

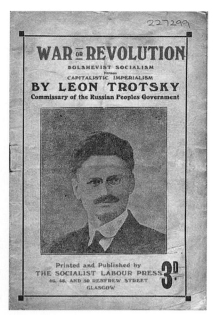

Fig. 17 *The front cover of Trotsky's pamphlet, **War or Revolution**, published in 1918, in which he set out his view that only permanent, worldwide revolution could ensure the survival of the Soviet Union*

The role of ideology in the power struggle

Although the power struggle was in essence about personalities, the different ideas about the future of the revolution and the development of the economy were also critical.

The future: World Revolution v. Socialism in One Country

At the heart of the dispute between Trotsky and Stalin in 1924 was the question of how the Bolshevik Revolution should be protected. During the Civil War, Western powers had sent troops to aid the enemies of the Bolsheviks and it seemed likely that these capitalist countries would attempt to crush the world's only socialist State. Trotsky believed that the answer was a permanent revolution, spreading the revolution across the world. Lenin and Trotsky had established the Comintern in 1919 and its aim was to promote revolutions around the world. Trotsky believed that aiding socialist revolutions around Europe would mean that the Soviet Union would not be isolated as the country would create socialist allies. Stalin was dismissive of Trotsky's ideas.

Activity

Source analysis

Study Source 4.

1. In what ways does Stalin undermine Zinoviev and Kamenev's commitment to worldwide revolution?

2. Is there any other way he could have criticised the policy?

Recently, in the Political Bureau [Politburo], Kamenev and Zinoviev defended the point of view that we cannot cope with the internal difficulties due to our technical and economic backwardness unless an international revolution comes to our rescue. We, however, along with the majority of the members of the Central Committee, think that we can build socialism, are building it, and shall continue to do so, regardless of our technical backwardness. We think that the work of building will proceed far more slowly, of course, than in the conditions of a world victory; nevertheless, we are making progress and will continue to do so. We also believe that the view held by Kamenev and Zinoviev shows a lack of faith in the internal forces of our working class and of the peasant masses who follow its lead. We believe that it is a departure from the Leninist position.

4 *J. V. Stalin, **Concerning Questions of Leninism**, 25 January 1926*

Stalin partly developed his idea of Socialism in One Country because he did not like Trotsky and was in competition with him to replace Lenin. However, he also recognised that the policy was over-optimistic and unpopular. Attempted revolutions in Germany and Hungary had been crushed and it was clear that attempts by the Soviet Union to inspire workers' uprisings could lead to war. Stalin recognised that war was impossible economically and psychologically; the country and the people had been shattered by the combined impact of the First World War and the Civil War. Socialism in One Country was a patriotic policy that showed faith in the Soviet people. Stalin portrayed Worldwide Revolution as a policy that put the needs of other countries before those of the Russian people. Trotsky's Jewish background marked him as a disloyal outsider among many party members anyway, and his international policy only seemed to confirm his treacherous nature.

The victory for Socialism in One Country further adapted Marxist–Leninism. Under Stalin, the Comintern became concerned with defending Soviet interests abroad rather than with spreading revolution. After the fall of Bukharin, its status under Stalin declined.

The economy: the NEP v. rapid industrialisation

Stalin's rejection of rapid industrialisation and then adoption of the plan as and when it suited him in the power struggle has led to the view that Stalin was not concerned with ideology. Certainly he changed his position to help him win the power struggle. However, Stalin had been a firm supporter of Lenin, who had introduced the NEP. He therefore continued Lenin's policy while it was working (and he made it clear that he was continuing Lenin's policies while the United Opposition were betraying the memory of the founder of the Soviet Union).

By 1927, Stalin had grave doubts about the NEP. Many party members were openly complaining that the Bolshevik Revolution had been in vain, pointing to women clad in fox furs attending the theatre while wealthy owners of private enterprises visited prostitutes (seen as a sign of the exploitation of tsarist Russia). The NEP was providing a slow recovery but it was also creating a new wealthy middle class, with the support of Bukharin.

> Our policy towards the countryside should develop in the direction of relaxing and in part abolishing many restrictions that put the brake on the growth of well-to-do and **kulak** farms. To the peasants, to all the peasants, we must say: enrich yourself, develop your farms, and do not fear that restrictions will be put upon you.

5

N. Bukharin, 'The New Economic Policy and our Tasks',
***Bolshevik**, 1 June 1925*

> **Activity**
>
> #### Source analysis
>
> Study Source 5. Why do you think Bolsheviks like Stalin objected to Bukharin's policies for the countryside?

Furthermore, in 1927 there was a war scare: Britain had broken off diplomatic relations, France had broken off trade links, the Japanese were threatening war in the Far East and the future of international Communism looked insecure after the destruction of the Chinese Communist Party in the Shanghai Massacre.

Stalin believed the Soviet Union had to become strong enough to defend itself from invasion as soon as possible. This meant maximising the production of grain to export and raise the capital for a rapid industrialisation that would produce the iron, coal, steel, oil and electricity necessary for self-defence. However, in 1927–8 State grain collection fell again. Stalin decided to take the grain from the peasants, leading the expedition to the Urals and Siberia where he closed the peasant markets, seized grain and arrested those who resisted. He was supported in this by the left wing of the party, many of whom he had promoted during the power struggle with Trotsky, Zinoviev and Kamenev and whose loyalty he needed. Rapid industrialisation and the collectivisation of agriculture (combining small peasant farms into large co-operative or State-owned farms to increase yields) were measures that ended the capitalist compromise that was brought about by the NEP and made the Soviet economy socialist. It was necessary because Lenin had forced the Bolshevik Revolution early and the capitalist stage had been missed out. The

> **Key term**
>
> **Kulaks:** rich peasants who had grown wealthy from the NEP. The term literally means 'fist' in Russian and they were seen as greedy capitalist enemies of Bolshevism by the left wing of the party. In December 1929, Stalin decreed the 'elimination of the kulaks as a class'. Hundreds of thousands of kulak families were deported to Siberia. Many historians believe the kulak was a myth; there were no 'rich' peasants. Instead the Bolsheviks were applying the term to anyone who opposed collectivisation.

> **Did you know?**
>
> The Chinese Nationalist Party and the Chinese Communist Party had worked together to liberate China from the rule of the Chinese emperor. However, having invited the communist leaders to a meeting at Shanghai in 1927, the nationalists executed the communist leaders. This act gave them control over China. Mao Zedong was not at the meeting and therefore survived to reorganise the Chinese Communist Party in the 1930s. He then led the Communists to victory in a civil war and established the communist People's Republic of China on 10 October 1949.

political system of Socialism now created a socialist economic system, the opposite of Marx's theory. State control of the economy was a key feature of Stalin's totalitarian rule.

Activity

Revision exercise

Review this section to identify the main strengths and weaknesses of the five leadership candidates. Copy and complete the table below to summarise them.

Candidate	Strengths	Weaknesses	Key strengths and weaknesses
Stalin			
Trotsky			
Zinoviev			
Kamenev			
Bukharin			

Stalin's adaptation of Marxist theory in the 1920s

Lenin had already made the fundamental adaptation to Marxism when he skipped the stage of feudalism and forced a socialist revolution rather than waiting for revolution to happen spontaneously. As we have seen, from 1924 Stalin proceeded to adapt Marxist theory further:

- The invasion of Georgia had seen Stalin ignore Marxist ideas of internationalism in favour of the invasion and takeover of the republic in the interests of greater Russian Nationalism.

- The victory of Socialism in One Country over Worldwide Revolution was also a victory for Nationalism over internationalism.

- Stalin created the cult of Lenin, which in its elevation of the dead leader to a god-like status was contrary to Marxist ideas of 'leadership'. Marx believed in the dictatorship of the proletariat, which would give way to a communist Utopia where there would be no leadership and no State.

- Stalin adapted Marxist–Leninist ideas on leadership too, as Lenin had sought to rule through the Central Committee and had allowed free discussion until a decision was agreed. He was 'first among equals' in the Soviet Union but he did not assert his personal power as freely as Stalin, who ended any sense of collective leadership and instituted a personal dictatorship.

- The continuation of the NEP until 1927 was clearly inconsistent with Marxism. It should be noted that the introduction of collectivisation and industrialisation by Stalin were both partially intended to end the ideological compromise and more closely align policy with Marxism.

Activity

Revision exercise

Copy and complete the table to summarise the different leadership candidates between 1924 and 1928 and their policies using the bullet points below. Some points will need to be used more than once.

Candidate	Posts	Policy or position, 1924	Policy or position, 1926	Policy or position, 1928
Joseph Stalin				
Leon Trotsky				
Grigori Zinoviev				
Lev Kamenev				
Nikolai Bukharin				

- General Secretary of the Communist Party
- Commissar for War
- Editor of *Pravda*
- Chairman of the Comintern
- Head of the Moscow Party
- Head of the Leningrad Party
- Socialism in One Country

- Worldwide Revolution
- Not directly involved
- Continue the NEP
- Rapid industrialisation
- End the NEP and begin rapid industrialisation
- Expelled from the party

Summary questions

1. Explain why the Bolshevik Revolution was not a true Marxist revolution.

2. How important was the role of ideology in explaining Stalin's victory in the power struggle in the years 1924 to 1928?

Activity

Group activity

In groups, identify a list of reasons for Stalin's success in the power struggle. Try to find five pieces of evidence to support each reason.

Russian totalitarianism in the 1930s

Fig. 1 *The Worthy Successor of Lenin. Large-size portraits of Lenin and Stalin were commonplace from the 1930s, reinforcing the legitimacy of Stalin's rule by his association with Lenin*

In this chapter you will learn about:

- the meaning of the intolerance of diversity

- the reasons why the Soviet Union was intolerant of diversity

- the extent to which the Soviet Union was intolerant of diversity in the 1930s, with reference to economic, political, religious and cultural diversity

- Marxist theories of leadership and the cult of personality.

On 29 December 1929, Stalin celebrated his 50th birthday at his *dacha* at Zubalovo. The previous years had been difficult for the General Secretary, or GenSek. He had fought a struggle for control of the USSR at the same time as critical decisions were taken about the future of the Bolshevik Revolution. As he celebrated his birthday with allies like Vyacheslav Molotov and Lazar Kaganovich, Stalin could reflect that his main rivals were defeated, humiliated and, in the case of Leon Trotsky, exiled. Stalin had a right to feel self-satisfied. The success of the Stalin faction had been assured with the fall of Bukharin and the right, but these other leading Bolsheviks did not yet fully recognise that the next phase in Soviet government would not be the dictatorship of the proletariat but the personal dictatorship of the Red Tsar.

■ The intolerance of diversity

The intolerance of diversity – the refusal to accept any difference – is a key theme in totalitarian states. This includes different ideas as well as any form of individuality. It is a direct result of totalitarian regimes having an exclusive ideology, the implementation of which would create the 'perfect' state. If there were alternative views and beliefs, by definition they are not 'perfect', and therefore they should not be allowed to exist.

In the Soviet Union there was a strong ideological basis for refusing to allow individual freedom and diversity:

■ Marxism was a scientific theory that stressed that progress towards Utopia was inevitable. However, in the stage of Socialism, the 'dictatorship of the proletariat' would occur. This involved ending class divisions (diversity) by one of two methods: re-education and the creation of a new class consciousness, or extermination. This would ultimately lead to Communism, the 'Utopian State'. However, before this stage could be reached, it was necessary to subordinate the individual to the State to ensure that the state would triumph against the enemies of Socialism. It was believed that as the final stage of communism became ever nearer, capitalist enemies would struggle ever harder to prevent this socialist victory.

■ Marxism had not been followed in the Soviet Union. Most of the population were peasants. The Soviet State had to destroy their belief in an alternative vision of Utopia. Other sets of ideas, such as Trotskyism, were also dangerous and destructive forces that had to be eradicated as concepts.

■ It was essential that the country was united because of the threat of war presented by international Capitalism in the 1920s, the aggressive Nazi regime from 1933 and the USA and its capitalist allies in the 1940s and 1950s. There could be no argument or opposition when, according to Lenin, the survival of the world's first communist state hung by a 'hair's breadth'.

■ 'Stalinism' was also a personal ideology that rejected any opposition to the leader: like the 19th century tsars, Stalin believed he was the Soviet State. He also added a racial element to Soviet intolerance in that he promoted Russian Nationalism. At times, this spilled over into violent attacks on minorities, such as Ukrainians in the collectivisation drive and Jews in the purges.

Economic intolerance

The adoption of the NEP in 1921 had introduced diversity into the economy. The State accepted that the control it had tried to exercise through War Communism had failed and therefore private ownership of land and 90 per cent of industry was once again allowed. The NEP had been introduced to try to aid economic recovery, and by 1927 production had returned to 1913 levels before the extreme disruption of the First World War, Civil War and the policy of War Communism. But the NEP was a capitalist policy and Stalin's opposition to it had enabled him to defeat Bukharin.

In 1927, the party agreed to implement a **Five Year Plan** for industry. Stalin argued in 1931 that the Soviet Union was 50–100 years behind the West and that this deficit had to be made up in 10–15 years. The introduction of collectivisation would ensure that the level of agricultural productivity would increase and that the State would also be more successful in procuring (or collecting) the grain they were entitled to from the peasants.

State control of the economy was ensured through the State Planning Commission or Gosplan, which set targets for production, prices and wages; allocated manpower and resources; and produced the statistics that proved the success of the socialist economy. Gosplan also provided State control of the economy. This ensured there could

Cross-reference

To recap on **Marxist ideology** and stage theory, review page 10.

Cross-reference

The **NEP** and **War Communism** are discussed on page 12, and **Stalin's defeat of Bukharin** on page 25.

Key term

Five Year Plans: sets of targets for industrial production, but they did not specify in detail precisely how these targets would be achieved. It was left to managers on a regional, local and individual factory basis to work out how to reach their targets. In total, there were five Five Year Plans, three before the Nazi invasion in 1941 and two post-war:

■ First Five Year Plan Oct 1928 to Dec 1932.

■ Second Five Year Plan Jan 1933 to Dec 1937.

■ Third Five Year Plan Jan 1938 to June 1941.

■ Fourth Five Year Plan Jan 1946 to Dec 1950.

■ Fifth Five Year Plan Jan 1951 to Dec 1955.

The First Plan ended a year early because the State claimed all targets had been met. The Third Plan was abandoned when the Nazis invaded.

■ A closer look

Were the Five Year Plans an economic success?

Table 1 *Successes and failures of the first three Five Year Plans*

The First Five Year Plan

Successes	Failures
■ Huge increase in the production of heavy industry: oil production rose from 11.7 to 21.4m tonnes, coal production 35.4 to 64.3m tonnes. ■ New towns were built, such as Stalinsk, Magnitogorsk and Karaganda. ■ New tractor factories were built at Stalingrad and Kharkov.	■ Failure to fulfil the plan in almost all areas, e.g. the target for coal was 75m tonnes. ■ Decrease in the production of woollen cloth meant there was a shortage of clothes. ■ Inefficient distribution and planning meant machines rusted because factories were not completed or factories were flooded by the completion of a new dam. ■ A emphasis on quantity rather than quality meant substandard goods were produced. ■ Poor living standards: rationing was introduced, black-market food prices rose and there was a shortage of housing in industrial cities.

The Second Five Year Plan

Successes	Failures
■ Overfulfilment of some areas of the plan, e.g. steel and machine tools. ■ Huge increase in production: oil production rose to 28.5m tonnes, coal production to 128m tonnes. ■ Improvement in living standards: bread rationing was ended, real wages rose and electricity was supplied to almost all Moscow's citizens. ■ Prestige projects were completed, including the opening of the Moscow Underground. ■ The ability to manufacture machine tools is the mark of a sophisticated economy: imports fell from 78% in the First Plan to only 10%.	■ Targets were still not met in key areas: coal production was still below the target of 150m tonnes. ■ Living standards were still low because of the shortage of consumer goods. In 1935, there were no razor blades or frying pans in Leningrad shops. ■ The Baltic–White Sea Canal was opened but it epitomised the failures of Soviet planning. It cost 60,000 lives, was too narrow and shallow to be of use to the Soviet navy, and was bombed and closed early in the Second World War.

The Third Five Year Plan

Successes	Failures
■ Production continued to grow: coal production reached 150m tonnes by 1940. ■ The plan focused on war production and by 1941 the Soviet air force was the largest in the world. ■ Whole factories were dismantled and transported to the East where they were rebuilt away from the Nazi threat. ■ The Soviet Union's share of world manufacturing rose to 17.6% from 5%, giving them the second largest share in the world according to Hillmann's 1939 estimate.	■ The concentration on arms meant that living standards declined still further with real wages falling by 10%. ■ There was no increase in the production of oil and steel. ■ According to Bairoch's 1982 estimate, the Soviet Union's share of world manufacturing rose only to 9%, giving it the fourth largest share in the world.

be no relationship between the people and their employers which could undermine the loyalty that people felt towards the state: the state was their employer. In the countryside, Machine Tractor Stations were established which were responsible for supplying grain and hiring machinery to the collective farms. They were also meant to serve as a proletarian base in the countryside and were staffed by Bolshevik Party officials, members of the secret police and army units. The Soviet Union was trying to improve economic production but there was also a clear intention to increase political control through economic policy and to ensure that individualism was crushed by the all-powerful Soviet State.

A range of economic measures were used to enforce control over the people. Rationing for the cities had been introduced in 1929. In 1932, the death penalty was introduced to punish the theft of state property and internal passports were introduced to restrict movement, although on average industrial workers changed jobs every 17 months. In 1932, being absent from work without a good reason could lead to instant dismissal and the loss of home and ration card. By 1939, absenteeism was defined as being 20 minutes late for work and by 1940 it was punishable by a pay cut of 25 per cent for six months. Prison was used to punish any worker who left a job without permission. Strikes were banned and trades unions were used to control and discipline workers. Soviet workers were told where they would work and live, and for what price. They faced the accusation of being called a 'wrecker', 'saboteur' or 'Trotskyite' if they challenged their impossible targets for production or questioned the shortages of food, fuel or other essentials. The Soviet State proclaimed that the First Five Year Plan to develop industry had achieved its targets in four years and ended the plan early, despite the failure to achieve any of the targets for heavy industry. Dissenting voices were few and far between. Industrial experts who had argued that targets were unrealistic were arrested and placed on trial, as in the 1928 Shakhty trial of 53 technicians and engineers. A new world was being created by industrialisation.

> We were raised as the fanatical adepts of a new creed, the only true religion of scientific socialism. The party became our church. The works of Marx, Engels and Lenin were accepted as holy, and Stalin was the infallible high priest. Factories, mines, blast furnaces, locomotives, tractors, work benches, turbines were transformed into objects of a cult.

1 *Lev Kopelev, a party activist who worked in the factories*

Not everyone happily accepted the economic 'second revolution'. Labour discipline brought urban workers under control but peasant resistance was widespread. Small-scale actions saw Bolshevik officials assassinated but the extent of these was so great that Red Army units had to be deployed and, in one case, an air unit. This was seen by the Bolsheviks as a further civil war, fought to ensure the victory of Soviet power and Bolshevik ideology. Resistance to collectivisation was blamed on the bourgeois kulaks: those peasants who opposed collectivisation but were too poor to be described as 'kulaks' were considered to be 'subsidiary kulaks', that is they shared the capitalist views and values of the kulaks. The collectivisation campaign was therefore accompanied by the 'destruction of the kulak as a class', as decreed by Stalin in December 1929. In 1930, 115,000 kulak families were sent into Siberia in exile, a figure that rose to 265,800 in 1931. Moshe Lewin has estimated that the total number of deportations may have been as high as 10 million.

Activity

Source analysis

Study Source 1.

1 Why do you think Kopelev describes industrialisation, the party and Stalin in religious terms?

2 Why do you think the Soviet State wanted the people to see industrialisation as a 'creed'?

Cross-reference

The **kulaks** are introduced on page 27.

These measures ensured State control of the peasantry and grain production. In 1930, the Soviet State exported 4.76m tonnes of grain, rising to 5.06m tonnes in 1931. The grain was taken to raise foreign capital for investment in industry but it ensured a man-made famine in Ukraine, Kazakhstan, Don and Volga regions that historians generally accept killed approximately 7 million inhabitants. The very existence of the famine was denied, preventing aid through the League of Nations. One possible motive for this famine was to exact revenge on Ukraine, a region that had been independent between 1918 and 1922 and which had a stronger commitment to its own national identity than it did to Bolshevism. Ukrainian officials who objected to the requisition of grain were replaced by party officials from Moscow.

The introduction of internal passports prevented peasants leaving the collectives and seeking jobs in the cities. They became tied to the land as they had been under the tsars, as they were not issued with these passports. In August 1935, Stalin made a speech in which he stated that 'Life has become better, life has become merrier' as the end to rationing of bread, meat, fish, sugar and potatoes was announced. Denying the successful economic transformation became a crime. However, there were concessions to the peasants, forced on Stalin by circumstances. Private peasant plots were allowed from 1935 and became a crucial part of the economic system; by 1937, 50 per cent of vegetables and 70 per cent of milk came from these plots. Peasants frequently argued that a day's holiday for a local festival was traditional and then worked on their private plot rather than on the collective farm. Sheila Fitzpatrick has calculated that in some regions peasants spent more days a year on private plots than on collective farms. The party was also forced to make concessions to industrial workers, as a report from a British diplomat in 1936 made clear (Source 2).

Activity

Source analysis

Study Source 2.

1 How might this source be used as evidence of the failure to eliminate diversity?

2 How might this source be used as evidence for the intolerance of diversity?

In an individualist country like Russia the people had always understood working to improve their own lot; but they did not cotton on to the communist idea of working for the common good. So something had to be devised to induce them to work, and to work well.

A fundamental part of communism is equality, so equal wages were the order of the day, with the natural result that the amount of work done sank to the level of the idlest and worst men. That could not continue, so it was decided that wages would go by qualifications and by the amount of work done – that evil bourgeois idea that had so proudly been knocked out.

One of the 'slogans' issued by the Bolsheviks was even that 'Anyone who advocates equality is an anti-revolutionary, and is anti-State: so he will be dealt with accordingly.'

 2　　　　　*Extract from a report by M. MacKillop to the British Foreign Office, May 1936*

Political intolerance

Lenin had laid the foundations for political intolerance with the creation of the one-party state, which removed the formal political expression of alternative ideas. It should be noted, however, that there were only 12 years of legal political parties in the history of Russia/Soviet Union, and that political intolerance was actually the norm. There was also intolerance within the Bolshevik Party, again the legacy of Lenin's actions, as the 1921 Decree Against Factionalism had made it impossible to challenge

Central Committee of the Communist Party in 1917

http://marxists.org/

A. Rykov 1881–1938
Soviet Premier
Shot

N. Bukharin 1888–1938
Politburo
Shot

Y. Sverdlov 1885–1919
President CC
Typhoid

J. Stalin 1879–1953
General Secretary
Cerebral Hemorrhage

G. Zinoviev 1883–1936
Politburo
Shot

M. Uritsky 1873–1918
NKVD
Civil War

L.Trotsky 1879–1940
Commissar Red Army
Assassinated

L. Kamenev 1883–1936
Chairman CC
Shot

V. Lenin 1870–1924
Soviet Premier
Stroke

A. Kollantai 1872–1952
Ambassador Norway
Heart Attack

I. Smilga 1892–1938
Military Rev. Comm.
Shot

A. Joffe 1883 – 1927
Commissar Foreign Affairs
Suicide

V. Nogin 1894–1926
CPC
Natural causes

A. Bubnov 1883–1940
Directorate Red Army
Died in prison

F. Dzerzhinsky 1877–1926
Comm. NKVD
Heart Attack

M.K. Muranov 1873–1959
CC
Natural Causes

G. Lomov 1888–1938
VSNKh
Shot

S. Shaumyan 1878–1918
Baku CPC
Civil War

J. Berzin 1890–1935
NKVD
Strangled

V. Milyutin 1884–1937
VSNKh
Shot

S. Artem 1883–1921
Comm. NKVD
Train Crash

E. Stassova 1873–1966
Secretary CC
Natural Causes

N. Krestinsky 1883–1938
Comm. Intl. Affairs
Shot

P. Dzhaparidze 1880–1918
Baku CPC
Civil War

G. Sokolnikov 1886–1939
Commissar for Finances
Died in prison

A.S. Kiselev (1879–1937)
VSNKh
Shot

Fig. 2 *The fate of Lenin's government. By the end of 1940, only Stalin was left alive from Lenin's original government in 1917*

the official party line. In 1936, Stalin introduced a new constitution for the Soviet Union. Known as the 1936 Constitution, it was prepared by Bukharin although Stalin took all the credit. It guaranteed personal freedoms but it also increased the powers of central government, leaving the republics with only minor responsibilities. The constitution clearly pointed out that the party was the key institution and that the party's interests came before any personal or group interests. It also noted that the struggle with the exploitative classes had now ended and that the foundations of Socialism had therefore been achieved. As political parties were the expression of class interest and classes no longer existed, the constitution recognised only one legal party, meaning that the Bolshevik

Key chronology

The purges

1933–4	Purge of the party: 1 million members expelled.
1934 February	17th Party Congress ('Congress of Victors').
1934 1 December	Assassination of Kirov and the extension of NKVD power.
1934 13 December	**Arrest of Zinoviev and Kamenev.**
1936 August	First Show Trial of Zinoviev, Kamenev and 14 other Old Bolsheviks.
1936 August	Replacement of Yagoda by Yezhov as head of the NKVD.
1936 December	Stalin's Constitution.
1937 January	Second Show Trial of Pyatakov, Radek and 15 other Old Bolsheviks.
1937 June	Military tribunal finds Tukhachevky guilty of treason.
1938	Third Show Trial of Bukharin, Rykov, Yagoda and 17 Old Bolsheviks.
1938	Replacement of Yezhov by Beria as head of the NKVD.
1939	18th Party Congress announces the end of the purges.

Party's monopoly of power was constitutionally ensured. The destruction of the kulaks as a class was also partly a political act, in that Stalin was destroying a group who believed in capitalist ideas. In doing so he showed a rare affinity with Trotsky, who had argued 'Either the revolution destroys the peasantry or the peasantry will destroy the revolution.'

The purges

The most extensive expression of political intolerance came in the purges of the 1930s. In the Soviet Union, several purges of the Bolshevik Party took place. In the 1920s and the early 1930s, the term was used to describe the updating of party membership, which meant the expulsion of individuals who were considered to be suspect in their loyalty to the party. However, between 1936 and 1938 the Great Purge took place, which was a violent cleansing of the party and society. The Bolshevik Party turned on party members who were politically suspect; they might have had a Menshevik past, or have supported Trotsky, Zinoviev, Kamenev or Bukharin in the power struggle, or their crime may be no more than to have politically suspect members of their family. Expulsion was replaced by punishments of arrest, torture and execution.

The initial party purges had begun following criticism of Stalin by Martimyan Ryutin, an Old Bolshevik who called Stalin 'the evil genius who had brought the revolution to the brink of destruction' in a paper to the Central Committee. Around 1 million of the 3 million party members were now expelled as 'Ryutinites'. The loss of the party card was a serious matter as it meant the loss of job, work and home. The treatment of Ryutin made it clear that Stalin would not accept criticism of official party policy. At this stage, only ideas were not tolerated; Stalin's demand that Ryutin and his family be executed was resisted by a majority in the Politburo, led by Sergei Kirov and Sergo Ordzhonokidze. For Stalin, the destruction of individuals who challenged his rule was essential to ensure the destruction of their ideas. The murder of the Leningrad Party boss Sergei Kirov on 1 December 1934 at the Smolny Institute, the Leningrad Party headquarters, was the event that triggered the Great Purge and allowed Stalin to achieve his maxim of 'no man, no problem'.

Key profile

Sergei Kirov

Sergei Kirov (1886–1934) had joined the Bolshevik Party in 1904, becoming a member of the Central Committee in 1923 and replacing Zinoviev as the head of the Leningrad Party in 1926. He supported Stalin against Bukharin in the power struggle. He was shot on 1 December 1934 by Leonid Nikolaev. His death was the trigger for the purges. Historians are still divided on whether Stalin had Kirov killed. The beneficiary of his death, however, was clearly Stalin.

Kirov had offered a clear threat to Stalin's position. The 17th Party Congress held in February 1934 was the 'Congress of Victors', a reference to the success of the First Five Year Plan and the economic transformation of the country. In this climate, the Leningrad delegates believed it was time to carry out Lenin's wishes from his testament and 'retire' Stalin. They privately offered Kirov the post of General Secretary, which he rejected, telling Stalin of the offer. According to Anton Antonov-Ovseyenko, Kirov told Stalin: 'You yourself are to blame for what happened. After all, we told you things couldn't be done in such a drastic way.' The voting for membership of the Central Committee confirmed that Congress generally saw Kirov as an alternative to Stalin. Only 3 votes were cast against Kirov, while 292 were cast against Stalin. The pro-Stalin elections chairman asked Kaganovich what to do; the loyal Kaganovich ordered him to destroy 289 ballot papers so there were only 3 votes against both Stalin and Kirov. According to Antonov-Ovseyenko, Kirov predicted his own doom, warning friends that his head was now on the block.

Fig. 3 *Kirov and Stalin*

Key profile

Lazar Kaganovich

Lazar Kaganovich (1893–1991) was a Ukrainian Jew who joined the Bolsheviks in 1911. He supported Stalin during the power struggle and was made a member of the Politburo in 1930. He was given responsibility for transport and heavy industry, and supported the purges wholeheartedly, allowing his brother to be arrested during the Second World War.

Kirov's assassination gave Stalin the opportunity to crush both alternative ideas and the people who were putting them forward. On the same day, Stalin issued the Emergency Decree Against Terrorism, which gave the **NKVD** the power to arrest, question, torture and execute without trial anyone suspected of terrorist activities.

A closer look

The activities of the NKVD

The main job of the secret police is to round up people who are looked on with disfavour by the Government. There are of course a certain amount of what we would call criminals, but the great bulk are so-called political prisoners.

Political prisoners are of various sorts. The rich peasant or kulak was of course a criminal because he was better off and harder working than his neighbours. Anyone who was unfortunate enough to be the child of a former landed gentleman, a merchant, an officer etc. became of course a class prisoner. Any peasant who refused to be collectivised, and, to avoid that, destroyed his live stock, and numerous other classes became 'political prisoners' and were sent off by tens of thousands to work in the great timber districts in the North.

I mentioned before the shortage of engineers and technicians in the country. Bearing that in mind, the secret police got a brain wave. It brought charges against the best engineers, technicians etc. of 'wrecking' machinery and other such anti-State activity.

Those engineers etc. became NKVD prisoners. Having thus secured a supply of good engineers, the NKVD let it be known that it was willing to draw up plans, estimates etc. for new works, buildings etc. at the ordinary fees. The NKVD pocketed the fees, and the arrested engineers drew up the plans, so it was quite a profitable show for the NKVD.

That having been so profitable, and bearing in mind the huge amounts of prisoners of all sorts it had – that would provide unpaid labour – some genius thought – why not take up big contracts, the engineers to draw up the plans and supervise, and the prisoners to do the work.

Activity

Challenge your thinking

Historians still debate whether Stalin ordered the execution of Kirov.

1. Read Chapter 4 of Anton Antonov-Ovseyenko's, *The Time of Stalin: Portrait of Tyranny*, 1981, for evidence that Stalin was behind the murder.

2. Counter this by reading the appendix of J. Arch Getty's, *Origins of the Great Purges*, 1985, which argues that Stalin was not behind the murder.

3. Compare the evidence the two historians use. Which argument do you find the most convincing?

Key term

NKVD: Stalin's secret police. The GPU had been replaced by the OGPU in 1923 and the NKVD in 1934. Genrikh Yagoda was the head of the NKVD from 1934 until his replacement in 1936 by Nikolai Yezhov, who was replaced himself in 1938 by Lavrenti Beria. Both Yagoda and Yezhov were themselves victims of Stalin. Beria survived Stalin but was arrested almost immediately after his death.

Accordingly, the NKVD was 'entrusted' with constructing that huge and most-important strategic work, the construction of the Baltic–White Sea canal, to enable warships to get from the Baltic into the White Sea.

The plans were prepared and tens of thousands of prisoners were turned on to the work. They were kept at it day and night and all the year round, although the canal was being built in a most appalling climate.

The canal was finished in fabulously quick time. When it was finished huge numbers of words were written in the Soviet papers about the NKVD as the saviour and reformer by kind methods of the 'criminal classes'. The kind NKVD had allowed those misguided criminals to regain their souls and become decent people again by permitting them to join in helping improve the welfare of their country. No mention was made of the awful death-roll that occurred.

This experiment was so successful, that it was felt that, when important strategic work was required to be done in a hurry, quite the best thing was to allow the NKVD to help some more of the criminal classes to repent of their errors.

3

Extract from a report by M. MacKillop to the British Foreign Office, May 1936

Initially, known opponents of the regime in Moscow and Leningrad were arrested; Zinoviev and Kamenev were accused of being part of the conspiracy and tried in secret for moral complicity in the murder. Both were sentenced to five years' imprisonment. Eighteen months later they were put on trial in the first Show Trial, charged with collaborating with Trotsky and conspiring to murder Kirov. They were found guilty and executed. The Show Trials enabled Stalin to publicly destroy those who offered alternative ideas. Conspiracy with the exiled Trotsky was a favourite accusation, and Trotsky's assassination by Stalin's agent Ramon Mercader in Mexico in 1940 meant that only Stalin remained alive from Lenin's first Soviet government of 1917. Stalin had ensured there was no political diversity.

Stalin had also taken revenge on the Congress of Victors, which had preferred Kirov. In all, 98 out of the 139 members of the Central Committee elected at the 17th Party Congress were executed, along with 1,108 of the 1,996 delegates who had attended. In addition, the regional communist parties were purged. Beria arrested 30,000 officials and executed 10,000 in Georgia between 1936 and 1938, including two State prime ministers. All the Ukrainian Politburo members were arrested. Finally, the armed forces were purged, with three out of five marshals of the Soviet Union executed. Around half the Officer Corp was arrested, with 5,000 being executed, although 30,000 were released following the disastrous Winter War with Finland. These purges ensured that Stalin's political power could not be challenged, but Stalin also saw them as destroying those who stood for a different set of ideas, as the murder of Tukhachevsky makes clear. Like the other two marshals executed, he had worked with Trotsky in the Civil War. The scale of repression during the purges is still not clear. Today, the KGB admits that 681,192 political executions took place. An estimated 1 in 3 Leningrad citizens were arrested and 1 in 18 of the population overall. By 1941, the Gulags

■ **Exploring the detail**

The Show Trials

The Show Trials were public trials of leading Bolsheviks. In total, 53 Old Bolsheviks (who had joined the party before the revolution) were tried and executed. Zinoviev and Kamenev were the leading figures prosecuted in 1936, followed by Pyatakov and Radek in 1937 and Bukharin, Rykov and Yagoda in 1938. Tomsky 'cheated' Stalin by committing suicide. The 'trials' consisted of accusations and confessions, which were essential to convince the population that if Old Bolsheviks were plotting against the State, enemies could be everywhere and that therefore everyone should be permanently vigilant.

(the labour camp system) contained an estimated 8 million prisoners serving an average sentence of 10 years. The prisoners were mainly purged party members. The harshness of conditions in the camps ensured very high levels of mortality.

■ Key profile

Mikhail Tukhachevsky

Mikhail Tukhachevsky (1893–1937) was the most talented of Stalin's generals, who made his reputation during the Civil War and particularly the Russo–Polish War of 1920–1. He was made Marshal of the Soviet Union in 1935. Stalin was jealous of his status and feared he could use the Red Army to depose him. Tukhachevsky was arrested in 1937 on bogus charges of plotting with the Japanese and Germans, although it has been suggested by the historian Vladimir Rogovin that he was genuinely plotting to remove Stalin.

Stalin's motives for the Great Purge have been debated. Historians like Robert Conquest have argued that Stalin carried out the purges to explicitly destroy potential opposition. His vengeance on those who had opposed him in the 1920s and at the 1934 Congress of Victors was responsible for the destruction of the party. Stalin was realistic enough to recognise the threat to the Soviet Union from the West or, increasingly, Nazi Germany, and was therefore making sure that there would be no rival leader to challenge him if the anticipated war was as disastrous as the First World War; he was not playing the part of the Tsar in the sequel. Yagoda was replaced by Yezhov, who was charged with the instigation of the Great Purge. The impact of the Great Purge was to transform the party from one consisting of 55 year olds who were old comrades of Lenin and lacked the necessary respect for Stalin, to a new generation of 35 year olds who understood that obedience to Stalin was all. For this reason, terror was a systematic part of Stalin's rule, designed to crush all opposition and diversity. In July 1937, the NKVD set targets for arrests and executions by region; 72,500 were to be executed and 177,500 arrested. Truth and lies, innocence and guilt ceased to have any meaning as obedience became all. The destruction of Bukharin makes this clear. During the confessions of Zinoviev and Kamenev at their Show Trial, both Bolsheviks had admitted that they were part of a wider conspiracy against the party. Bukharin had been questioned about this involvement with oppositionists but his protestations of innocence were accepted and he was told that the investigation was to be discontinued. However, in December 1936 the investigation was renewed. On 4 December 1936, he gave a speech to the Central Committee which developed into accusations and questioning. Bukharin asked why he had been released if he was considered to have been involved. Kaganovich replied, 'We were referring to the legal aspect of the matter. It's one thing to speak of legal matters, quite another to speak of political matters.' Bukharin may therefore have been innocent of the specific charges but he was guilty of crimes against the party, in that he was not supporting the party line that all oppositionists should be destroyed. By refusing to fully cooperate in the murder of former colleagues, Bukharin was failing to act in the best interests of the party. Stalin sat and listened to the evidence; his interjections in proceedings were to make jokes. The Great Purge was therefore part of a process of crushing not just opposition but also concepts like truth, evidence and reality.

Activity

Challenge your thinking

Review the evidence in this chapter.

1 Which interpretation of the purges do you find the most convincing? Explain why.

2 Consider the question of Soviet totalitarianism. How does your answer to Question 1 influence your understanding of how totalitarian the Soviet Union was under Stalin in the 1930s?

This view has been challenged by historians like J. Arch Getty and Robert Thurston, who have argued that the purges were the result of complex social and economic circumstances. Stalin was reacting to circumstances: he feared for his own life after the assassination of Kirov and gave the NKVD greater powers to protect the party leadership. To justify these powers, the NKVD found conspiracies and those arrested then provided more information (under torture) that drove the process on. The replacement of Yagoda with Yezhov was not part of a decision to act against the party. Instead, it followed an explosion at a mining complex in Siberia; Yagoda had failed to prevent an act of terrorism and Yezhov was known to excel at ferreting out conspirators. Industrial managers were informed on by workers who were frustrated by the lack of raw materials that hindered their ability to exceed individual targets and gain the status of *Stakhanovite* – elite workers who received higher wages and other privileges. Gulags were responsible for 10–15 per cent of Soviet GNP by 1939 and therefore the economy relied on purging. Individuals also took the opportunity to settle scores and remove rivals for jobs and sexual partners. The lover of the wife of the head of the Leningrad NKVD, Filip Medved, unsurprisingly found himself sent to a labour camp. The NKVD targets demonstrated lack of control, for it is a grim irony that this target is one of the few that the Soviet Union succeeded in overfulfiling. The purges had snowballed out of Stalin's control. Bukharin was destroyed by his rivals for Stalin's patronage. His failure to play the game made it impossible for Stalin to defend him, although it was suggested in a contemporary play that Stalin sent Bukharin to Paris in 1936 to give him a chance to defect and save himself.

Religious intolerance

Marx saw religion as an error, as it was a false understanding of the world. There was nothing beyond the material world that could be seen and felt. He thought that the revolution would come in its own good time and that religion would eventually wither away. Lenin was much more actively opposed to religion. As he had forced revolution on a country that had not yet passed through the necessary stages that Marx had identified, he saw getting rid of religion as a matter of great urgency. Lenin began his attacks on the Church in the spring of 1918. Leaders of the Orthodox Church were murdered, often quite brutally: the Metropolitan Vladimir of Kiev was mutilated, castrated and shot, and his stripped corpse put on public display; Archbishop Vasily was crucified and burned. Acts of terror were commonplace against priests, monks and nuns who were crucified, forced to drink molten lead from the Communion chalice or drowned in holes in ice. Lenin commanded the Cheka to shoot those who failed to attend work because they were observing a religious holiday. In 1922, the 80,000 Orthodox churches were stripped of their gold, silver and jewels, and ancient books and bibles were burnt.

In the 1920s, the NEP brought some religious toleration, but the 'second revolution' of industrialisation and collectivisation led to renewed attacks on the Church. Industrialisation was a new secular faith, as Lev Kopelev describes in Source 1 on page 33. Meanwhile, the full flowering of totalitarianism was taking place under Stalin and the Bolshevik Party was committed to destroying organised religion and religious beliefs, as no alternative to the one true set of ideas could be allowed. The creation of collective farms saw churches turned into grain stores as part of a deliberate attempt to break the grip of religion in the countryside. The attack on the Catholic Church in Ukraine was also

Exploring the detail

Religion in the Soviet Union

The Soviet Union contained a range of different religious faiths. The religion of the ethnic Russians was Greek Orthodoxy, the eastern European branch of Christianity. The Orthodox Church had been an unswerving supporter of the Tsar and was therefore seen as the enemy of the Bolshevik Revolution. Ukraine was Catholic in faith whereas the Asian republics were mainly Muslim. There was still a sizeable Jewish minority in the Soviet Union, although many Jews had fled from Russia to the West following the Bolshevik Revolution. Leningrad and many other large cities contained all of these faiths and churches, as well as a wide range of other more minority religions.

part of the drive to bring the republic under control. A new law passed in 1929 made it illegal to engage in religious activity outside churches and only officially licensed congregations were permitted to meet. The League of the Godless, established in 1925, saw its membership grow to 1 million in 1929. The Muslims of the Soviet Union were so harshly treated that by 1930 it was reported to the Central Committee that Islam in the Soviet Union was on the verge of complete destruction and disappearance off the face of the Earth. It was estimated that 10,000 out of 12,000 mosques had been closed. In the Muslim Asian republics, religious leaders were accused of working with kulaks to resist the regime and were treated accordingly.

Even so, in April 1931 a British diplomat in Leningrad, Reader Bullard, wrote in his diary that the churches in the city were 'crammed' for the Russian Easter. This could not continue and the 1930s saw churches destroyed and anti-religious propaganda. Children were indoctrinated with a vicious contempt for priests. Anti-religious museums were opened in churches, containing artistic works showing the corruption of priests as well as scenes of poverty in cities in religious countries such as London in Britain. Churches were subject to oppressive levels of taxation and the government then seized the church when these debts could not be paid. All but 87 of Moscow's 500 Orthodox churches were closed. The Cathedral of Christ the Saviour in Moscow was destroyed to make way for the new Palace of the Soviets, and the Archbishop's Palace at Novgorod became a rest home for scientists. In July 1937, Yezhov identified categories of people who were carrying out anti-Soviet activities and set quotas for arrest and execution by region. Prominent on his list were the clergy. As a result, between 1937 and 1939 105,200 Orthodox priests were executed and a further 87,500 arrested. By 1939, only about 100 churches remained open and only 12 out of 163 bishops survived. Many Jewish members of the party were subject to denouncement during the purges because of their religion. As early as 1934, Bullard was recording that there was only one Catholic priest in Leningrad for 36,000 Catholics. Despite this, in the census of 1937, 57 per cent of the population described themselves as having a religion. The militant atheism that the Bolsheviks preached could not break the traditional superstition and popular religion. After the Nazi invasion in June 1941, Stalin reopened churches and used religion as a unifying factor to mobilise support for the Bolshevik regime.

Cultural diversity

Control of the press and the arts ensured that only the official doctrine would be communicated to the people. *Pravda* and *Izvestiya* were the two main newspapers, responsible for printing the party message.

> Following the Soviet press, one finds it extraordinarily difficult to try and judge how things really are going on. The papers are of course controlled and the Bolshevik Government are firmly convinced that they have created heaven on earth, so all their geese are swans, and are written up as swans.

4
Extract from a report by M. MacKillop to the British Foreign Office, May 1936

Radio stations were controlled by the state. A new artistic style was officially prescribed called 'Socialist Realism'. This style had to be followed

Fig. 4 *Examples of Socialist Realism: (top) Red Army Parade after the painting by Konstantin Yuon, 1923; (bottom) a Russian collectivised peasant in the 1930s*

in all forms of creative work. The Union of Soviet Writers was established in 1932 and novels that did not conform to the official style were not published. Artistic and intellectual freedom was therefore destroyed, being replaced with poor quality works. *How the Steel was Tempered*, the autobiographical novel by Nikolai Ostrovsky, was a typical example. Published in 1934, it told the story of Pavel Korchagin, a party member with a peasant background who struggled to become a writer and teacher. Along the way, he chose the party over his first love, middle-class Tonya Tumanova, whom he considered to be guilty of cheap individualism. The novel was adopted as a school text in 1935 and sold 5 million copies over 10 years.

In a country where the population was overwhelmingly illiterate, cinema was of even greater significance to the Bolsheviks. Lenin recognised this, remarking to the People's Commissar for Enlightenment, Anatoli Lunacharsky, that 'Of all the arts, for us cinema is the most important.' The 1920s, however, did see creativity, like the work of Sergei Eisenstein, although when *Potemkin* was premiered in 1926 it lasted only two weeks before its replacement by Douglas Fairbanks in *Robin Hood*. Stalin was not prepared to allow this pandering to popular taste. In 1930, cinema was reorganised and films were expected to follow socialist realistic themes, with the threat of exile and death for those who made errors. Many directors like Eisenstein stopped making films. Foreign films were no longer imported. *Chapyev*, released in 1934, was a particularly successful film, attracting audiences as well as stressing the correctness of the Bolshevik Revolution and the moral correctness of the Bolshevik victory in the Civil War during which the film was set. The most popular film of the 1930s was *The Happy Guys*, also released in 1934, which was a musical comedy that helped generate a feel-good factor. Stalin himself took a close interest in the cinema and approved scripts. The 1936 release *Circus* featured a song with the lines 'I know of no other country/Where a man so freely breathes'. Later in the 1930s, as war appeared likely, films like *Alexander Nevsky* (1938) were made which celebrated the medieval victory of the Russians over the Teutonic knights from Germany. The message was essential and had to be spread. By 1940, there were 28,000 cinemas in the Soviet Union.

Soviet children were controlled through education and party youth organisations: the Pioneers for under 14s and Komosomol for those aged 14–28. Komosomol's membership was 10.2 million by 1940. Compulsory primary education was introduced in 1930 and by 1941 there were 35 million children in schools. At the time of the Bolshevik Revolution, it was estimated that as few as 25 per cent of the population could read. As a result of educational changes, the Soviet press claimed that there was a 90 per cent literacy level, although literacy was defined as being able to write your name. In the mid-1930s, it was not unusual for a school of 250 children to have just a single textbook, which was kept locked up by the teacher. There was a shortage of pencils and, although pens were in greater supply, there was no ink. In country districts, teachers were regarded as 'bourgeois' because they were not occupied in manual labour and therefore the village council gave them virtually no rations and delayed paying their salaries. Inevitably there was a shortage of teachers in village schools and therefore the effectiveness of education was reduced.

Under Lenin, more tolerant attitudes had developed towards Russian women, and women in Lenin's Russia enjoyed genuine equality and freedoms such as being able to obtain an abortion or divorce their husband. The 1936 Constitution guaranteed their social and political rights and gave the impression that they were the most liberated women

Fig. 5 *A still from the film* Alexander Nevsky *by Sergie Eisenstein, 1938. This historical drama was both a popular story and a reminder to the Russian people that German invasion was likely*

in the world. However, the position of women in Russia had actually changed drastically under Stalin. The women's section of the party was shut down by Stalin in 1930, a clear statement that he saw politics as a male sphere of life. Stalin wanted to increase the birth rate and so, in 1936, abortion was made illegal except on medical grounds. The mother became a symbol of stability in Soviet Russia. Medals were given to mothers of large families, with mothers of 5 children receiving a 'medal of motherhood' and mothers of 10 children becoming 'mother heroine of the Soviet Union'. The sexual freedom of the 1920s also disappeared in the 1930s, with contraception no longer available, prostitution condemned and homosexuality made illegal in 1934. Despite these measures, the birth rate failed to increase in the 1930s. This was partly explained by Stalin's view that women represented a mass of cheap labour. By 1939, 5 million Soviet women were working on building sites and between 1928 and 1940 the numbers of women employed rose from 3 million to 13 million. They were paid less than men and frequently found themselves forced to take dangerous and physically hard jobs in heavy industry and the chemical industry.

Activity

Source analysis

Study the text on cultural diversity and Figure 4.

1 What do you think are the main features of Socialist Realism?

2 Why do you think Stalin sought to control artistic style?

3 Why do you think the film *Circus* contained a song with the lines quoted above?

Activity

Challenge your thinking

Study the text on pages 42 and 43.

1 Why do you think Stalin restored traditional values in the Soviet Union in the 1930s?

2 What was the purpose of Soviet education? Did it achieve its purpose?

The treatment of national minorities reveals Stalin's intolerance of ethnic diversity. He had argued with Lenin and the Party Congress as early as 1923 over the position of the non-Russian people. Stalin felt that ethnic differences were the greatest threat to socialist unity. Once 'Red Tsar', he put this into practice with the purges of non-Russian Bolsheviks in the republics to ensure the regions were loyal to Moscow and Bolshevism and not to their own ethnic group. The excessive grain collections from

Cross-reference

The **grain collections** from Ukraine are discussed on page 34.

Ukraine were deliberate measures to destroy the resistance of a region whose loyalty Stalin suspected. Great Russian heroes like Ivan the Terrible and Peter the Great were celebrated whereas statues to national heroes in the republics were pulled down.

Limits to intolerance

It would appear that Stalin was successful in creating a totalitarian State because the intolerance of diversity was absolute. However, there were limits to the intolerance of diversity, which were forced on Stalin by circumstance.

■ **Activity**

Using the evidence on pages 31–44, identify examples of diversity that suggest there were limits to Stalin's totalitarianism.

■ Marxist theories of leadership and the cult of Stalin

The cult of personality

The worship of the leader, or the cult of personality was a key feature of the Soviet Union from 1929. Reverence for leading members of the party was not new. Lenin himself had always rejected any hero worship, complaining once about how he hated reading about himself in the papers: 'Wherever you look they write about me. I consider this un-Marxist emphasis on an individual extremely harmful. It is bad and harmful.' On his death, however, he had become an even greater symbol of Bolshevism than he had been alive. His body was embalmed and placed in a mausoleum in Red Square, to be visited by millions of Soviet citizens and foreign visitors each year. The funeral oration given by Stalin also played a key role in deifying Lenin.

■ **Key profile**

Vyacheslav Molotov

Vyacheslav Molotov (1890–1986) joined the Bolsheviks in 1906. He became a full member of the Politburo in 1926 as a consistent supporter of Stalin throughout the power struggles of the 1920s. He was rewarded with the post of prime minister in 1930. Effectively Stalin's number two, Molotov co-signed death lists with Stalin. He raised no objection to the arrest and imprisonment of his own wife in 1949 but, despite his loyalty to Stalin, it is likely that only Stalin's own death saved Molotov from the fate he had consigned so many others to in the 1930s.

■ **Activity**

Source analysis

Study Source 5.

1 How does Stalin give the impression that Lenin was a god-like figure?

2 How do you think this speech linked Stalin to Lenin?

In leaving us, comrade Lenin commended to us to hold high and pure the great calling of the Party Member. We swear to thee, Comrade Lenin, to honour thy command.

In leaving us, Comrade Lenin commanded us to keep the unity of the party as the apple of our eye. We swear to thee, Comrade Lenin, to honour thy command.

In leaving us, Comrade Lenin ordered us to maintain and strengthen the dictatorship of the proletariat. We swear to thee, Comrade Lenin, to exert our full strength in honouring thy command.

5   *Extract from Stalin's funeral oration*

Stalin was already referred to as *Vozhd* by those who worked with him within the party secretariat. When these allies of Stalin used the term, it meant 'the boss', referring to Stalin's position as General Secretary as well as his control over appointments within the party. *Pravda* started to push the use of the name nationally from 1929, where it also became synonymous with 'leader'. In 1925, Petrograd was renamed Leningrad in deference to the dead founder of Bolshevism. Other leaders, like Kirov and Molotov, were recognised in the same way. Stalin's contribution to the Soviet State was also recognised: the city of Tsaritsyn was renamed Stalingrad in 1925, and Stalinsk and Stalinabad also appeared on the map. After Stalin's victory in the power struggle, he no longer had to take joint billing with other leading Bolsheviks. *Pravda* began to systematically develop the cult of Stalin when it devoted the entire edition of 29 December 1929 to him. Articles, letters, poems and pictures all praised the 'Lenin of today' who was now guiding the USSR to the Utopian future.

Excessive praise of Stalin became the norm over the next 24 years. He acquired the status of living God in the USSR. He was considered to be capable of doing no wrong, to be all-seeing, all-knowing and all-powerful, constantly acting in the best interests of the Soviet people. Source 6 is typical of the way in which Stalin was viewed by the Russian people.

> J. V. Stalin is the genius, the leader and teacher of the Party, the great strategist of socialist revolution, helmsman of the Soviet State and captain of armies ...
>
> Everyone is familiar with the cogent and invincible force of Stalin's logic, the crystal clarity of his mind, his iron will, his devotion to the Party, his ardent faith in the people, and love for the people. Everybody is familiar with his modesty, his simplicity of manner, his consideration for people, and his merciless severity towards enemies of the people ...
>
> Stalin is the worthy continuer of the cause of Lenin, or as it is said in the Party: Stalin is the Lenin of today.

| 6 | *Adapted from A. Alexandrov et al.,* ***Stalin: A Short Biography***, *1947* |

■ **Activity**

Source analysis

Study Source 6. How does Alexandrov's use of language create the cult?

(Hint: look at individual words he uses and their meanings and connotations.)

Key themes of the cult of Stalin

The expression of the cult of Stalin's personality can be found in a wide range of media, from naming more than 30 towns and cities after him to poetry, literature, paintings, posters and statues. When he attended the Bolshoi Ballet in 1934, *Pravda* reported: 'The appearance of the ardently loved *Vozhd*, whose name is linked inseparably with all the victories scored by the proletariat, by the Soviet Union, was greeted with tumultuous ovations' and 'no end of cries of "Hurrah" and "Long live our Stalin!"'

Why did the cult of Stalin develop?

> The Russian people is really a tsaristic people. It needs a tsar.

Stalin's comment to his brother-in-law gives us a clear insight into one of the key reasons for the development of the cult, but there were a range of reasons behind the development of such an all encompassing cult:

 There was a psychological need for a single leader to follow and worship. The tsars had been considered to be the 'little father' (*batyushka*) of the Russian people. As God's representative on Earth, they embodied all that was holy and omnipotent and were worshipped as such. The typical Russian peasants' home would contain a cross

■ **Activity**

Study the section on the cult of Stalin and Figure 6. What roles is Stalin presented as fulfilling in the USSR?

The cult of Stalin

Fig. 6 *The cult of Stalin*

and a cheap icon of the tsar, symbols of the two pillars of faith. The Russian peasantry now transferred their allegiance to a new 'little father', with a picture of Stalin replacing the tsar and the cross. It mattered little that the Bolsheviks and Stalin were responsible for the murder of the last tsar and had banned the Orthodox Church.

■ Stalin himself played a key role in creating his own cult by deifying Lenin. Lenin too had filled the crucial psychological role of guide and leader for the Russian people, in spite of his hatred for such veneration. As we have seen in Source 5, Stalin directly linked himself to Lenin. The 'Lenin of today' therefore benefited from the cult of Lenin.

■ The psychology of adulation is also complex. It is possible that, as the cult grew, it became more difficult to resist as the average Soviet citizen wished to behave in the same way as their neighbours and to take part in the same mass activities. It is also likely that, once people had invested their emotions and commitment in Stalin, they did not want to have to face up to the reality of him as it would mean their worship had been meaningless.

■ Soviet propaganda played a crucial role in creating the cult, from the gigantic busts and portraits of Stalin at every corner and every crossroads to speeches on artistic and scientific subjects which were also peppered with the glorification of Stalin. All the examples of Soviet propaganda on page 42 were typical of the way the cult was created and maintained.

■ Stalin clearly benefited from the cult. He could impose his views and demand absolute submission without having to argue a case because he was the *batyushka* and therefore his word was law. This suited him psychologically as he could not personally accept any criticism. Stalin had demanded the death penalty for Ryutin and his family in 1932 after Ryutin's public criticism of Stalin.

■ It was easier to follow an individual than a set of ideas. The complexities of Marxism and the Soviet version of Marxist–Leninism required the cult. It was not easy to explain to the uneducated masses the rationale for government decisions, particularly when they contradicted previous policies. The masses accepted policies because Stalin said they were a good idea and he knew best, particularly valuable when the Nazi–Soviet Pact was signed and then the Germans invaded 22 months later.

■ Although many Soviet citizens suffered during the 1930s, millions were also grateful to Comrade Stalin. Famine devastated Ukraine and the purges traumatised millions, but they disproportionately affected Leningrad, the party and those in 'bourgeois' professions. *Pravda* stressed that 'life was getting more joyous' and living standards made some improvements. The Soviet people had to have someone to express their thanks to for the material improvements in their lives and the successes of the regime, and they wanted to thank a real person rather than an abstract concept. The people were grateful for the end to rationing in 1935, for the order in their lives, for their education, for the systematic unmasking of the enemies of the people discovered during the purges and for the victory in the Great Patriotic War. Furthermore, each of these successes reinforced the genius of Stalin.

Marxist theories of leadership and limits to the cult

Despite the universal praise that Stalin received, he himself often rallied against it, writing a strong rebuttal in response to a letter of praise from a party member in 1934 (Source 7).

You speak about your devotion to me. Maybe the phrase just slipped out. Maybe … But if it didn't just slip out, I would advise you to discard the principle of devotion to individuals. It is not the Bolshevik way. Be devoted to the working class, to its party, its State. That is what is needed and what is good. But don't get mixed up with devotion to people, which is just an empty and superfluous fad of intellectuals.

 7

Extract from a letter from Stalin to a Bolshevik Party member, 1930

It is difficult to believe Stalin's words given the extent of worship that took place. If he objected to the cult, it seems logical that he would have used his tremendous power to bring it under control. However, his daughter, Svetlana Alliluyeva, believed Stalin himself was a prisoner of the system: the party and the country needed Stalin to worship, regardless of whether he wanted to be worshipped. She claimed her father despised the cult as hypocrisy, remembering him twitching with annoyance and complaining with angry contempt that 'they open their mouths and yell like fools' when they shouted slogans. She has written that she was 'horribly embarrassed' by the cult and that she always feared Stalin would explode and say something inappropriate.

Ideologically, there was also a key limitation to the cult, as Stalin himself indicates in Source 7. The cult was totally contrary to Marxism. Marx anticipated the stage of Socialism beginning with the dictatorship of the proletariat, with the most advanced sections of the working class ruling in the interests of all the workers. The rule of an individual was therefore wholly incompatible with Marxism. Lenin had adapted Marxism, with the party replacing the working class as the group who took power, but there was still no place for the rule of the individual and therefore the worship of the leader in Marxist–Leninist ideology. Lenin had never taken the title of 'leader' and had advocated a collective leadership for the USSR in his Political Testament. Stalin's cult was therefore always moderated by the continuing reverence for Lenin and the proletariat in the USSR.

Learning outcomes

Through your study of this section you should be in a position to assess the importance of Marxist ideology to the Bolshevik Revolution and to assess the extent to which the Soviet Union was a Marxist State. You should understand the events of the power struggle to succeed Lenin and be able to reach a judgement on why Stalin emerged victorious. You should have an understanding of how Stalin's victory affected Soviet ideology and begin to consider how Stalin might have had an impact on the development of Soviet totalitarianism in the 1930s.

You should be in a position to assess why the cult of personality developed in the Soviet Union and understand how far it was consistent with Marxist ideology. You should be aware of the limits to the cult. You should understand the extent to which the economic, political, religious and social events of the 1930s demonstrate that the Soviet Union was intolerant of diversity. You should be aware of the reasons for the intolerance of diversity, as well as recognising the limits to intolerance. Consideration of both the cult of personality and the intolerance of diversity should help you to reach a judgement on how totalitarian the Soviet Union was in the 1930s.

Cross-reference

Lenin's Political Testament is discussed on page 18.

Questions

1 How and why did Stalin create the cult of Lenin?

2 How far was Stalin responsible for creating his own cult?

3 Why was the cult incompatible with Bolshevik ideology?

4 Why do you think the cult was an essential part of totalitarianism?

Practice questions

(a)   Explain why Stalin did not allow cultural diversity.   *(12 marks)*

Study tip It is important that you avoid describing examples of the intolerance of cultural diversity. You need to focus on those general reasons for the intolerance of diversity that also apply to cultural diversity. You should also consider if there were any particular reasons why freedom of cultural expression was not allowed. Think of the significance of cinema, the press, education and youth organisations. Remember that you need to think about the relative importance of the reasons you have found. You could also demonstrate the high level skill of judgement by showing you understand how these reasons link together, for example the influence of Stalin's personality as well as Bolshevik ideology.

(b)   'Stalin's cult of personality was the result of the people's desire for a leader to worship.' How far do you agree or disagree with this statement?   *(24 marks)*

Study tip The question is asking you to consider the reasons for the development of the cult of personality, so review pages 44–48. Remember that you will get few marks for describing examples of the cult. In planning your answer, you need to ensure that you consider both the reason suggested in the question as well as other possible reasons. After you have identified all the reasons you will cover, consider which reason was the most significant. It might help you to think about whether you see Stalin as all-powerful or someone who lacked control over various aspects of the Soviet system. If you see him as all-powerful, you will probably argue that Stalin created the cult for the benefits it brought; if you see him as less in control of events, you might argue that it was the people's desire for a leader to worship that was significant. What evidence from this chapter could you use to suggest that Stalin did not create the cult?

3 Fascist ideology and the establishment of the first Fascist State

Fig. 1 *The respectable fascist. Mussolini leading a Fascist march in 1921, dressed as an Italian gentleman to reassure the property-owning classes*

In this chapter you will learn about:

- the circumstances that led to the development of fascist ideas
- the ways in which fascist ideology changed between 1919 and 1939 and why these changes took place
- the central features of fascist ideology
- whether Fascism is revolutionary or reactionary
- the reasons for the rise of Fascism, including the attraction of fascist ideology, the role of Mussolini, the weakness of Liberal Italy post-war and the fear of Communism
- the establishment of the one-party state.

■ Fascist ideology

The fascist takeover of Italy began on 29 October 1922 when King Victor Emmanuel III offered Benito Mussolini the post of prime minister. The success of Mussolini could not have been easily anticipated. In the elections of 1921, Mussolini's Italian Fascist Party had won only 35 seats in the Italian parliament. Mussolini's successful accession to power was followed by the establishment of a one-party state, the creation of the cult of Il Duce ('the Chief') and a policy of the intolerance of diversity.

Underpinning these actions was the totalitarian ideology of Fascism. We have seen that in the Soviet Union there was conflict between the ideas of Karl Marx and the practical considerations that meant that Lenin and Stalin had to adapt these ideas. In Italy, there was no such 'bible' of fascist ideology. Fascist ideology changed frequently, with the theoretical statements of Fascism being written after Mussolini had been in power for several years. This has led the historian Denis Mack Smith to argue that 'Fascism was not a system of immutable [unchanging] beliefs, but a path to political power.'

Benito Mussolini

Benito Mussolini (1883–1945) was born in the hamlet of Verano di Costa in the Romagna region of central Italy, the son of a blacksmith. He was a journalist and revolutionary socialist before the First World War. He was expelled from the Italian Socialist Party because he favoured Italy joining the First World War. He founded his own newspaper and, after war service, the political movement of Fascism. He was appointed prime minister in October 1922 and established a one-party state in Italy, which he described as 'totalitarian'. He led Italy into the Second World War in 1940. He was deposed in 1943 but rescued by SS paratroopers, ruling the Nazi puppet State – the Republic of Salo – until 1945, when it collapsed. Mussolini was hung by Italian communists.

Fig. 2 *Mussolini*

The development of fascist ideas

The First World War was the key event of the 20th century. It destroyed the Russian, German, Austro-Hungarian and Turkish empires, and saw them replaced by parliamentary democracies that could not cope with the post-war challenges, in particular the social and economic problems. It also created resentment at the way in which the world was reordered in many countries. Finally, it left millions of ex-servicemen, brutalised by war but with no role or security in the peacetime world. All of these circumstances were critical to the development of fascist ideology in Italy. In addition, the war was responsible for the establishment of the world's first communist regime in the Soviet Union, and the reaction to Communism was also a critical component in the development of Fascism.

Although Fascism drew on many 19th century ideas, Mussolini was the father of fascist ideas. Originally a revolutionary Socialist, he was appointed editor of the socialist newspaper *Avanti* ('forward') in November 1912, and he unsuccessfully stood for election in the 1913 national election. The war was central to the development of Mussolini's political ideas. He argued in favour of Italian entry into the war, as a result of which he was expelled from the Socialist Party. Mussolini founded a new newspaper, *Il Popolo d'Italia* ('the People of Italy'), which backed Italian involvement in the war. He was called up and fought in the Italian army before being invalided out following serious injury in a training accident with a grenade-throwing machine in 1917. Mussolini founded the Fasci di Combattimento ('League of Combat') at the Piazza San Sepolcro in Milan in March 1919, in front of a crowd of 118 war veterans and former socialists. Other *fasci* soon spread to about 70 cities and towns, with local organisations and local programmes.

Italian Fascism and Mussolini's rise to power

1883	Birth of Mussolini.
1912	Mussolini becomes editor of *Avanti*.
1914	Mussolini leaves *Avanti* and founds *Il Popolo d'Italia*.
1915	Italy enters the First World War; Mussolini conscripted.
1917	Humiliating defeat at Caporetto.
1918	Victory at Vittorio Veneto.
1919 March	Mussolini forms the Fasci di Combattimento.
1919 September	D'Annunzio seizes Fiume.
1919 November	Fascists fail to win any seats in the election.
1920	Fascism starts to win support across the Po valley and northern regions.
1920 August	Strikes in northern cities; climax of *biennio rosso*.
1921 May	Fascists win 35 seats in the election.
1921 November	PNF founded by Mussolini.
1922 August	General Strike crushed by Blackshirts.
1922 October	March on Rome; Mussolini appointed prime minister.

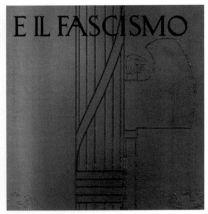

Fig. 3 *The Fascist Party took its name from the symbol of the party, the Fasces. This was a bundle of rods and an axe, bound together, which were carried before a judge in Ancient Rome to show his power to punish*

■ **Activity**

Source analysis

Study Figure 3. What message do you think the fascist symbol was meant to convey?

■ **Key term**

Liberal Italy: the name given to the kingdom of Italy after it was created in 1861. The new State was a constitutional monarchy. The dominant force in the new State were the Liberals. They wished to break down Italian regionalism, modernise the backward Italian economy and reduce the influence of the Catholic Church. These measures would end poverty and create a State that was unified in practice as well as theory.

■ **Activity**

Source analysis

Study Sources 1 and 2.

1 What do these two speeches tell us about the methods of Fascism?

2 What does Source 2 tell us about why fascists hated communists?

The political programme of the national movement of fascists shared many features with both the new Italian Socialist Party (PSI) and the Italian Popular Party (PPI): they were all republican and nationalist, and showed a concern for better welfare provision for Italian people. The Fascist Party aimed to win support from ex-First World War soldiers and the working class. However, as there was little that was distinctive about their programme, the Fascists were defeated in the November 1919 national elections, failing to attract significant support; even in Milan where the party had been founded, Mussolini polled less than 2 per cent of the vote. The most defining feature of Fascism seemed to be what it was against: trades unions and the PSI, as well as capitalism and big business, the monarchy and the Church! This has led some historians to see Fascism as an entirely negative movement and there is some debate about the extent to which Fascism was a genuine ideology. What is likely is that the impact of the First World War created a desire for something different in Italy. Italo Balbo wrote in 1932 that 'When I returned from the war, just like so many others, I hated politics and politicians who had betrayed the hopes of the soldiers, reducing Italy to a shameful peace.' The politicians who were blamed were the elected governments of **Liberal Italy** and the alternative for many seemed to be the new movement of the workers that had been successful in taking power in Russia: Communism. However, Mussolini was an Italian Nationalist and he hated Communism. Therefore, Fascism developed as an alternative to the internationalism of Communism and to the failure of liberal democracy. Fascism was clearly neither communist nor democratic.

Fascist ideology, 1919–39

By November 1921, the movement had become a national political party, the Partito Nazionale Fascista (PNF). Mussolini tried to win power through the political process and to do so he changed the political programme of the Fascists. Fascism now focused on winning support from the property-owning middle class rather than the working class. The proposed wealth tax mentioned in the 1919 party programme disappeared and, far from attacking the Catholic Church, Mussolini argued that the freedom of the Church would be guaranteed. It has been suggested that Mussolini had cynically moved to where the money was, adopting a programme that focused on antisocialism and defending business and Capitalism from the threat of the trades union movement and the socialists; the Socialist Trades Union (CGL) saw its membership grow from 250,000 in 1918 to over 2 million by 1920.

> Fascism breaks forth irrepressibly in every corner of Italy, while the proletariat, nauseated, disillusioned, 'massacred', begins to disband.

1   *Mussolini speaking in 1920*

> Bolshevism is lying prostrate in its death throes, mortally wounded. Without the beatings, the revolver shots, and the arson of the Fascists – when would the terrible drunken Russian frenzy of Italian Bolshevism ever have evaporated?

2   *Mussolini speaking in 1922*

Mussolini had certain core ideas that were at the heart of Fascism. Once he was in power he sought answers to practical problems. These policies were later justified as being the 'fascist programme' that developed from Fascist ideas. Mussolini argued that 'Fascism is not only a party, it is also a regime; it is not only a regime but a faith; it is not only a faith but a religion.' Mussolini therefore saw Fascism as an ideology. At the heart of the ideology were ideas of Nationalism, militarism and violence, as well as the original totalitarian idea, the belief that only Fascism could solve Italy's problems and create a great state, and therefore it had to be the only ideology. The extreme nationalism of Fascism led to the belief that Italian people were entitled to land in Africa at the expense of inferior races, although Italy's anti-Semitism from 1938 was more as a result of the close relationship with Nazi Germany rather than any ideological hatred of Jews. Mussolini also developed an economic alternative to capitalism and socialism in the form of the Corporate State. In an entry for an Italian encyclopaedia in 1932 and *The Doctrine of Fascism*, Mussolini defined Fascism. It is important to remember that this definition was retrospective and that therefore Mussolini was as much describing fascist policies as a coherent set of ideas. Furthermore, although Mussolini was credited with having written the text, much of the work was completed by Giovanni Gentile. It provides a clear statement of some aspects of fascist ideology.

Fascism, the more it considers and observes the future and the development of humanity, does not believe in perpetual peace. War alone puts the stamp of nobility upon the peoples who have the courage to meet it.

Fascism is the complete opposite of Marxian socialism, which believes that history can be explained through the conflict of interests among the various social groups (classes). Fascism believes in heroism; that is to say actions influenced by no economic motive. Fascism denies that class war can be the main force in the transformation of society.

Being anti-individualistic, the Fascist system of life stresses the importance of the State and recognises the individual only where his interests coincide with those of the State. It is opposed to classical Liberalism as Liberalism denied the State in the interests of the individual; Fascism reasserts the rights of the State. Fascism is totalitarian and the Fascist State includes all values, interprets, develops and adds power to the whole life of the people.

For Fascism, the growth of empire, that is to say the expansion of the nation, is an essential sign of health. Peoples which are rising are always imperialist; and rejection of imperialism is a sign of decay and death. But empire demands discipline, the co-ordination of all forces and a deeply felt sense of duty and sacrifice: this fact explains many aspects of the practical working of the regime and the necessary severe measures which must be taken against those who would oppose this inevitable movement of Italy in the twentieth century.

3　　　　　*Adapted from B. Mussolini, **The Doctrine of Fascism**, 1932*

Activity

Source analysis

Study Source 3.

1 According to Mussolini, what are the key features of Fascism?

2 According to Mussolini, what does Fascism oppose?

3 Reach a judgement on whether Fascism is mainly a 'positive' or a 'negative' ideology.'

The central features of fascist ideology

The key features of fascist ideology were:

- ■ **a totalitarian system of government**. Mussolini invented the concept of 'totalitarianism' and the slogan 'Everything within the state, nothing outside the state, nothing against the state.' Individual freedom was dangerous as this allowed people to act against the interests of the state.
- ■ **the heroic leader**. Fascism believed that change would be brought by the actions of an heroic individual, Mussolini, whose will would transform society. Democracy was nothing more than collective

Cross-reference

To recap on Mussolini's invention of the concept of **totalitarianism**, look back to the introduction on page 1.

To learn about the **racism** inherent to fascist ideology that developed as a result of extreme Nationalism, see pages 78–80.

Key term

Blackshirts: the fascist paramilitary organisation or *Squadre*, which carried out violent attacks on socialists, and trades union members and buildings. They dressed in black shirts and gave the traditional Roman salute.

Cross-reference

To learn more about Mussolini's **Third Way**, read page 73.

irresponsibility as the majority could rule effectively and with strength simply because it was the majority. Actions were more important than words, and the heroic leader would be the one whose actions would lead the nation rather than a political manifesto motivating the masses into action.

- **extreme nationalism**. Mussolini wished to return Italy to the glory of the Roman Empire, so an aggressive foreign policy including wars of conquest would be necessary. There was a racial element to this aggressive Nationalism. He sought to extend the Italian Empire in Africa, a traditional aim of Italian foreign policy. The actions of the Italian army in both Libya (1928–33) and Ethiopia (1935–6) were brutal, displacing 100,000 Libyan Arabs to concentration camps and gassing and massacring the Ethiopians. In both cases, racial superiority was used as a justification. Anti-Semitism was not, however, at the core of Fascism.

- **militarism**. The military actions in Africa typified Mussolini's desire to transform the character of the Italian people by militarising the population. The intimidation of political opponents by the **Blackshirts** was more than a means to political power, as it emphasised Mussolini's belief in the need for strength. Mussolini believed that it was war that drove forward history and therefore it was 'better to live one day as a lion than 100 years as a sheep' and that 'war is to man what childbirth is to woman'. The creation of 'an army of 8 million bayonets' and 'an air force that would block out the sun' would be accompanied by the militarisation of children through education, where teachers wore military uniform and children learned military discipline. Mussolini's military actions in the 1930s were increasingly because of his belief in the transformational power of violence rather than because of strategic need; Italian aid to Franco in the Spanish Civil War crippled the Italian economy and was unpopular, and the annexation of Albania in 1939 was unnecessary as Albania was already an Italian puppet State.

- **hatred of communism**. Belief in the greatness of the Italian nation meant that Mussolini despised the internationalism of Communism. The loyalty of Italian socialists and Communists was considered to be to Moscow and the Soviet Union rather than the Italian State; the PSI's flag was the Italian national flag with the Soviet 'hammer and sickle' added to the top. Mussolini rejected the idea that economic factors drove on history, believing that the heroism of individuals like himself was the critical force. Fascism also believed in creating harmony among all Italians rather than class warfare.

- **corporatism**. Mussolini believed Fascism was a 'Third Way' between liberal democratic capitalism and communism. As such, it was both a political and an economic system, and the Corporate State was the economic system that was an alternative to capitalism and socialism. It developed over the period 1925–39, aiming to create harmony between workers and employers through the creation of corporations led by fascist officials. The Ministry of Corporations was created in 1926, headed by Mussolini himself.

Fascist ideology: revolutionary or reactionary?

The question has also been raised as to whether Fascism was a new movement that aimed to transform Italy or a movement that was reacting against the changes brought by industrialisation, democracy and the post-war world. Mussolini certainly tried to appeal to different groups at different times, offering different and sometimes contradictory policies.

This has suggested to some historians that Fascism was therefore no more than a pragmatic political programme that sought to maximise support rather than having an ideology that was consistently followed.

Activity

Revision exercise

The historian Alexander De Grand identified five sub-ideologies within Fascism. Complete the table below to indicate who you believe each sub-ideology was designed to appeal to and whether you consider each sub-ideology to be revolutionary or reactionary. Revolutionary refers to the aspects of ideology that intended to make significant changes, modernising Italy. Reactionary refers to the aspects of ideology that were against modern ideas and change.

Sub-ideology	Who was this sub-ideology invented to appeal to?	Reactionary or revolutionary?
1 **National Syndicalism**, aimed at creating syndicates of workers and employers to run industry, and was generally republican and anti-clerical		
2 **Rural Fascism**, which saw the traditions of the countryside as the basis of Italian life rather than the cities, industry and the modern world		
3 **Technocratic Fascism**, which accepted industrialisation and modernisation		
4 **Conservative Fascism**, a traditional programme based on the alliance between those who owned property, land, industry, the Catholic Church and the monarchy		
5 **Nationalist Fascism**, with its emphasis on expansionism, the recreation of an Italian Empire at the expense of inferior races and a totalitarian political system to provide the unity required for war		

The rise of Fascism

Understanding of the rise of Fascism and the appointment of Mussolini as prime minister on 30 October 1922 requires consideration of two separate but clearly interrelated issues. First, why did Liberal Italy, which had existed since the unification of Italy in 1862, disintegrate and, second, why was Mussolini the beneficiary of this collapse?

The weakness of Liberal Italy post-war

Liberal Italy had never enjoyed the support of all of the population after unification. The limited franchise (only 2 per cent of the population could vote), strong regionalism including division between the industrial north and rural south, and the lack of support for the regime from the papacy, meant most Italians saw the government as something that did not represent them and did little for them. In 1912, the Prime Minister Giovanni Giolitti attempted to end the impression that the government was in the corrupt hands of a small self-perpetuating elite by extending the franchise to all men over the age of 30 (men over 21 who were literate or had served in the army were also given the vote).

Key profile

Gabrielle d'Annunzio

Gabrielle d'Annunzio (1863–1938) was a First World War hero who has often been seen as the originator of many fascist ideas. He had been a poet and author before the First World War. As a fighter pilot, he was famed for a 700 mile round trip to drop leaflets on Vienna. He became obsessed with *Italia irredenta* and took matters into his own hands in 1919 when he seized Fiume. Here he established a regime that seemed to be the pre-cursor of Fascism. He set up the Corporate State, introduced Blackshirts, the Roman salute, moved the crowd with emotive speeches from the balcony and used militia to brutally repress opponents. He could have been a genuine rival to Mussolini but after Fiume he retired to his home on Lake Garda to write poetry. In 1937, Mussolini made him head of the Italian Royal Academy, a collection of the 60 greatest intellectual and artistic figures in Italy.

This change had made little impact when the First World War started. Although Italy had been an ally of Germany and Austria-Hungary since the 1882 Triple Alliance, it did not enter the war in 1914, as Italy was unprepared for war and particularly vulnerable to the British navy. In 1915, Italy did join the war, but on the side of the Triple Entente following the promise of territorial gains in the secret Treaty of London. Italy's war was not a great success, with the Battle of Caporetto in October 1917 being a national humiliation with half a million Italians either captured or deserting. In total, over 1 million Italians were killed or injured. The victory at Vittorio Veneto in 1918 was of limited significance to the outcome of the war, but it did raise expectations that Italy would receive rich rewards at the peace conference. Italy expected to receive possession of **Italia irredenta** ('unredeemed Italy'), as well as territory from the Turkish Empire, colonies in Africa and payment of a war indemnity. The Paris Peace Conference did not award Italy the war gains expected; although it gained South Tyrol, Trentino and the Istrian Peninsula including the city of Trieste, it did not gain the city of Fiume or any German colonies. The First World War became known as the 'mutilated victory'.

The Prime Minister Vittorio Orlando could not survive the national humiliation of the peace treaties and he resigned in June 1919. In September 1919, Gabriele d'Annunzio, a war veteran, staunch nationalist and poet, led an army of volunteers who seized the city of Fiume on the Dalmation coast. He held the city for 15 months. His supporters wore black shirts and used the traditional Roman salute.

This seemed to be clear evidence of the success of direct action rather than the failure of the weak and unpopular political process. It also suggested that the government was powerless to stop such actions. The November 1919 election, conducted under the system of **proportional representation**, only served to further emphasise the contrast between

Key terms

Italia irredenta: Italian-speaking areas of the Austro-Hungarian Empire that had remained part of Austria at the time of Italian unification. Acquiring these areas in the Tyrol and around Trieste were Italian war aims agreed as part of the Treaty of London.

Proportional representation: the system of election used in both Liberal Italy and Weimar Germany. Political parties receive a number of seats in direct proportion to the percentage of the vote they win. This encourages large numbers of political parties to stand for election and often results in governments made up of more than one party (coalitions).

Fig. 4 *Italy in 1919: the post-war settlement and Italia irredenta*

revolutionary action and the political process. The two largest parties were the PSI and the PPI, who between them shared a majority of the seats but who refused to work together in government. This ensured that the political system was unstable; there were six prime ministers between the end of the war and 1922.

These constant changes in leadership were a consequence of the extreme social and economic problems facing Italy, as well as ensuring that these problems could not be solved. Post-war there was a national debt due to war loans being taken out, mainly from the United States. This and a serious shortage of food and raw materials resulted in inflation, with the cost of living increasing by 50 per cent. At the same time, the short post-war economic boom ended and the demobilisation of troops, coupled with the need to restructure industry to focus on peace-time production, led to a huge increase in unemployment, which reached 2.5 million. The bankruptcy of large industrial companies such as Ansaldo that had been responsible for munitions production was a symbol to nationalists of the failure of the government to protect Italian patriots.

The fear of Communism

The middle class and industrialists had another reason to resent the government. The end of the war had seen the relaxation of the labour discipline imposed to ensure national solidarity during the war, accompanied by the release from prison and return from exile of socialists and trades unionists. The result was increased labour militancy. Many workers believed that the Bolshevik Revolution in Russia would soon spread to Italy. Trades union membership grew and the Socialist Trades Union (CGL) seemed to offer a particularly potent threat with their 2 million members by 1920, but the Catholic confederation also had 1.2 million members and the anarcho-syndicalists of the Italian

> ### Cross-reference
>
> **Weimar Germany** is covered on page 92.

> ### Key chronology
>
> **Italian prime ministers, 1917–22**
>
> | | |
> |---|---|
> | 1917 October | Vittorio Orlando |
> | 1919 June | Francesco Nitti |
> | 1920 June | Giovanni Giolitti |
> | 1921 July | Ivanoe Bonomi |
> | 1922 February | Luigi Facta |
> | 1922 October | Benito Mussolini |

Biennio rosso: the two 'red years' of 1919–20, during which the threat of the trades union and socialist movements seemed likely to lead to a Russian-style revolution.

Exploring the detail

Key *Ras* and their locations

- Roberto Farinacci, Cremona: here, fascists had a reputation for extreme brutality. They terrified the population into obedience, allowing Farinacci to make himself mayor of Cremona in 1922, an act that angered Mussolini.

- Italo Balbo, Ferrara: organised the *Celibano* group (named after their favourite drink, cherry brandy) who acted as strike breakers for local landowners, as well as beating up Socialists and Communists. His invasion of Portomaggiore in June 1921 with 4,000 *Squadre* led to two days of violence that left the dead unburied in the streets.

- Dino Grandi, Bologna: elected to parliament aged 24 in 1919, but quickly acquired a reputation for leadership of the Bologna *ras* and for uncompromising treatment of opponents.

Syndical Union claimed 300,000 members in September 1919. Strikes and rioting were frequent, with 1.5 million strikers in 1919. The Italian Socialist Party (PSI) grew in support from 50,000 pre-war to 200,000 in 1919 and, worryingly for the property-owning classes, it rejected a reformist programme and joined the international communist movement. The ***biennio rosso*** reached a climax in August 1920 when workers occupied factories and shipyards in several cities in the north. In Turin factory councils were set up, similar to Russian soviets. In the countryside, many ex-labourers had returned from the war and simply seized land they previously had rented. The government was powerless to act and accepted the seizures.

Mussolini reacted to the fear of both property owners and industrialists in the cities and landowners in the countryside, changing the fascist programme so that the central feature was anti-Communism. He certainly had nothing to lose as the Fascists had failed to win even a single seat in the 1919 election. The fascist *Squadre*, each of around 40 men led by an ex-army officer, attacked socialists, broke strikes, and damaged the offices of the socialist newspaper *Avanti* and the offices of the PSI and CGL. Between November 1920 and May 1921, 200 died and 800 were injured. At the same time, the *Squadre* grew from 20,000 to 200,000 members. It was at this point that they adopted the black shirts and Roman salute that D'Annunzio had pioneered. Support for the Fascists grew, beginning with peasants and landowners in the Po valley. Across the regions of Emilia and Romagna, antisocialist, nationalistic fascist groups began to take over local government, establishing *Ras* (local fascist bosses).

Fascism also found support among the professional classes, middle classes and the young, attracted by the dynamism of the movement. Furthermore, support came from an unusual source. Prime Minister Giolitti had lost control of the situation and therefore called an election for May 1921, inviting Mussolini to fight the election as part of the governing coalition that would be nationalist and antisocialist. The violence of the fascist movement was therefore legitimised and Mussolini was given credibility as a national politician. The Fascists won 35 seats, which gave them disproportionate power in the new coalition as Giolitti's National Bloc would struggle to rule without

Fig. 5 *Benito Mussolini, centre right, at the fascist convention in Naples, 1922. On the far left is General Emilio De Bono and next to him is Italo Balbo*

Mussolini's support. Mussolini tried to work as a democratic politician, signing a pact with the PSI to end violence. Prominent *Ras* objected to the change in policy and Mussolini resigned as leader of the fascist movement. However, within days he had won back the support of the movement and in November he tore up the pact, indicating that violence would remain a fascist strategy.

The role of Mussolini

The role of Mussolini in the final year before he became prime minister in October 1922 was critical. Before 1922, the local *Ras* had become so powerful in their regions that they were almost independent; the fascist movement can be described as 'movements'. In November 1921, Mussolini made two important moves: he united the movements as a single political party, the PNF, and returned to the policy of *Squadre* violence. The fascist violence seemed to suggest that the communist threat was growing and this, together with parliamentary weakness, suggested that Italy was ungovernable. In May, the socialist council of Bologna was driven out by the Fascists. On 1 August 1922, a general strike began and Mussolini made it clear through *Il Popolo d'Italia* and public speeches that if the government failed to restore order, the Fascists would crush the strike themselves. On 2 August, strikers in Genoa, Ancona and Leghorn were defeated and on 3 August the Fascists took control of Milan, burning the offices of *Avanti* to the ground, driving out the socialist government and running the trains after the transport workers went on strike. These successes convinced Mussolini that power could be taken by force, and on 13 August the Fascist Party Congress approved this policy. In September, Mussolini told a crowd at Udine that 'Our programme is simple: we intend to govern Italy.'

Fig. 6 *The growth of fascist support: Italy 1919–22*

The *Ras* certainly favoured action and so Mussolini began to plan the March on Rome. The intention was for three columns of Fascists to march on the city on 28 October to take power. In fascist myth this became the event where Fascism triumphantly took power in Italy. The reality was very different. Mussolini himself was in Milan, trying to negotiate fascist inclusion in the cabinet. Far from confidently expecting victory, Mussolini's train ticket to Rome sat in his pocket alongside another ticket to Switzerland and safety. Facta had acted ineffectually throughout the summer, but he now assured himself of the support of the army and prepared to act against any 'march'. The King approved plans to defend the city and the cabinet approved plans to resist Fascism. Around 30,000 troops and police awaited the fascist columns, which had been stopped outside the city.

■ **Key profile**

Luigi Facta

Luigi Facta (1861–1930) was the last prime minister of Italy before Mussolini. He was elected to the Chamber of Deputies in 1892 as a Liberal. He served as finance minister before the First World War and was appointed as prime minister in February 1922. He proved to be indecisive in dealing with the political crisis of 1922. He was sacked for failing to deal with fascist violence in the summer of 1922, but reappointed when it became clear no one else could form a government. He only finally acted against Mussolini at the eleventh hour, but the King refused to agree to his plans to defend Rome and instead dismissed him a second time. He was finance minister in the coalition government led by Mussolini and was made a life senator by Mussolini in 1924.

At 9am Facta met King Victor Emmanuel III to get martial law formally declared. The King backed down, having changed his mind overnight. A range of reasons have been suggested, including the King's fear that his cousin, the Duke of Aosta, might lead a revolution to usurp him as well as the influence of those at court and in his family who were sympathetic to Fascism. He was also visited during the night by army generals who advised the King that the loyalty of the army could not be guaranteed, and the prospect of civil war was probably what led Victor Emmanuel to act as he did. It meant Mussolini could not be stopped. Salandra, a trusted adviser of the King, failed to form a coalition government including the Fascists because Mussolini would not be satisfied with merely seats in the cabinet. Left with no choice, Victor Emmanuel asked Mussolini to form a government on 29 October. Mussolini finally caught the train from Milan, changing from his black shirt into a suit, symbolic of the mix of violence and legal measures he had used to secure power. Finally, the March on Rome took place on 30 October, a symbol of the seizure of power but otherwise an event of no consequence.

The attraction of fascist ideology

The success of Mussolini in acquiring power was partly due to the attraction of fascist ideology. Mussolini's triumphant proclamation following his appointment as prime minister highlighted some of the key features of Fascism.

> Fascists! Italians! The hour of decisive battle has struck. Four years ago this day the National Army launched a supreme offensive that led to victory. Today, the Army of Blackshirts seizes again the mutilated victory. The martial law of Fascism goes into full effect.
>
> The Army must not participate in the struggle. The Fascists renew again their highest admiration for the Army of Vittorio Veneto. Neither do the Fascists march against the police and guards, but against the political class of feeble, weak-minded men who, in four years, have not been able to give a true government to our nation.
>
> The bourgeoisie should know that the Fascists want to impose a unique discipline on the nation, and help all forces destined to increase the economic expansion and welfare of the nation. The labourers and workers have nothing to fear from Fascist power. We shall be generous with unarmed opponents and relentless with others.

One passion inflames us: that is to contribute to the salvation and greatness of the country. Long live Italy! Long live Fascism!

4

Mussolini's fascist proclamation, 28 October 1922

 Activity

Revision exercise

Review the sections on fascist ideology, the weaknesses of Liberal Italy, the fear of Communism and the role of Mussolini. Copy and complete the table below to identify the specific appeal of fascist ideology.

Key issue	Fascist ideology	Key supporters
Political instability		
Corrupt democracy		
The 'mutilated victory'		
National divisions		
Squadre violence		
National debt		
Unemployment		
Direct action of D'Annunzio		
Union power		
Biennio rosso		

 Activity

Talking point

In pairs, argue either that Mussolini's rise to power was mainly due to his actions or that his rise to power was mainly due to the circumstances in Italy between 1919 and 1922. Each member of the pair then explains his or her arguments in three minutes while the partner listens. The pairs then swap roles. Write down all the arguments put forward by your partner.

The establishment of the one-party state

Mussolini's appointment as prime minister did not create a Fascist Italy. Although he held the critical positions of Minister of the Interior and Minister of Foreign Affairs, the 14-man cabinet contained only four Fascists. The remaining 10 members, mainly Liberals, Catholics and military leaders, were convinced that Mussolini could be used to crush the threat of the left. After this crisis passed, they believed that either Mussolini would become a respectable politician, tamed by the trappings of power, or he could be dismissed. Mussolini had been appointed by the King and therefore he could be dismissed by the King just as easily. The Fascists were still a minority in the Italian parliament where their 35 seats represented only 7 per cent of the popular vote. However, by the end of 1925 all other political parties had been banned and a one-party state had been established. Mussolini was able to achieve this through a combination of factors. This revolution was more easily achieved because it was partly endorsed by the King and parliament. The use of violence was also critical, and the murder of the socialist deputy Giacomo Matteotti on 10 June 1924 represented a key turning point.

Activity

Source analysis

Study Source 4 and re-read the section on fascist ideology. Identify the features of fascist ideology present in the proclamation of 28 October.

Key chronology

The establishment of the dictatorship

1922 November	Power to rule by decree for 12 months.
1922 December	Creation of the Fascist Grand Council.
1923 January	Creation of the Fascist militia.
1923 November	Acerbo Law passed.
1924 April	National election leads to the Fascists becoming the largest party.
1924 June	Murder of Matteotti and the Aventine Secession.
1925 December	Legge Fascistissime bans other political parties.
1926 October	Formal decree confirms the one-party state.

Fig. 7 *Preaching to the converted. Mussolini addresses the Constituent Assembly*

Initially Mussolini gave the impression that he would work within the constitution, telling the Chamber of Deputies at the end of 1922 that he did not wish to close parliament and replace it with a government of Fascists. He stressed that the strength of the Blackshirts would allow him to close parliament but that he did not wish to do so, arguing, 'I formed a coalition government … in order to gather in support of the suffering nation all those who, over and above questions of party and section, wish to save her.' The response from parliament was to grant Mussolini emergency powers to rule by decree for 12 months. The Socialists and Communists voted against the decree, but it was supported by the Liberals and the Catholics, both of whom preferred a strong fascist government to a left-wing takeover. At the same time, Mussolini was taking two important steps to consolidate power. In December 1922, he set up the Fascist Grand Council, which would be responsible for presenting policy to the government. Mussolini himself would choose members of the council, ensuring that he controlled the movement and the creation of fascist policy. At the same time, he took a decisive step to bring all the *Squadre* under his control. He created a new State militia from the Blackshirts called the Volunteer Militia for National Security (MSVN). They were paid by the state and took orders from Mussolini as leader of the party and prime minister. The militia enabled Mussolini to use the threat of violence against opposition politicians and any *Ras* who tried to oppose him. Three opposition politicians were murdered in 1923 and 50 were violently attacked.

The King was prepared to allow Mussolini to rule by decree for 12 months, but he was not prepared to pass the decree that proposed to grant a two-thirds majority of seats in the Chamber of Deputies to the largest party providing they won over 25 per cent of the vote in a national election. The measure was therefore introduced into parliament in November 1923, a month before the power to rule by decree expired. Mussolini saw this measure as essential so he turned his attention to passing the law through parliament. His assurances that the law would end the weakness of coalition governments and provide Italy with a strong government convinced all but the socialist and communist deputies. This measure became known as the Acerbo Law, named after Giacomo Acerbo, a close ally of Mussolini, and was passed by a 100-vote majority in both Houses of Parliament. Mussolini now needed to make use of the law and elections for the Chamber of Deputies were held in April 1924. He won two great foreign triumphs before the election. The murder of an Italian general sent to Greece to decide on the boundary between Greece and Albania was the sort of humiliation that Liberal Italy would have accepted. Mussolini, however, demanded an apology and compensation, and when it was not forthcoming he ordered the bombardment of the Greek island of Corfu. Greece paid compensation of 50 million lire. In addition, the Pact of Rome was signed with Yugoslavia, and the disputed city of Fiume was returned to Italy. The King awarded Mussolini the title 'Cousin to the Sovereign'. In April 1924, the Fascists polled more than 4.5 million votes against less than 3 million for the opposition parties, with 66 per cent of the vote translating to 374 seats out of 535. The intimidation of voters by the Blackshirts and vote rigging both helped to ensure success, but the result was decisive. The Fascists had won two-thirds of the vote even without the manipulation of the Acerbo Law. Mussolini was now free of parliamentary restraint.

The decisive event of this period took place on 10 June 1924 when the socialist deputy Giacomo Matteotti was murdered by fascist thugs.

Activity

Challenge your thinking

1. Identify a list of reasons why the Italian parliament passed the Acerbo Law.

2. Which reason was the most important? Explain why.

3. Which reason was the least important? Explain why.

Cross-reference

Fiume is shown in Figure 4 on page 57.

A closer look

The murder of Matteotti

The fascist success in the 1924 elections for the Chamber of Deputies had partly been the result of ballot rigging and intimidation, especially in the south of Italy. The new election laws had included the Bochini system, with the secret ballot in the rural south being replaced by open ballots by the show of hands. This ensured the MSVN could intimidate voters into lowering their hands. Secret ballots were maintained in urban areas, probably because foreign visitors were more likely to visit the cities than the countryside. Giacomo Matteotti, a Socialist Party deputy, collected evidence of the violence and intimidation and published it in an article called 'The Fascists Exposed'. He followed this up with a courageous speech in the Chamber where he condemned the actions of the Fascist Party, the Blackshirts and Mussolini. Matteotti became a marked man. On 10 June 1924, Matteotti was abducted from outside his house. He struggled as he was bundled into a seven-seater Lancia and driven away, attracting the attention of a bystander who took the registration number of the car and informed the police. The police were able to trace the car and the owner, but Matteotti had disappeared. The abduction led to a public outcry, inflamed by the press which still felt independent enough to report the disappearance and pass comment. A fascist gang, the Ceka, had carried out the kidnap and murder, so Mussolini was directly blamed. Some members of the party returned their party cards, reflecting the nationwide criticism.

Fig. 8 *The murder of Giacomo Matteotti sparked outrage across Italy and Europe, as the front page of this French newspaper makes clear*

Mussolini ordered an investigation into the abduction, which was initially conducted by independent judges. However, during the investigation Matteotti's body was discovered in a shallow grave about 20 km (12 miles) from Rome. The summer of 1924 has been seen as a moment of danger for Mussolini in his consolidation of power. Orchestrated opposition to fascist rule through a general strike or opposition from the army could have brought down the government. The socialist deputies in the Chamber could not have brought down Mussolini by parliamentary means as all the opposition parties totalled only a third of the deputies. Instead, they withdrew from the Chamber, and a group of around 100 deputies met separately. This action mirrored the withdrawal of the Roman plebs to the Aventine Hill in 494 BC in protest at the aristocratic abuse of power, and so this action of protest against the Fascists became known as the Aventine Secession. The King could have ended Mussolini's rule

Fig. 9 *Mussolini and Victor Emmanuel III in 1922. The King's refusal to act against Mussolini in 1922 or 1924 allowed Il Duce power*

there and then. However, as in October 1922, he was more concerned about the danger of Socialism and refused to act. As time passed, Mussolini became more confident. His fear that he would be removed receded because no one had the power or the desire to overthrow him. In January 1925, he began to establish a dictatorship. A second investigation into the murder was carried out by a fascist tribunal that exonerated Mussolini.

Although no evidence was ever found that directly linked Mussolini to the murder of Matteotti, he was at least morally responsible for the death. The fascist thugs responsible knew they were acting in the interests of their leader and fascist violence had gone unchecked by Mussolini from the early days of the Fasci di Combattimento. Cesare Rossi and Filippo Marinelli – both close allies of Mussolini – were thought to have pushed the Ceka to act. It is possible that these supporters acted to rid Mussolini of the 'troublesome socialist' in the same way that Henry II's troublesome priest Thomas Becket was murdered in 1170 or indeed Sergei Kirov was murdered in the Soviet Union in 1934.

In January 1925, Mussolini acted decisively. He told the Chamber, 'Italy wants peace and quiet, work and calm. I will give these things with love if possible and with force if necessary.' The fascist deputies cheered their approval. Freedom of the press, of association and of speech all disappeared. The liberal newspaper *Corriere della Sera* was taken over by the Fascists. Political opponents were attacked, forced to eat live toads or drink castor oil. Four attempts on Mussolini's life in 1925 and 1926 gave him the opportunity to crush all opposition. The first attempt was by a socialist and this provided the excuse to act against the Socialist Party. In December 1925, the Legge Fascistissime was passed which banned opposition political parties. The deputies who had withdrawn from the Chamber in the Aventine Secession were refused re-admittance and informed that they had forfeited their seats by their revolutionary act. Mussolini became answerable only to the King and not to the Chamber, and on 31 January 1926 government by decree was legalised. In October 1926, a formal decree was passed that banned all other political parties. It was merely constitutional confirmation of a reality that had existed for nearly two years.

Cross-reference

The murder of **Kirov** is discussed on pages 36–37.

Exploring the detail

The murder of Thomas Becket

Thomas Becket was Henry II's chancellor of England, the leading position in the 12th century State. In 1162, Henry appointed his loyal friend the Archbishop of Canterbury to bring the Church under Henry's control. To his fury, Becket put loyalty to God before Henry. In 1170, Becket was in exile in France. Henry II cursed his former friend over dinner one evening, asking his knights, 'Who will rid me of this troublesome priest?' Four knights travelled to France and murdered Becket. The King's outburst was not a direct order, but it led to Becket's death as the knights set out to prove their loyalty to the King. It has been suggested that the murders of Matteotti and Kirov may have been the result of followers trying to please their leader.

Activity

Revision exercise

Copy and complete the table below.

Reason for the consolidation of power	Examples
Use of legal power	
Use of terror	
Support of the King	
Mistakes of opponents	

Summary questions

1 In what ways was the First World War significant in the development of Fascism?

2 Why was the fear of Communism strong in Italy between 1919 and 1924?

3 Why was Liberal Italy unpopular with many Italians?

4 Identify the ways in which Fascism was attractive to workers, peasants, ex-First World War soldiers, Catholics and the elite.

5 Identify three key strengths of Mussolini that helped him become prime minister.

6 In what ways did the King help Mussolini between 1922 and 1925?

7 How far had Mussolini overcome the limits to his power as prime minister by the end of 1925?

Italian totalitarianism in the 1930s

In this chapter you will learn about:

■ the reasons why Fascist Italy was intolerant of diversity

■ the extent to which Fascist Italy was intolerant of diversity in the 1930s, with reference to political, economic, religious and cultural diversity

■ Il Duce and the cult of Mussolini in relation to fascist ideology.

Fig. 1 *The totalitarian dream – fascist from cradle to grave*

Activity

Challenge your thinking

Study Source 1.

1 Identify the reasons why Mussolini argued that Fascism was intolerant of diversity.

2 Which areas of Italian politics and society do you think Mussolini would seek to control?

■ The intolerance of diversity

The many practical expressions of Fascism, such as the party organisation, educational systems, discipline can only be understood when considered in relation to its general attitude towards life. The Fascist system of life stresses the importance of the State and recognises the individual only in so far as his interests coincide with those of the State.

The Fascist conception of the State is all-embracing; outside of it no human or spiritual values may exist. Fascism does not merely aim at remoulding the forms of life, but also man himself and his character and his faith. To achieve this purpose it enforces discipline and makes use of authority.

1 *Adapted from B. Mussolini, **The Doctrine of Fascism**, 1932*

There are a number of reasons why Fascist Italy was intolerant of diversity:

■ Italy was founded in 1861 as a liberal democracy and constitutional monarchy. The problems that existed post-unification grew out of the unsolved issues of regionalism and uneven economic division. However, it was an essentially tolerant society. Fascist Italy therefore had very few roots in the ideology of Italy's past and Mussolini reacted against Italy's recent past.

■ Fascism stressed the subordination of the individual to the state. The fascist belief in duty and sacrifice in pursuit of a common goal was crucial and precluded any alternative, individual beliefs. The common goal was, of course, the Utopian State that all totalitarian dictators pursue. Mussolini wanted to create a new heroic Italy. To do this, he believed he would have to create new Italians. All other beliefs were wrong and threatened to undermine the creation of a perfect state.

■ Socialism/Communism was inherently wrong as men were not equal and the nation state, not the international movement, was what mattered. The loyalty of Italian Socialists and Communists to Moscow meant the left was guilty of treason.

■ Liberal democracy had created all of Italy's problems from 1861 to 1922. Individuals were not equal, so there was no need for every man to vote. Democracy actually meant collective inertia and weakness. Under liberal democratic Italy, Italians had been forced to suffer a humiliating defeat by an Abyssinian army in 1896. Nothing demonstrated the weakness of democracy more than the nation's defeat by an African army that fought with bare feet. Post-war, the government had failed to solve the economic problems and Italy had descended into strikes and violence.

■ It was essential the country was united in pursuit of a common goal because that goal was war. Clearly, at a time of war there was no room for argument or opposition, otherwise Italy's drive to be a great power would be undermined.

■ Ironically, although Mussolini was intolerant of Socialism and Communism, it could be argued that the intellectual roots of Mussolini's intolerance can be found in Marxism. Mussolini was a Socialist until the First World War, and as such he had absorbed the belief that the state needed to control all aspects of life to ensure the perfect state could be created or, perhaps, reborn. From this arose his conception of the totalitarian state where nothing exists outside the state.

■ The nationalism of Fascism led to racism. Although racism was not as central to Fascism as it was to Nazism, there was a similarity in that the belief in the racial superiority of the Italian people expressed itself in the belief that they had a right to territory in Europe and North Africa. The Italian nation's desire for resources, living space and the status of being a great imperial power led to the seizure of Fiume and the conquest of Abyssinia and Albania. In addition, the policy of **ethnic cleansing** was carried out in Libya. Italian Jews were also persecuted from 1938. However, the lack of a racial ideology to underpin the legislation introduced helps to explain why Italian Jews were not persecuted to the extent that Jews in the rest of Europe were.

■ Fascist Italy was certainly intolerant of political diversity. Mussolini announced his intention to rule as a dictator on 3 January 1925 and from that point political diversity was steadily destroyed, both in theory and in practice. The establishment of the one-party state was

■ **Cross-reference**

An explanation of the concepts of **Socialism** and **Communism** can be found on page 14.

■ **Key term**

Ethnic cleansing: the policy of removing members of a rival ethnic group from a particular region or territory. The policy involves the relocation or execution of all men, women and children in the territory. Relocation often involves forcing people into camps where they starve to death or die as a result of disease. The term has been used to describe the actions of the Serb forces against the Bosnian Muslims in the war in Yugoslavia in the early 1990s.

achieved following the failure of the opposition and the King to act in the aftermath of the Matteotti crisis. It is not unreasonable to argue that the establishment of the one-party state and the intolerance of political diversity were fundamentally popular in Italy, at least until 1940 and Italy's entry into the Second World War. The basis of this intolerance of diversity was Mussolini's belief in totalitarianism: 'Everything within the state, nothing outside the state, nothing against the state.' However, the extent of economic, social and religious intolerance are all open to question and might suggest that Fascism was not as totalitarian as Mussolini liked to believe.

Cross-reference

Racism in Nazi ideology is discussed on pages 94–97.

More information on the conquest of **Abyssinia** can be found on page 79.

To recap on the **Matteotti crisis**, look back to page 64.

A closer look

Liberal Italy

The Napoleonic Wars had destroyed many traditional structures of European government and allowed the idea of the nation state to develop, but the defeat of Napoleon was a setback for Italian Nationalists. The northern Italian states returned to Austrian rule at the end of the Napoleonic Wars in 1815 and Metternich, the chancellor of Austria, showed his contempt for the idea of an Italian nation by declaring that Italy was no more than a 'geographical expression'. However, after 1815 a cultural and literary movement, the *Risorgimento*, called for the creation of a united Italy. From 1859, the kingdom of Piedmont-Sardinia united the other independent Italian states in the north and forced the Austrians to withdraw from Lombardy. Garibaldi, an Italian Nationalist, had conquered Sicily and southern Italy and was persuaded to hand over the territory to the new king of Italy, Victor Emmanuel II, who had been king of Piedmont-Sardinia. Victor Emmanuel was crowned king of Italy in 1861. Italy was fully unified in 1870 when Rome was incorporated.

The causes of Italian unification have been the source of historical debate. Italian Nationalists have argued that the unification was the inevitable consequence of the rise of national consciousness that took place in the first half of the 19th century. However, some historians have argued that Piedmont-Sardinia, the largest and most advanced Italian state, actually annexed the rest of Italy. The new Italian nation state guaranteed individual freedom and, although the franchise was limited, it was also a democracy. Liberal Italy's opposition to the Catholic Church is a good example of the general toleration of the regime, as the hostility was based on the Catholic Church's refusal to accept economic modernisation and religious freedom.

Political diversity

The establishment of the one-party state destroyed any official political diversity. The next 15 years saw the suppression of political opposition. However, it has been argued that Mussolini's main motivation was not so much the fascist revolution as the pursuit of personal political power. For this reason, control over the government and the Fascist Party itself were also essential features of political intolerance.

Suppression of political opposition

Mussolini had declared his intention to rule by decree in January 1925 when he declared, 'I am the State' and by 1926 parliament had no control over policy. In the 15 years between 1925 and 1940, 100,000 decrees were passed. As the fascist grip on Italy tightened, he declared, 'I am the government. Italy will obey me as she has never obeyed before.' Elections ceased in all but name. With opposition parties banned, unions and employers submitted names to the Fascist Grand Council, which then chose 400 representatives. Voters decided whether to elect or reject the list in its entirety. A new electoral law was introduced in May 1928 that restricted the franchise. Replacing universal manhood suffrage was a franchise that aimed to prevent the least wealthy from voting – the group that by definition was the most likely to oppose Fascism. Only those who paid taxes of more than 100 lire a year were entitled to vote. As a result of this measure, the numbers of Italians entitled to vote fell from 10 million to 3 million.

■ **Cross-reference**

Information on the **Lateran Treaty** can be found on page 75.

The first election under this system was held in March 1929 when the surprise was not that 2,864,000 voted in favour of the list but that 136,000 felt able to vote against it, despite the presence of Blackshirts outside and frequently inside polling stations. The Catholic Church led the way and it was estimated that the Lateran Treaty helped to deliver thousands, if not hundreds of thousands, of voters. Even 95.3 per cent of the vote was not sufficient for Il Duce, so the results in this and subsequent elections were rigged to show a 98 per cent approval rate. The new deputies made a mockery of parliamentary consent for legislation, simply roaring their assent to measures introduced. Ultimately, there could be no clearer recognition that parliamentary democracy had fully consented in its own murder than the fact that in January 1939 parliament abolished itself, to be replaced by the Chamber of Fasces and Corporations, which was equally a sham. In 1928, King Victor Emmanuel had accepted his own impotence when he agreed that in the future the choice of the prime minister would lie with the Fascist Grand Council. Local government was also abolished and elected mayors were replaced by fascist appointees.

■ **Activity**

Source analysis

Study Source 2. What reason does Nitti give to explain why political oppression was so readily accepted in Fascist Italy?

The ignoble phenomenon of a dictatorship is a shameful blot on European civilisation. Reactionary minds, which are indignant at red dictatorships, have only sympathy with 'white' dictatorships, which are equally, if not more, bloodthirsty, no less brutal and unjustified by any ideal, even a false one.

The Fascist government abolished in Italy every safeguard of the individual and every liberty. No free man can live in Italy, and an immoral law prevents Italians from going to a foreign country on pain of punishment. Italy is a prison where life has become intolerable ... Without a free parliament, a free press, a free opinion and a true democracy, there will never be peace.

2 *Francesco Nitti, 1929. Nitti had been prime minister from 1919 to 1920*

The destruction of parliament was accompanied by establishment of control over the civil service, the army and the judiciary. Mussolini resisted radicals within the party who wished to replace existing post holders with fascist appointees. Instead, he promoted generals to the much sought-after rank of field marshal and enhanced the status of the army through his militarisation of the country and foreign policy adventures in the 1930s. The civil service was also exempt from action, even though it was estimated that in 1927 only 15 per cent of the bureaucracy were members of the Fascist Party. Mussolini recognised that essentially the army and the civil service were naturally supportive of any regime that resisted radical change, and were particularly defensive against the threat of socialism. Given the affinity of these organisations with Fascism, it was no hardship for many members of both to join the PNF as a way of advancing their careers. The judiciary was dealt with slightly differently. The initial investigation into the Matteotti murder had demonstrated to Mussolini that he needed tighter control over those who dispensed justice to ensure that they understood the need to dispense fascist justice. Dozens of judges were sacked and the legal system was perverted to allow imprisonment without trial. Mussolini was happy to personally intervene in cases and the judiciary was increasingly happy to let him.

Further initiatives were introduced to help suppress political opposition. Known opponents were kept under surveillance. It has been estimated that in a typical week 20,000 visits, searches or arrests took place. Critical to these was the Organisation for Vigilance and Repression of Anti-Fascism (OVRA) – the secret police – which was established in 1926. The OVRA sounded more intimidating than might have been the case, given that it was staffed by only 375 agents. The Special Military Tribunal for the Defence of the State was established in November 1926. It adopted military procedures and penalties although it was used to try political opponents, and therefore it had the ability to impose the death sentence, which had been abolished in 19th century Italy. The tribunal met in secret and there was no right of appeal. Until the final fall of Mussolini, it heard an average of 2,000 cases a year, although until 1940 there were only nine executions. Penal camps were established on the Lipari Islands off the southern coast which ensured that dissidents were tracked down and removed from society. In total, 5,000 opponents were imprisoned or banished for a total of 28,000 years. Many fled Italy, including political opponents like Francesco Nitti (prime minister 1919–20) and Sturzo, who had founded the PPI. Some 3,350 exiles fought for the Spanish Republic in the Spanish Civil War in the Garibaldi brigade that was formed in November 1936. Carlo Roselli was one of the founders of 'Justice and Liberty', a group that aimed to unite all non-communist political opponents. High profile gestures like dropping anti-fascist pamphlets from planes enraged Mussolini and the leaders were arrested. Roselli escaped from the Lipari Islands and edited the group's anti-fascist journal *Justice and Liberty* from Paris. He was assassinated by Mussolini's agents.

Control of the party

The intolerance of political diversity also had consequences for the Fascist Party. The Fasci di Combattimento had been established in 1919, but it was made up of local movements with local policies, and the PNF only united in 1921. The development of the party meant that there were different regional organisations that did not always follow the official party line. There were also *Ras* who enjoyed the support of the regional parties. Together, these factors threatened the unity of the party and the primacy of Mussolini. In addition, the party had to come to terms with the different expectations of its members, as not all Fascists had the same understanding of what the 'fascist revolution' and 'Fascism' meant in practice. Party extremists, led by Roberto Farinacci, wanted to see a fascist takeover of the state, with organisations like the bureaucracy being purged and Fascists appointed. As veterans of street fights themselves, they were also keen to use the *Squadre* to forge the revolution in blood. Some, the national syndicalists, saw the role of the party as being to transform the economy through the creation of fascist unions that would offer a 'Third Way' between capitalism and socialism. The 'white revolutionaries' who saw Fascism as a defence against socialism wanted little to do with either an economic or a social transformation. There were further non-ideological sections in the party. These pragmatic Fascists were at once both the easiest to control and the hardest to sustain. This group had joined the party for personal advancement and sought reward for their support. They were also likely to fade away if Mussolini ceased to be successful and if other leaders or movements offered a more attractive alternative. Mussolini had to bring some order and common understanding to the movement. Just as he was not prepared to tolerate diversity outside the party, he was not prepared to tolerate any diversity within the party that threatened his position and status.

Mussolini had the ability to control the party. He chose the Party Secretary, who in turn nominated the party directorate, which met weekly, as well as the 92 provincial secretaries. Mussolini changed Party Secretary frequently to prevent anyone creating their own power base. The extremists were brought under control through the inspired decision to make Farinacci Party Secretary in January 1925. Farinacci centralised the Fascist Party and closed the provincial press, and in doing so brought the *ras* under control and ensured they could not act independently by using the violence of the *Squadre*. He was forced to resign in April 1926, by which point Mussolini's position was much more secure. The October 1926 revised Party Statute affirmed the strength of Il Duce as it officially made Mussolini head of the party, made all party posts subject to selection by Mussolini and confirmed the Fascist Grand Council (selected by Mussolini) as the body that made policy. The party itself was purged, with around 170,000 Fascists expelled because of their extremism. By 1939, party membership numbered 2.6 million, but these members were mainly opportunists and bureaucrats who built a career through possession of a party card. New jobs were created through the establishment of new ministries and government organisations, often with little actual work required. Other forms of public employment were also dependent on membership of the party, and in the 1930s teachers and university professors had to swear an Oath of Loyalty. Of the 1,250 professors active during this period, only 11 refused. These careerist Fascists had no interest in challenging Mussolini and no commitment to any particular set of ideas. There was no violent purge of the party such as the one that took place in the Soviet Union under Stalin. The OVRA did not become a State within a State such as the NKVD was under Stalin or the SS became under Hitler. The Italian police force remained under the control of the State and not the party. Most individual *Ras* were too concerned with fighting each other to challenge Mussolini, although Italo Balbo, one of the few *ras* who may have had ideas beyond his station, was sent to Libya where he died in a mysterious plane crash.

Economic diversity

Unlike Communism, Fascism was not an ideology that contained explicit ideas for economic reform. Mussolini's early incarnation as a Socialist was long dead by October 1922 and the support he had received from the Conservative establishment was mainly because the Fascists offered physical protection from socialist and communist reform. There was a wing of the Fascist party that expected economic revolution, but its vision of national syndicates was not shared by Mussolini and the taming of the party by Farinacci reduced its influence. However, Mussolini's belief that the Fascist State was all-encompassing and totalitarian clearly implied that there would have to be economic reconstruction.

■ **Activity**

Revision exercise

Draw a diagram showing the relationship between the Fascist Party and the State. You could start by placing Mussolini at the top or in the centre of your page.

> We are a State which controls all the forces of society. We control moral force, we control political forces, we control economic forces; therefore we are a full-blown Corporative State.

3   *Mussolini, 1926*

If private enterprise was allowed to continue unchecked, there were two potential challenges to Fascism. The exploited workforce might decide its best interests would be served by violent opposition to the regime, possibly through the trades unions. The existence of the MSVN, the OVRA and the support of the army meant that Mussolini could feel confident of crushing a workers' uprising. There was also the possibility of individual workers feeling greater loyalty to the company where they had worked for many years than to the State. It was therefore important that as well as breaking union power, the bond between individual and employer was destroyed. Another danger of private enterprise was that it would not provide the necessary progress that Mussolini desired; if production did not grow, Italy would not be able to follow the sort of aggressive foreign policy he had in mind.

The early economic actions of the Fascist State suggested they were little more than the protectors of Capitalism. Trades unions were banned and the right to strike was abolished in the 1925 Vidoni Pact. Employers were given the power to fix wages (1923) and conditions of employment (1925). Protective tariffs had been raised which benefited Italian heavy industry and the government paid subsidies, gave tax concessions and intervened to save firms and banks from bankruptcy.

The reorganisation of the Italian economy took place from 1926 to 1939 as the Corporate State was established. In theory, Mussolini aimed to find a genuine 'Third Way' between Capitalism and Socialism. Capitalism created conflict in society because workers were exploited, but Socialism removed incentives from the workers who would collect their wages regardless of how hard they worked. The Third Way would solve these problems (Table 1).

Table 1 *Capitalism, Socialism and the Third Way*

Ideology	Harmony?	In the interests of the State?	The lesson of history
Capitalism	Impossible – workers would be exploited. The working class would strike and try to seize power	Capitalism would ensure that what was produced was profitable but not necessarily what the State needed – why produce guns when you are making money from radios?	Capitalism had led to the strikes of the post-war period as the socialist unions won over exploited Italian workers
Socialism	Impossible – the lack of incentives for workers would lead to those who worked hard resenting those who took their wages in return for minimal effort	Socialism would reduce productivity as workers would have no incentive to work if their wages were guaranteed. They would also resist change, such as retraining workers to produce weapons rather than radios	The Soviet Union had been crippled by the Bolshevik Revolution and the Civil War. The Soviet Union was no longer a great power
Corporate State	Possible – harmony would be ensured through the meeting of workers and employers as fascist officials would prevent stalemate	Fascist officials would ensure that the decisions reached were in the best interests of the State	A new way had to be found. Only a leader like Il Duce could find a solution. Foreign academics and politicians recognised the advantages of the Third Way

The Ministry of Corporations, established in 1926, had overall control of the Corporate State, and Mussolini himself was the minister. In 1930, a National Council of Corporations was set up, with representatives from the employees, employers and the party. In 1934, the Third Way was fully established. Each sector of the economy would have two governing boards, known as syndicates – one for employees and one for employers – which met separately and jointly. Each syndicate was controlled by fascist officials. These corporations would be responsible for governing their sector of the economy, deciding on wages, working hours, holidays and other conditions of employment. The economy was divided into seven sectors: industry, agriculture, commerce, banking and finance, internal transport, the merchant marine and the intellectual community. Each sector was then subdivided so in total there were 22 categories: for example, metal workers were grouped in the ninth category and the sugar-beet industry was represented in the fifth category. In 1939, the Chamber of Fasces and Corporations was set up, based on the original National Council of Corporations and replacing the Italian parliament. This was to ensure that the government of Italy would be based directly on economic interests.

In reality, the Corporate State did not deliver quite what was intended. It certainly created job opportunities for members of the party. These corporate officials were able to enhance their state salaries with bribes from employers to ensure their support. Taps were put into buildings but the pipes were never laid as the money to pay for them had been pocketed by fascist officials. The Corporate State therefore operated in the interests of the employers, with repressive labour laws introduced; for example, the eight-hour day was replaced by a nine-hour day. The threat of repression kept workers in line and Confindustria, the representative body of larger employers, was able to buy considerable freedom for its members.

Religious diversity

■ Cross-reference

Marx's criticism of the Church is discussed on page 15.

The Bolsheviks had attacked religion and the power of the different Churches across the Soviet Union. The basis of this position was the fundamental opposition to religion as an alternative set of ideas that could win the loyalty of Soviet people. Mussolini himself was an avowed atheist: he married in a civil ceremony in 1915 and had even written an anti-clerical novel, *The Cardinal's Mistress*, as a young man. Early fascist ideology was, therefore, anti-Catholic. However, when Mussolini reinvented Fascism, he went out of his way to promise the Catholic Church that its independence would be respected. In 1925, he even married his wife Rachelle in a church in Milan.

Mussolini was being pragmatic. Liberal Italy had been in conflict with the Pope for 60 years. When Italy was created in 1861, Rome was not part of the new State. The constitutional monarchy with its belief in freedom and democracy objected to the Catholic Church and its traditional values, which seemed to hold Italy back. Removing the political power of the Pope over Rome was critical to the Liberals as they sought to create a nation State where the people would be loyal to Italy, not the Pope. However, French troops protected the Pope. In 1870, the outbreak of the Franco-Prussian War led to the French troops being withdrawn, which had enabled Italian troops to complete the unification of Italy. The Pope lost political control over Rome. Therefore, at the heart of Liberal Italy was a conflict between the state and the Catholic Church, which ensured that Italian people's loyalties were torn in two competing directions.

Mussolini recognised that there was more to gain by appearing to be the defender of the Catholic Church and by working with the papacy than by forcing people to choose between Fascism and Catholicism. In fact, there was a similarity between the intolerance exercised by Fascism and the intolerance exercised by the Catholic Church, which also rejected the notion that there was an alternative to their religious views. The basis of the shared intolerance was the hatred of Communism. The Church had seen the Bolshevik approach to the Church in general and to the Catholic Church in Ukraine in particular, and captured priests had been one of the largest groups executed by the Bolsheviks during the Civil War. Mussolini's appeal to the King in October 1922 was the protection he offered against the extremism of the left, and the Church was no different to the rest of the Italian elite which saw Mussolini as their saviour from the red threat. This explains the support from the PPI for Mussolini's temporary dictatorial powers, the Acerbo Law and its willingness to work with Mussolini from 1922 to 1924. The murder of Matteotti did lead to the PPI having second thoughts about the nature of Mussolini's regime, but by then it was too late to oppose Mussolini's political domination of Italy.

It was essential that Mussolini avoided the mistake of Liberal Italy and allowed Italians to be fascists and Catholics. Initially the support of Pope Pius XI was won through the restoration of Catholic education in State schools and through the increase in State payments to priests.

■ Cross-reference

Mussolini's appeal to the King in October 1922 is covered on page 60.

Key profile

Pope Pius XI

Pius XI (1857–1939) was pope from 1922 to 1939. He offered little opposition to Mussolini and Fascism in the 1920s, being grateful that Mussolini offered protection from Italian and international Communism which was anti-religion. The high point of relations with Mussolini came with the Lateran Treaty, but in 1931 he issued a letter, 'Non Abbiamo Bisogno', in protest at the pagan worship of Fascism by Italians. In 1937, he attacked both the Nazi regime and Communism, and was critical of the anti-Semitism of Mussolini's Italy. In all cases he objected to the un-Christian inhumanity of man towards man.

A plan of Giolitti's government in 1922 to make registration of share ownership compulsory and to tax income from shares had spelled financial doom for the Catholic Church, Italy's biggest shareholder. The proposal disappeared after Mussolini's appointment as prime minister, while the Banca di Roma in which the Church was the largest shareholder was saved from bankruptcy by the intervention of the fascist government. These measures were successful in that the Pope decided that there was no longer a need for a separate Catholic political party and withdrew support for the PPI in 1923. However, this did not go far enough, so Mussolini set out to solve the 'Roman question' and in February 1929 concluded the Lateran Treaty with the papacy. The treaty granted the Pope absolute sovereign power over an area of 108.7 acres in the centre of Rome. The Vatican City therefore became an independent State governed by the Pope. In addition, a Concordat defined the relationship of the Fascist State and the Catholic Church. The treaty was finalised with a payment to the Pope of 750m lire in cash and 1,000m lire in government bonds.

■ Exploring the detail

The Concordat

The Concordat specified that:

- Catholicism was the State religion of Italy
- religious education would take place in all primary and secondary schools
- church marriages were to be recognised as legal by the Fascist State
- divorce was to be allowed only with the consent of the Church
- the Church would give up any claim to rule beyond the Vatican City
- the Fascist State could object to the appointment of archbishops and bishops on political grounds.

The Lateran Treaty gave a priceless lift to Mussolini's prestige. He could present himself as the only man who had been able to solve the dispute that had divided Italian society for 60 years. It also ensured that belief in Fascism was consistent with belief in Catholicism and Mussolini avoided forcing Italians to choose where their loyalties lay. Following the Lateran Treaty, the Church made clear its political support for Fascism. In the March 1929 election, cinema footage showed Cardinals La Fontaine of Venice, Gamba of Turin and Maffi of Pisa leading their clergy from the celebration of Mass to the polls to vote in favour of Fascism. It was this political support that Mussolini had intended the treaty would secure. Pius XI supported the Italian invasion of Abyssinia in 1935–6 and Italian involvement in the Spanish Civil War from 1936 to 1939.

However, fundamentally the existence of the Catholic Church was an affront to Fascism. Mussolini was forced to tolerate the Church and this undermined his hold on Italy. The Pope was a rival for the affection of the Italian people. Furthermore, Catholic organisations and the values of the Church came into conflict with Fascism. In 1931, the Pope opposed Mussolini's attempts to suppress Catholic Action, a Catholic leisure organisation, calling Fascism a 'pagan ideology'. A compromise was reached whereby Catholic Action's activities were confined to those of a religious nature and former members of the PPI were not allowed to be leaders. The changes did the movement no harm and its numbers swelled from 250,000 in 1930 to 388,000 in 1939. The Pope also objected to the introduction of anti-Semitic measures, declaring, 'Spiritually, we are all Jews.' However, the death of Pius XI in February 1939 prevented a damaging clash between Church and State. The new pope, Pius XII, never criticised Mussolini's policies publicly.

Cultural diversity

A discussion of cultural diversity in Italy embraces a wide range of elements of Italian life. The arts and the intellectual communities were part of the cultural world that the Fascists increasingly controlled. University professors were forced to swear an Oath of Loyalty to the regime or lose their post, and all but 11 did so. The historical philosopher Benedetto Croce lost all university positions and saw his books removed from university and school syllabuses, but he was allowed to continue writing and publishing. His *History of Italy from 1871 to 1915* countered the fascist attack on Liberal Italy and claimed that Fascism was the 'parenthesis', or break from the main flow, in Italian history, not the years of the Liberal State. Sixty academics became members of the Italian Royal Academy, chosen by Mussolini. The composer Puccini was won over in this way and publicly supported the regime. Cultural diversity also relates to the different values of Italian society and Mussolini sought to transform values through control of education, leisure and Italian families. The intolerance of cultural diversity even came to mean attacks on those who were not ethnically Italian.

Education, leisure and the family

Mussolini believed that the Italian people needed to be transformed. The recent history of Italy was of a nation that had been pushed around because its ruler and people had failed to resist greater powers. The 'mutilated victory' was considered to be clear evidence of this. Mussolini viewed war as essential as it 'turned the blood-stained wheels of history'. As we have seen here, he stated that 'war is to man what

Cross-reference

The conquest of **Abyssinia** is described on page 79.

Questions

1 How successful was Mussolini in his relations with the Catholic Church?

2 How damaging do you think toleration of a rival set of ideas was to Mussolini's desire for a totalitarian State?

childbirth is to woman' and that it was 'better to live one day as a lion than 100 years as a sheep'. He therefore set out to militarise the Italian nation through propaganda, the use of language (such as describing the policy of increasing Italy's birth rate as the 'Battle for Births') and a social policy that significantly changed the culture of Italy. School teachers were forced to join the Fascist Party and wear uniforms to work. A picture of Mussolini in military uniform appeared in every classroom. 'Fascist Culture' became a compulsory subject, and Italian history, literature and the study of Latin were introduced to all schools. The study of history became simplified after 1936 when a single history textbook became compulsory, which made clear not only the Italian contribution to the world of artists like Michelangelo and explorers like Christopher Columbus but also the debt Britain, France and the USA owed to Italy, which had won the First World War. School organisation was also changed and single-sex schools were enforced.

Outside the school gates, youth organisations were created to ensure continuous exposure to fascist values. In April 1926, the national youth organisation Opera Nazionale Balilla ('the Balilla') was formed for boys aged between 6 and 18. As well as swearing an oath to serve Mussolini and Fascism, members had to memorise the creed of the movement.

Fig. 2 *A 1931 cover of **Gioventri Fascista**, the newspaper of the Italian fascist youth movement*

I believe in Rome the Eternal, the mother of my country, and in Italy, her eldest daughter, who was born in her virginal bosom by the grace of God; who suffered through the barbarian invasions, was crucified and buried, who descended to the grave, and was raised from the dead in the 19th century, who ascended into heaven in her glory in 1918 and 1922 … I believe in the genius of Mussolini, in our Holy Father Fascism, in the communion of martyrs, in the conversion of Italians and in the resurrection of the Empire.

4 *The creed of the Balilla*

The Piccole Italiane was set up for girls aged 9 to 14 and the Giovani Italiane for girls aged 15 to 17. Both these organisations provided instruction in fascist ideology and the genius of Mussolini, as well as opportunities to play sport, go camping, and take part in artistic and musical activities. There was also military training and members wore military-style uniforms. By 1937, there were 7 million members of the Balilla. The Opera Nazionale Dopolavaro (meaning literally, 'after work') was set up in 1925 to coordinate the leisure time of adults, and took control of a wide range of social organisations. By 1932, it controlled all football clubs, 1,350 theatres, 2,208 drama societies, 8,265 libraries, 3,324 brass bands and 2,139 orchestral societies. Membership stood at 4 million in 1939 and the organisation was genuinely popular; a little fascist rhetoric was a price worth paying for day trips, cheap holidays, local entertainment and sports facilities. Fascism stressed the traditional role of women, subservient to men, and returned them to the home to fight the 'battle for births'. The youth movements trained girls for their future role as mothers. A 'mother and child day' was introduced in 1933 and working mothers received

■ **Exploring the detail**

Anti-Semitic measures

■ Foreign Jews were banned from Italian schools.

■ All Jews who had arrived in Italy after 1919 were given six months to leave, meaning Jews who had fled from Nazi Germany or Austria had to move on again.

■ Jews were forbidden to join the Fascist Party or the army.

■ State employment was denied to Jews, so all Jewish teachers were dismissed.

■ Jewish property was confiscated and Jews could not be managers of businesses employing more than 100 workers.

■ Marriages between Jews and Italians were forbidden.

■ Cross-reference

The *Anschluss* is explained on page 116.

maternity leave and state benefits. Women gained the vote in local elections in 1925, although this reform was undermined by the fact there were no more local elections. Women continued to be allowed into higher education, to study to become teachers, for example, but they could not teach subjects that were particularly important to the regime; as a consequence, men taught history, Latin and philosophy, but the sciences were taught by women. However, the reality for most middle-class women was that opportunities were restricted. In 1938, a law was passed limiting the number of women in the workplace to 10 per cent and women were forced into appropriate employment as secretaries and telephone operators, for example.

Racial policy

Jews

Although Mussolini was an extreme Nationalist, this did not lead to discrimination against ethnic minorities in Italy in the immediate aftermath of his appointment as prime minister. The Jewish community stood at around 50,000, or 0.1 per cent of the population, and was particularly well integrated. One in three adult Jews was a member of the Fascist Party, the mayor of Milan was Jewish and Mussolini had a Jewish mistress, Margherita Sarfatti. Mussolini himself stated in 1932, 'Anti-Semitism does not exist in Italy. Italians of Jewish birth have shown themselves to be good citizens and they fought bravely in the war.' In 1935, he ridiculed the anti-Semitism of Nazi Germany. However, by 1938 Mussolini's attitude had changed and Italian Jews came under attack. In July 1938, the Manifesto of Racist Scientists asserted that there was a pure Italian 'Aryan' race and Jews did not belong to it. Discriminatory measures followed in September and October 1938.

Mussolini's new-found anti-Semitism was clearly influenced by Hitler and Nazi policies. After 1936, he and Hitler brought their nations ever closer, united by a common hatred of the left and by their desire for expansion. In March 1938, Mussolini allowed Hitler to carry out the *Anschluss* with Austria, having prevented it only four years earlier.

The inevitable consequence of the closer relationship between Mussolini and Hitler was the introduction of anti-Semitism into Italy, despite the fact that this created conflict with the Pope. It is also likely that Mussolini's aggressive foreign policy made war increasingly likely, and that at a time of war it was not possible to tolerate 'racial aliens' who might not have been entirely loyal to the fascist regime. However, it is difficult to believe that these measures would have been easily accepted without at least some level of complicity from the Italian people. The Italian historian Michele Sarfatti has argued that Italy did not become anti-Semitic overnight. He points out that the myth of a Jewish–Bolshevik conspiracy was a common theme in fascist literature in the 1920s and in the 1930s as much anti-Jewish printed material appeared in Italy as in any other European country except Nazi Germany. The anti-Semitic legislation of the 1930s was the natural conclusion to this wave of hatred. The ultimate consequence of discrimination would be the complicity of Mussolini and the fascist regime in the Holocaust, with 7,000 Italian Jews murdered.

Africans

■ A closer look

The conquest of Abyssinia

The Roman Empire was an inspiration to Mussolini who saw himself as a new Caesar, recreating the glories of the past. Mussolini was desperate to extend the Italian Empire. The militaristic nature of Fascism demanded that the empire was extended through war and conquest. Before the First World War, European powers had engaged in a scramble for Africa. By the 1930s, there were only two independent African countries left. One was Ethiopia (Abyssinia), which was strategically and psychologically important to Italy. Abyssinia was the largest country in the Horn of Africa, the north-eastern tip of the continent. It lay between the Italian colonies of Eritrea and Somaliland. Furthermore, the defeat of the Italian army in 1896 by the Abyssinians was a national humiliation that represented a low point for Liberal Italy. Mussolini was intent on revenge, as well as desiring the colony for the manpower it could provide for the Italian army and the additional land it could provide for Italian migrants. He was convinced by 1935 that Britain and France were more concerned with the growing threat of Nazi Germany and, in October 1935, half a million Italian troops invaded. The Emperor of Abyssinia, Haile Selassie, fled the country. He appealed to the League of Nations as the international body charged with settling disputes between countries. Italy was condemned as the aggressor and economic sanctions were introduced by League members against the Italians. However, Britain and France, the leading members of the League, were concerned about pushing Mussolini towards Hitler, so the sanctions did not include oil and Britain did not close the Suez Canal to Italian troop ships. Italy's victory was therefore assured. The conquest of Abyssinia once again made Rome the heart of a great empire. Fascist propaganda linked Mussolini with the glories of the Roman Empire and few pointed out that the Roman Empire making covered most of western Europe and parts of the Middle East and Africa, making the Fascist Empire a pale imitation of Rome's.

Fig. 3 *The Fascist Empire in Africa after the conquest of Abyssinia, in a postcard from August 1936. The Fasces symbol is used to unite Italy and its colonies in Africa: in the north Libya; and in the north-east Eritrea, Abyssinia and Somaliland*

The Italian Empire in Africa consisted of Libya, Eritrea, Italian Somaliland and, after 1936, Abyssinia. The actions of fascist governors and Italian armies suggest there was a racial intolerance of Africans based on the belief in the racial superiority of 'Aryan' Italians over Arabs and black Africans. In Libya, the 100,000 Arab population was driven out of the interior and families were placed in concentration camps, where 50,000 died. From 1911, when Italy invaded Libya, to the mid-1930s the population fell from 1.2 million to 800,000. Poison gas was used against local leaders who refused to accept Italian rule. The conquest of Abyssinia saw further use of poison gas, massacres of civilians and bombing of non-military targets. After the victory in 1936, Mussolini introduced race-based legislation in Italy and its colonies by prohibiting relations between Italians and Africans. Massacres took place after attacks on Italian rulers. In total, Ethiopian historians have estimated the death toll as somewhere between 300,000 and 600,000 between 1935 and 1941, the years of fascist control.

Fig. 4 *Haile Selassie is knocked off his throne by an Italian tank in a postcard from 1935. The wooden throne is contrasted with the mechanisation of the Italian army to highlight the cultural and economic backwardness of Abyssinia*

Germans and Slavs

The territories in north-east Italy acquired as a result of the Paris peace treaties contained two substantial ethnic minorities. There were 228,000 Germans in the South Tyrol, and 327,000 Slovenians and 98,000 Croats in Istria. The policies imposed in these regions were aggressively nationalistic with the intention of destroying the language and culture of these ethnic groups. Italian became the official language of these regions. Italian teachers replaced local teachers; in Istria, Italian teachers were forced out of schools and terrorists bombed public buildings. State institutions used Italian, which meant non-Italian speakers lost their jobs in government, the civil service and the courts. German and Slav surnames were Italianised. There was greater resistance to Fascism in these regions than anywhere else in Italy and the Church continued to preach in native languages. The small number of political executions in Italy between 1925 and 1940 included five Slavs convicted of political terrorism. The position of those of 'German blood' who lived in Italy was a potential source of conflict between Il Duce and Germany's Führer, Adolf Hitler. Hitler declared after the *Anschluss* that his ambitions for uniting German people did not extend south of the Alps and there was no campaign to 'liberate' Germans who were ill-treated by the Italian government, yet he had justified his annexation of the Sudetenland from Czechoslovakia as necessary to save Germans from persecution.

Limits to intolerance

Despite fascist ideology and Mussolini's claims, it is clear that practical considerations meant Italians enjoyed a great deal of toleration and Italy contained many features of a pluralist state.

Cross-reference

Figure 4 on page 57 is a map of **Italy's territorial acquisitions** following the Paris treaties.

Nazi ideology and **race** are discussed on pages 94–97.

The *Anschluss* is discussed on page 116.

Activity

Revision exercise

Review the section on the intolerance of diversity and copy and complete the table below.

	Intolerance	Limitations
Politics		■ The existence of the monarchy meant people had another secular figurehead to follow ■
Economy	■ Trades unions were banned ■	■ ■
Religion	■	■ The existence of rivals for people's affections and commitment in the form of the Pope and the Catholic Church meant that an alternative ideology did exist ■
Culture	■ Italianisation of South Tyrol and Istria ■	■ ■

Il Duce and the cult of Mussolini in relation to fascist ideology

Following Mussolini's appointment as prime minister and the symbolic March on Rome that marked the fascist takeover, he began to project an image of himself as the saviour of Italy. He was already Il Duce – 'the Chief' – of the PNF. He now created an image of himself as Il Duce of Italy in a similar way as Stalin had created a leadership cult in the Soviet Union, although Mussolini unashamedly encouraged his cult. It has been suggested by one of Mussolini's foremost biographers, Denis Mack Smith, that Fascism was merely theatre and Mussolini's talents lay mainly in acting the role of Il Duce, supported by a propaganda machine that emphasised the fascist slogan 'Mussolini is always right.' The cult of the leader was clearly a central feature of Fascism in action and at the heart of fascist ideology.

The development of the cult

The development of the cult was also the story of the development of Mussolini's personal dictatorship, which ensured he was genuinely the father of the nation. His political power could be ensured if he replaced government through the existing political organisations, namely parliamentary government through the Chamber of Deputies and the Cabinet, with government through the PFI organisations, while simultaneously asserting his control over the *Ras* and the PFI. By 1939, the Chamber of Deputies was simply rubber-stamping Mussolini's decisions. The Cabinet was constantly given orders by Mussolini, although it was increasingly difficult to find someone to give orders to, as by 1929 Mussolini held eight Cabinet posts including Prime Minister, Minister of Foreign Affairs, Minister of the Interior, Minister of War, Minister for the Navy, Minister for the Air Force, Minister for Corporations and Minister for Public Works. By 1933, the number had grown to 14. The creation of the Fascist Grand Council in 1922 gave him immense power, as he determined membership of the council as well as when it met and what it could discuss. Elections within the party ended and Mussolini alone determined who held which post. This enabled him to increasingly sideline potential opponents. Roberto Farinacci from Cremona, who was Secretary General of the PFI, was dismissed and replaced by the colourless Achille Starace, who offered no threat to Mussolini. Italo Balbo was sacked from the Air Ministry in 1933 on the pretext that the air force was only a third of the strength that Balbo had claimed, although Mussolini was more concerned that his popularity might make him a rival. Balbo was sent to Libya as governor, away from Rome and real power. Outside the party, the King was the Head of State and could have controlled Mussolini, but he seemed to have no desire to do so. He accepted that Mussolini replaced him as Commander-in-Chief of the army in times of war and chose to act against Mussolini only in 1943 when Italy was about to be defeated in the Second World War. After the fourth attempt to assassinate Mussolini, the death penalty was introduced for contemplating an attempt on his life. In a new legal code of 1931, it became a crime to criticise Mussolini.

Fig. 5 *Il Duce preaches to his followers*

Cross-reference

Mussolini's appointment as prime minister and the **March on Rome** are detailed on page 60.

Key features of the cult

Mussolini was portrayed as the national saviour, sent to save Italy from the disasters of liberal democracy and the strong man who would resist the threat of the left. He was the new Caesar who would make Italy a great power again. On a more mundane level, he was also the greatest of all mortal men, a role model to all Italians. He played the role of both father and lover, stripped to the waist and worked in the fields as a common man, and was pictured studying literature or art as a renaissance man as well as displaying his prowess as a racing driver, fencer and swimmer; he was even filmed wrestling lion cubs. Two activities were particularly popular in Italy in the 1930s, so Mussolini was shown skiing expertly as well as gaining his pilot's licence in 1939.

His dedication to Italy was a key feature. His office on the second floor of the government building in the Palazzo Venezia was over 18 m (60 ft) long and contained a desk in the corner and a huge ornate fireplace. Visitors would find him seated at the desk working; party and military visitors were expected to quick march across the room to meet Il Duce. The light in his office was left on all night to give the impression he worked throughout the night for Italy, although in fact he went to bed

Fig. 6 *The cult of Il Duce traced a direct line from the caesars of Ancient Rome to the great modern leader Mussolini*

early and slept for nine hours every night. In 1931, Starace introduced the salute to Mussolini as leader to start all meetings of the Fascist Party. Mussolini was far more concerned with creating an image of himself as the man of action who would save Italy than ensuring Italy was governed effectively. He preferred to remain ignorant in discussions with the Nazi government than to employ an interpreter and admit his lack of fluency in German.

Fascist government became the government of Il Duce. He met with key ministers every day, and initialled official reports with a blue 'M' but never commented on their content, preferring to make decisions over the telephone or in conversation. There was no formal structure to government. The Fascist Grand Council could not replace the government because it only met at Mussolini's command. He preferred to announce policy to the crowds who gathered beneath the balcony of the Palazzo Venezia. His ability to move a crowd and generate enthusiasm was second to none.

The use of propaganda to spread the cult

Mussolini was 1.67 m (5 ft 6 in) tall and balding, yet he was able to project the image of a powerfully built man with great physical strength. The triumph of the cult was therefore also the triumph of fascist propaganda; pictures of him riding around the riding track at his house, Villa Torlonia, were taken at an angle which suggested that the small fences were actually major hurdles. The measures taken to control the media were a typical feature of a totalitarian regime. From 1925, the press came under Mussolini's control. The Liberal newspapers dared not risk taking on the government and sacked offending editors. The Press Law of December 1925 stated that only registered journalists could write for the papers. Editors knew Mussolini read the papers himself every day, so self-censorship became the rule. Government subsidies were introduced for the press and the press office sent out detailed instructions on what to print about Mussolini's speeches. By the end of the 1930s, regulations had been established by the Ministry of Popular Culture that directed newspapers, radio and cinema on how Mussolini should be presented. For example, newspapers had to spell his name with capital letters and he was never to be presented with priests.

Fig. 7 *Mussolini as the warrior leader*

In 1937, the Ministry of Popular Culture was established. Radio broadcasting was State owned and, with 1 million radio sets by 1938, this was a crucial means of conveying the message. Cinema was a key tool. The most popular films were American imports, but these were censored and official newsreels were shown as part of the same show. Cinecitta, the Italian Hollywood, came under fascist control and produced both entertainment films and those praising the achievements of Fascism such as *Luciano Serra Pilota* which had strong family connections with Il Duce; his son Vittorio helped to make it and Mussolini suggested the title.

Fascist propaganda demonstrated undeniably that Mussolini was the great saviour. The success of Italian foreign policy was a rich source of evidence that Il Duce was the special one. In the 1920s, he had attended the Locarno Conference with Britain, Germany, France, Belgium, Poland and Czechoslovakia. He arrived by flying boat and his landing on the lake at Locarno was covered by hoards of journalists funded by the State. The Locarno Pacts fixed the western borders of Germany as guaranteed by Britain and Italy. Mussolini achieved great power status by association with Britain and was delighted when the British Foreign Secretary Austen Chamberlain described Il Duce as 'a wonderful man working for the greatness of his country'. He was even more delighted that the comment was reported across Europe; back in Italy, newspapers gleefully reported the high esteem in which their Duce was held by the rest of Europe. The conquest of Abyssinia in 1936 was a twin triumph as Mussolini won revenge for Italy after the humiliation of the defeat in 1896. His triumphant announcement that 'Ethiopia is Italian' and that once more Rome was the centre of an empire marked the height of his and Fascism's popularity.

Mussolini also benefited from Italy's great sporting success in the 1930s. When Italy won the 1934 football World Cup, he handed out medals to his winning team. The Italians also won the 1936 Olympic football tournament and the 1938 World Cup, and the triumph of Italian sport was a success that added glitz to Mussolini's gold.

> The newspapers also suggested that the Duce was infallible. 'Mussolini is always right' became a popular phrase, an idea the dictator encouraged with such utterances as 'often I would like to be wrong, but so far it has never happened and events have always turned out just as I foresaw'.
>
> **5**   *M. Robson, **Italy: Liberalism and Fascism 1870–1945**, 1990*

Activity

Challenge your thinking

Review the section on the cult of Mussolini and read Source 5.

1 Identify the reasons for the development of the cult of Mussolini.

2 Try to identify reasons why the cult of Mussolini might have been limited in its success.

Cross-reference

Nazi ideology is considered on pages 94–97 and page 129 covers the influence of Nietzsche's ideas on the **Nazi Führerprinzip**.

The cult of Mussolini and fascist ideology

One of the key reasons for the development of the cult was the status of the leader within fascist ideology. Fascist ideology is confused because it developed over time, but a consistent strand is the belief that Il Duce was a man apart. The philosopher Friedrich Nietzsche had argued that evolution would not simply stop and that therefore humanity in the 19th century would not be the same as humanity in the 20th century. He therefore developed the concept of the 'superman', which both Fascist Italy and Nazi Germany picked up and incorporated into their ideas. The evolution of man into 'superman' was accompanied by the belief in the 'will to power'. In Fascism this came to mean the ability of Il Duce, the 'superman', to mould Italy and the world through his will. This will was greater than the power of the people, for people-power meant liberal democracy and national weakness. Nietzsche was a rationalist, that is he sought logical explanations for events rather than religious or supernatural explanations. He proclaimed that 'God is dead.' His ideas went far beyond the simplistic ideas that Mussolini and Hitler seized upon and would have been appalled to be considered a founder of Fascism; he was an individualist who did not intend his ideas to be applied to states. However, the roots of the fascist belief in their superman, Il Duce – able to shape the world through the strength of his will – can be found in Nietzsche's work, as can the creation of a new secular religion with Mussolini the 'God-like' leader of the movement.

The worship of the leader was also an inevitable by-product of Fascism's rejection of alternative forms of government. Mussolini's Third Way extended beyond the economy and the Corporate State to become a vision for the development of Italy. This was reflected in theories of leadership. He sought a 'Third Way' because Communism was evil and capitalist democracy was weak. The Third Way needed to be significantly different not only in the organisation of the economy but also in its theory of leadership. Communism gave power to the working class before the state would fade away, so leaders were less important than the spontaneous actions of the masses. Capitalist democracy gave the masses the power to govern through the ballot box. The Third Way was therefore strong leadership through individuals, who recognised the best interests of the nation and had the will to act to secure these interests; they would wage war in the interests of the nation, for example, because they had the strength to take such a decision. It is not a particularly sophisticated idea to believe in the leadership of individuals, but the fascist obsession with the heroic history of Italy, and the Roman Empire specifically, helps explains why Il Duce wished to be a modern Caesar and worship of the leader became part of Fascism. Mussolini's obsession with the militarisation of Italy was also responsible for the place of his cult within fascist ideology. He stated that 'The Fascist Party is an army. You enter to serve and obey.' The army contains a chain of command with the commander at the apex who should be obeyed at all times. Clearly, Mussolini saw a comparison between the trained obedience of the army and the need to train the Italian people to obey in the same way. The militarisation of society was to transform the nature of the Italian people but it was also about creating obedience to the leader.

Limits to the cult

Despite the great success of the cult of Il Duce, Mussolini always had to share the stage with two major rivals. The loyalty of the Italian people to the Catholic Church had led him to abandon his pre-war atheism and conclude the Lateran Treaty in 1929. Undoubtedly this was a sensible political move because it meant he avoided having to directly compete with the Pope for the adoration of the people. However, it also meant he was not the only focus for the Italian people. The popes were also infallible, that is they refused to accept they could ever be wrong when they pronounced on matters relating to Catholic religion or morality. This was clearly an issue for Mussolini when Pope Pius XI spoke out against anti-Semitic policy, because if the Pope was right on this spiritual matter, Mussolini was clearly wrong. The Pope was also the head of an international movement with loyal disciples in every European country, which gave him a status and charisma that was

Fig. 8 *Victor Emmanuel III, Mussolini and Pius XI. A postcard commemorating the signing of the Lateran Treaty*

greater than Il Duce's. Postcards were produced to commemorate the Lateran Treaty, which featured a picture of the Pope flanked by pictures of Mussolini on his right and the King on his left. Mussolini was furious and had the postcards banned.

Such an image also showed that the King was a rival. Victor Emmanuel may have granted Mussolini power and refused to act against him during the Matteotti crisis, but he was no more a Fascist than the staunchly republican Mussolini was a supporter of the monarchy. Although the King allowed Mussolini to govern, he could still rely on the loyalty of the Italian people. His reputation was enhanced by his role as Commander-in-Chief during the First World War and he was associated with

Fig. 9 *Mussolini the military leader. One of the many faces of Il Duce*

the great Italian victory at Vittorio Veneto in 1918. The middle classes and the peasantry in the south maintained their traditional respect for the monarchy. Three groups never wavered in their support for the King and remained royalist: the aristocracy, the upper middle class and the army. The army and navy remained 'the Royal Army' and 'the Royal Navy', and the King insisted that the traditional army salute was not replaced by the fascist salute. In a dispute between Mussolini and the King, only the air force would have backed Mussolini.

Learning outcomes

Through your study of this section you should be aware of the development of fascist ideology, the different interpretations of fascist ideology, and its contribution to Mussolini's rise to power. You should also be able to reach a judgement on the relative importance of the weaknesses of Liberal Italy, the fear of Communism and the role of Mussolini himself in explaining his appointment as prime minister in October 1922.

You should understand the reasons why Fascism was intolerant of diversity, what intolerance of diversity meant in relation to politics, the economy, religion and culture, and the extent to which Italy was truly intolerant in the 1920s and 1930s.

You should understand how and why the cult of Il Duce developed, including its place in fascist ideology, and the key features of the cult. You should appreciate the impact of the King and the Pope on the extent of the cult.

Activity

Revision exercise

1 Review your reasons why the cult of Mussolini developed.

2 Add any additional ideological reasons you have identified after reading the section on the cult of Mussolini and fascist ideology.

3 Review your reasons why the cult of Mussolini might have been limited in its success.

4 Add any additional reasons you have identified after reading the section on limits to the cult.

Practice questions

(a) Explain why Mussolini failed to secure power
before October 1922.   *(12 marks)*

Study tip It is often difficult to argue a negative, so a useful tip is to consider what is the positive question that could have been asked, which is 'Why did Liberal Italy survive until October 1922?' This should make identification of the reasons slightly easier. Consider why Fascism was weak as well as any strengths of Liberal Italy. Remember to look for the most important reason and try to think about how reasons interlink. Mussolini had limited support in the 1921 election, where the governing coalition's tactic of working with him seemed to have worked because he signed the pact with the PSI abandoning violence.

(b) 'How far were the mistakes of others responsible
for Mussolini becoming prime minister in
October 1922?   *(24 marks)*

Study tip It is important that you plan this answer carefully, as you need to think about who are the 'others' that need to be considered. The King is an obvious starting point but Facta, Giolitti and even Orlando could be considered. Clearly, other factors will need to be covered to demonstrate balance and judgement. The appeal of Fascism, the social and economic circumstances and the fear of revolution generated by the growth of workers' actions and PSI support are all important. So too is the role of Mussolini in terms of creating the fascist movement and also his actions in 1922. Remember that your answer should not just cover reasons generally, but link them to the actual appointment of Mussolini. This means that the post-war economic and social problems must be related to the political crises and the lack of any alternative to Mussolini by October 1922. This approach will also ensure you demonstrate judgement by showing how the factors you are covering link together.

5 Nazi ideology and the establishment of the Nazi State

In this chapter you will learn about:

- Nazi ideology with reference to Nationalism, Socialism, race and anti-Semitism, and the *Volksgemeinschaft*

- Hitler's rise to power from 1928 to January 1933: the economic crisis in agriculture and industry, the attraction and strengths of the Nazis and Nazism, the failures of democracy and the role of the elite

- the establishment of the dictatorship from January 1933 to the army 'Oath of Loyalty'.

Cross-reference

To review the fascist **March on Rome**, re-read pages 59–60.

The origin of the term **Weimar Republic** is outlined on page 92.

Fig. 1 *The memorial in front of the Reichstag, Berlin, to the 94 Social Democrat deputies who voted against the Enabling Act that gave Hitler dictatorial powers in March 1933. They all died in concentration camps*

In 1928, a secret government report concluded that the Nazis and Adolf Hitler had 'no noticeable influence'. The Nazi attempt to seize power in November 1923 by aping the fascist March on Rome had led to Hitler's arrest and imprisonment. Although Adolf Hitler was able to rebuild the party on his release from prison in 1925, economic stability in Germany led to increased political stability. Extremist parties like the Nazis appeared to have missed their chance. In the 1928 elections to the German parliament, the Reichstag, the Nazi Party saw its support decline to 3.4 per cent of the vote and only 12 seats. It appeared that both Hitler and the Nazi Party would be consigned to the footnotes of history. Less than five years later, Hitler was sworn in as the fifteenth chancellor of the Weimar Republic on 30 January 1933.

The next 18 months saw the transformation of a theoretical democracy into a one-party dictatorship in which Nazi ideology was increasingly put into practice. Initially, Nazi ideology was a confused and contradictory set of ideas based on the 1920 25-point programme and Hitler's 1925 autobiography *Mein Kampf*. Once the Nazis were in power it became clear that, although some of these contradictions continued to exist, the Nazi values central to Hitler were given free reign and extremist actions took place because of a commitment to a set of extremist values. Hitler's popularity as 'Führer', fear of the Nazi terror state and the fact that many Nazi ideas were genuinely popular with large sections of the German population allowed an intolerance of diversity that would have genocidal consequences from 1941.

■ Key profile

Adolf Hitler

Fig. 2 *Adolf Hitler*

Adolf Hitler (1889–1945) was born in Braunau Am Inn in the Austrian Empire, the son of a customs official. He had little formal schooling and after the death of his mother he moved to Vienna in 1907, where he failed to win a place at the Viennese Academy of Fine Art in successive years. In 1913, he moved to Germany where he eagerly greeted the outbreak of war, enlisting and serving with some distinction until he was hospitalised following a gas attack. He joined the German Workers' Party (DAP) in 1919, placing his stamp on the party and leading the renamed Nazi Party attempt to seize power in the Munich Putsch in 1923. After serving less than a year of his prison sentence for treason, he abandoned the violent path to power and worked through the political system. The party fortunes were transformed by the Wall Street Crash and the agricultural depression, and by 1932 the Nazi Party was the largest party in Germany. Failure to find a democratic political solution without the Nazis led to Hitler being appointed chancellor on 30 January 1933. Hitler's domestic and foreign policies were initially popular, with unemployment being conquered and the Treaty of Versailles reversed. Policy became increasingly extremist and, by the end of 1941, Germany was at war with the British Empire, the Soviet Union and the USA, while diverting resources away from the war effort into the pursuit of genocide against Europe's Jews. Defeat in the war destroyed the Nazi regime and Hitler committed suicide in April 1945.

■ Key chronology

Nazism and Hitler's rise to power

1889	Birth of Hitler.
1907–13	Hitler living in Vienna.
1914	Outbreak of the First World War; Hitler enlisted.
1918 Oct	Hitler leaves the trenches after being gassed.
1918 Nov	Germany surrenders.
1919	Germany signs the Treaty of Versailles.
1919	Hitler joins the German Workers' Party (DAP) in Munich.
1920	25-point programme formulated.
1920	DAP renamed National Socialist German Workers' Party (NSDAP), or Nazi Party.
1921	Hitler leader of NSDAP.
1923 Nov	Munich Putsch.
1924	Hitler writes *Mein Kampf* while in Landsberg prison.
1928	Nazis win 12 seats in the Reichstag election.
1929 Oct	Wall Street Crash.
1930 Sept	Nazi electoral breakthrough; 107 seats in the Reichstag election.
1932 April	Hitler comes second in the presidential election.
1932 July	Nazis are the largest party with 230 seats in the Reichstag election.
1932 Nov	Decline in support to 196 seats in the Reichstag election.
1932 Dec	Failure of von Schleicher's anti-Nazi coalition.
1933 Jan	Hitler appointed chancellor of a coalition government.
1934 Aug	Hitler combines posts of chancellor and president and becomes the Führer.

■ Nazi ideology

Nazism was a combination of Nationalism and Socialism. The name 'Nazi' was a combination of both 'nationalist' and 'socialist', emerging in response to the name 'Sozi' which was used to describe the German Social Democratic Party (SPD).

Revision exercise

Look back to the section on ideology in the introduction (pages 4–8), Marxism in Chapter 1 (pages 13–15) and Nationalism in Chapter 3 (page 54).

Identify which of the bullet points below are nationalist and which are socialist. Copy and complete the table.

	Nationalist	Socialist
Government by the working class		
Aggressive foreign policy		
Belief that your nation is the best		
End to private ownership of business		
Desire to create an empire		
Belief in racial superiority		
Money distributed fairly according to need		
Belief that workers are exploited		
Belief that people of the same blood should be united		

Cross-reference

Details of Hitler's concept of the *Volksgemeinschaft* can be found on page 96.

Fig. 3 *'The storm sweeps through the land.' A Bavarian National Party poster of about 1923 against the spread of Russian Bolshevism. All nationalist parties were anti-communist; the Nazis were not offering a unique selling point*

There is a clear parallel between the development of fascist ideas and the development of Nazism. The First World War was as critical in Germany as it had been in Italy. Germany, however, had been defeated and the resentment of a defeated power was a central feature of German Nationalism, along with the fear and hatred of the new Russian disease, communism. Nazism shared many features of other German nationalist political parties; to be a German in 1918 was to be a nationalist, with the exception of revolutionary socialists and communist movements. Nazism was not a new set of ideas. The combination of ideas and their extremism, however, were in many ways new. Hitler's contribution must also be acknowledged, to the extent that it does make sense to discuss Nazism as 'Hitlerism'. There has always been a fundamental contradiction between a movement that sought to be both 'nationalist' and 'socialist' but Hitler suffered from no such confusion. He was able to bring the two concepts together through his belief in the *Volksgemeinschaft* ('people's community'), but more significantly he was not the author of the socialist ideas of the early party. Once he had complete control of the party, and particularly once he was in power, his nationalistic, racist and anti-communist ideas became National Socialism.

The shaping of Nazi ideology

Nationalism and the legacy of the First World War

The First World War has been referred to as the war that made the Nazis. Therefore, understanding Nazi ideology requires an understanding of the international position of Germany in 1914, the expectation of the German people as war began and the treatment of Germany at the Paris Peace Conference following the war.

The German Empire in 1914 thought of itself as the world's greatest power. Ruled by Kaiser Wilhelm II, Germany was the world leader in new and emerging industries such as chemical and electrical engineering, as well as competing with Britain and the USA in the production of coal, iron and steel. The German army (the Wehrmacht) could claim to be the best in the world, as military conscription had created a trained reserve that was on a par with the regular army. Furthermore, every junior officer and NCO was trained to do the job of their superior; the Russian army may have been bigger than the Wehrmacht, but its men were untrained peasants. Germany had the second largest navy in the world, and the development of the new Dreadnaught-class battleships had closed the gap between Britain and Germany by making much of the British fleet obsolete. Germany had begun to acquire an overseas empire and, although the 13 colonies in Africa, Asia and the Pacific were of limited economic and strategic value, they confirmed Germany's status as a great power. Germany had also taken steps to improve the social and economic condition of the people and had introduced unemployment insurance and old-age pensions in the 1880s. Germany was also the land of great composers such as Beethoven and Wagner, great writers like Goethe and Schiller, and great philosophers like Marx and Nietzsche. Most of us would agree today that the dominant power of the 20th century was the USA but in 1914 the likelihood was that the 20th century would be the German century.

German entry into the First World War was greeted with widespread enthusiasm. The war would enable the country to break out of the encirclement faced from France and Russia and to ensure its dominance of continental Europe. There was no sense that Germany might be defeated in the war. The German army enjoyed immediate success, driving through Belgium and northern France and approaching Paris; the front line was so close to the city that Parisian taxi drivers transported French soldiers to the front. In the east, the Russian army was defeated in the autumn of 1914 at the battles of Tannenberg and the Masurian Lakes. Sebastian Haffner in his memoir of the inter-war years *Defying Hitler* (2002) has written of the psychological impact of the war starting in the summer and the glorious sunshine that he associated with German victories. None of the western campaign was fought in Germany, and after the German victories in the autumn of 1914 the eastern front was in Russia. Germany was never invaded, never defeated and almost broke through to Paris at the end of May 1918. When Lance Corporal Adolf Hitler was admitted to hospital in October 1918, he, like most German soldiers and civilians, had no reason to doubt that victory was at hand. The German surrender on 11 November 1918 was therefore incomprehensible to Germans. Scapegoats were sought for defeat and the myth developed that Germany had been 'stabbed in the back' by the **'November Criminals'**. The new Weimar Republic of Germany that was established was born out of defeat, associated with failure and, in the eyes of many Germans, governed by traitors. Sebastian Haffner was a seven-year-old boy when the war began. In his memoirs he contrasts the outbreak of war with Germany's defeat and the Weimar 'revolution'.

> ■ Key term
>
> **'November Criminals'**: the term used by nationalists to describe those who undermined the war effort and surrendered in 1918. The term was particularly applied to the first chancellor and president of the new Weimar Republic, Friedrich Ebert, and to the political party he led, the Social Democratic Party (SPD), as well as Communists. Ebert was a Jew, and extreme Nationalist and anti-Semitic political groups often extended the term 'November Criminals' to apply to prominent German Jews who they believed were less committed to the war.

It has been of ominous significance for the later history of Germany that in spite of all the terrible misfortunes that the war brought, its outbreak was associated in almost everyone's memories with a number of unforgettable days of great excitement, while the revolution of 1918, while it finally brought peace and freedom, only awakens dark memories in the minds of most Germans. The very fact that the war began in brilliant summer weather and the revolution in cold, wet November fog was a severe handicap for the revolution. Though November 1918 meant the end of the war, husbands restored to wives, and life restored to men, it recalls no sense of joy, only a bad mood, defeat, anxiety, senseless gunfights, confusion and bad weather.

1　　*Sebastian Haffner, **Defying Hitler**, 2002*

Key
- From German Empire
- From Austro-Hungarian Empire
- From Russian Empire
- From Bulgaria

Fig. 4 *Germany in 1919: the Treaty of Versailles*

Exploring the detail

The Weimar Republic

The new German republic was established in February 1919 in the town of Weimar, about 240 km (150 miles) south-west of Berlin. Berlin had been the scene of a communist uprising and although the 'Spartacists', as they called themselves, were crushed in January 1919 by Freikorps units, it was felt that Berlin was too unstable. The new Reichstag therefore met in Weimar and the new State was subsequently known as the Weimar Republic.

The Paris Peace Conference followed the war and the Treaty of Versailles was signed between the Allies and Germany in June 1919. Opposition to the treaty would be a central belief of German nationalists and of Hitler and Nazis specifically. The treaty was condemned in Germany as a 'diktat' (dictated treaty) as the German delegation was not allowed to negotiate the terms. Germany lost all non-German speaking territory under the principle of national self-determination, lost all its overseas colonies, and was forced to demilitarise the west bank of the River Rhine and 50 km (31 miles) of territory on the east bank. The German army, a symbol of pride to the German nation, was reduced to 100,000 men; Germany was restricted to six battleships and no submarines or military aircraft were to be built. Germans living in East Prussia found themselves divided from the rest of Germany by the Polish Corridor when the territory of West Prussia and Posen, which contained 2 million Germans in a mixed Polish–German population, was given to Poland to ensure Poland had access to the sea. The German cities of Danzig and Memel were placed under League of Nations control because of their strategic positions.

Germany was forbidden from uniting with the 7 million Germans living in the newly created Austrian State. In total, 12 million Germans were not part of the new Republic, as there were also 3 million Germans in the Sudetenland which was part of the newly formed Czechoslovakia. Germany was also forced to accept Article 231, which placed the blame for starting the war on Germany alone. As Austria-Hungary and Russia had mobilised before Germany, the 'War Guilt Clause' was a source of deep resentment, particularly as it was used to justify the payment of reparations to France, Belgium and Britain for the damage caused by Germany as a result of its aggression. In 1921, the reparations were fixed at 132,000 million gold marks (£11,000 million), payable in annual instalments. Not only was this the largest sum ever imposed following a war, it was felt by many to be impossible to pay. In 1921, the yearly repayments were estimated to be the equivalent of 40 per cent of German gross domestic product (GDP) by the English economist John Maynard Keynes.

A closer look

National self-determination and the Treaty of Versailles

The principle of national self-determination was one of the key ideas on which the president of the USA, Woodrow Wilson, wanted to base all the peace treaties. It meant that the future of disputed territory would be decided in line with the wishes of the people of that territory. Germany accepted an armistice on the basis that the principle would apply. As a result, they expected to lose Alsace-Lorraine to France as it had been annexed by Germany in 1871 following the defeat of France in the Franco-Prussian War. Germany had imposed the use of German in schools, changed the language of road signs and appointed German-speaking civil servants in Alsace-Lorraine, but the people still considered themselves to be French. Other non-German territory was lost, including Eupen and Malmedy to Belgium and northern Schleswig to Denmark. However, Germany expected that national self-determination would apply to German people who were not currently part of Germany and that they would be able to incorporate Germans who had been part of the Austro-Hungarian Empire until its collapse in 1918. Uniting Austrian-Germans with Germany would create the 'Greater Germany' that German Nationalists had longed for since the 19th century. Instead, the Germans discovered that national self-determination did not apply to countries that had lost the war. The Treaty of Versailles did not allow the 2 million Germans living in Poland to choose to join Germany. In the Treaty of St Germain, signed by Austria and the Allies in 1919, 3 million Germans became citizens of the new State of Czechoslovakia. Finally, both the Treaty of Versailles and the Treaty of St Germain explicitly forbade the unification of Germany and Austria. This union, known as the *Anschluss*, became one of the goals of many German nationalists and was part of the programme of Hitler and the Nazis.

Activity

Revision exercise

Look back to the section on the Treaty of Versailles and national self-determination on pages 92–93.

Use this information to copy and complete the table below to explain why the German people found the Treaty of Versailles so humiliating.

Reason for humiliation	Reason why this was so humiliating	Evidence from the Treaty of Versailles
Military terms		
Territorial terms		
War guilt		
Process		

Cross-reference

For more information on the *Anschluss*, look ahead to page 116.

To recap on **proportional representation**, re-read page 56.

Change in the political scene, 1918–19

German resentment of the Treaty of Versailles was widespread. However, it was not the only significant impact of the First World War that helped shape Nazi ideology. The war was also responsible for a change in the system of government. Kaiser Wilhelm II was forced to abdicate and the German Empire became a liberal democratic republic, with the newly elected Reichstag meeting in the town of Weimar. The system of proportional representation was used to elect the new government, leading to coalition governments of more than one party.

Germany's first experience of democracy was therefore one that was associated with defeat in the First World War and the humiliation of Versailles. In addition, it appeared likely that the Bolshevik seizure of power would be accompanied by a German communist takeover. Both the capital city Berlin and the southern state of Bavaria were the scene of short-lived communist States that were crushed by Freikorps, ex-First World War soldiers who saw Communists as traitors who had undermined the war effort in 1918 and who were now trying to establish a German Soviet Union. It was not lost on the right wing that half the leaders of the Bavarian 'Red' Republic were Jewish.

Early Nazi ideology

The 25-point programme

The ideology of the German Workers' Party was first presented in February 1920 in a speech made by Hitler in Munich. This 25-point programme was heavily influenced by the experience of the First World War and the nationalist desire to overturn the Treaty of Versailles, together with hatred of the democratic government that had signed the Treaty and of Communism which was considered to be anti-German. However, at this stage the party was also influenced by the desire of some members of the party to protect workers who were suffering as a result of the State failing to protect Germans at the expense of Jews and foreign capitalists. Hatred of Jews and the desire to discriminate against them in favour of those of 'German blood' was a view shared by many early Nazis and this idea of anti-Semitism was to become an increasingly important part of Nazi ideology. A summary of these ideas is presented as Source 2.

■ Cross-reference

The concept of a **Greater Germany** and the **Treaty of St Germain** are introduced on page 93.

1 All Germans should be united into a Greater Germany.

2 The Treaties of Versailles and St Germain should be overturned.

3 Germany should have land and territory (colonies) to feed its people and settle her surplus population. This land should be given to the German people because of their racial superiority.

4 Only those of German blood may be members of the German nation.

5 No Jew may be a member of the German nation.

6 Only members of the German nation may vote.

7 All non-German immigration must be stopped.

8 It must be the first duty of each citizen to work for the general good of the nation.

9 Education must ensure that all children understand the importance of the state and their role within the state.

10 No religious beliefs should be allowed that contradict German values.

11 All income unearned by work should be abolished.

12 Personal enrichment from war must be regarded as a crime against the nation. Therefore, all war profits should be confiscated.

13 The country requires a strong central government for the Reich.

14 The leader must be obeyed.

15 Parliamentary democracy has failed the German people. It is weak and leads to Communism.

16 Communism is evil. It places the working class before the nation.

2   *Extract from the German Workers' Party*
                                          25-point programme, 1920

Activity

Source analysis

Look back to the sections on ideology in the introduction (pages 4–8), Marxism on pages 13–15 and Nationalism on page 54. Study Source 2, which sets out the key points of the German Workers' Party programme in 1920.

1 Indicate which of the Nazi ideas are nationalist, socialist or anti-Semitic. Note that some ideas could be considered to be a combination.

2 Are there any other key themes you can identify as present in Nazi ideology?

Ideological developments

This initial statement of ideology was almost entirely the work of Hitler and Anton Drexler, although Hitler made sure his ideas came first, particularly points 1–4. The party was now renamed the National Socialist German Workers' Party (NSDAP), or Nazi Party. By 1921, Hitler was the leader of the party and the ideology of the party was developed in his autobiography, *Mein Kampf*, the first volume of which was published in 1925. *Mein Kampf* set out Hitler's political aims and ideas.

Key profile

Anton Drexler

Anton Drexler (1884–1942) formed the German Workers' Party in January 1919 in Munich. It was a party of workers and ex-servicemen, although Drexler himself had been unfit for military service. The party was nationalist and anti-Semitic, though some of the original members also held socialist ideas. Hitler attended a meeting in September 1919 and was persuaded to join the party. Hitler was the main asset of the party and Drexler became jealous. Inevitably, they clashed and Hitler resigned from the party. Other party members persuaded him to rejoin with effective total control and Drexler was sidelined.

Nazi ideology was not a coherent set of ideas. Karl Marx believed he had created a scientific theory, but Nazism was a range of ideas set out by different people at different times. The greatest area of confusion

German people should be united. The multi-ethnic Austro-Hungarian Empire where I was born was totally undermined by the lack of commitment of the different races to supporting the nation. This is why Austria was defeated in the First World War.

The Jew is Germany's greatest enemy. I remember seeing Jews in Vienna who looked and dressed differently to Germans. Jews are not a religion but a race and therefore they have no loyalty to Germany. Jewish businesses undermined the war effort by making profits from the production of war materials. The new government is dominated by Jews and Germany is suffering.

The job of the state is to protect German people and to secure their future by defeating inferior people and taking their land; otherwise the German people themselves will be defeated.

Democracy only leads to compromise and Communism. It will fail to provide the strong government Germany needs, so the workers will revolt and establish a communist state that is loyal to the Soviet Union not Germany.

Democracy is weak and un-German. Many people are ignorant and cowardly, and democracy can never replace the principle of leadership. One man knows better what is best for the nation.

The state knows what is best for the individual and therefore the state must have the power to act. Individual liberty is less important that strong central government.

Fig. 5

Nazi ideology: key themes

Activity

Thinking point

Why was Nazi ideology contradictory?

Key term

Lebensraum: meaning 'living space', the term was the Nazi idea that all Germans had a right to land. Germany's large population and relatively small territory meant that more land would have to be acquired. Living space would therefore be gained in Poland and Ukraine, with German families relocated to the east where they would run large farms with local (slave) labour. The Nazis idealised the German family living on the land and *Lebensraum* was an essential part of this vision.

lies in the fact that the party was both 'nationalist' and 'socialist'. This reflected the ideas of the early members. Hitler was a Nationalist, but other founding members who were workers were more concerned with protecting their rights. Drexler was mainly a Nationalist, but he thought the party should try to attract the support of German workers by winning them over from the German Socialist and Communist Parties.

The two ideas of 'Nationalism' and 'Socialism' were united in the idea of the *Volksgemeinschaft*, or 'people's community'. The Nazis sought to create a State that was exclusively German, including those Germans currently living outside Germany. At the same time, non-Germans would be encouraged to leave Germany. Those who remained would be outside the people's community and would therefore be exploited in the interests of those of 'German blood'. The German worker would therefore be protected not by redistributing wealth from the rich, but by redistributing wealth from non-Germans and by the State acquiring more land that could be given to Germans at the expense of non-Germans. This was the basis of the Nazi idea to acquire more territory abroad known as *Lebensraum*.

Alfred Rosenberg made further sense of Hitler's unconnected ideas by drawing to his attention the Jewish nature of Bolshevism. Rosenberg pointed out that Marx and Engels were Jews, Trotsky and other leading

Bolsheviks were Jews and therefore Communism was a Jewish plot to destroy the national identity and strength of Germany. Hitler's anti-Semitism, anti-Communism and desire for *Lebensraum* in Germany could all be united into one ideological goal, war with the Soviet Union. In 1939, Hitler said, 'Everything I do is directed against Russia.' This explains why he launched the invasion of the Soviet Union in 1941 even though it meant fighting a war on two fronts. Hitler would not have been Hitler if he had not invaded the Soviet Union.

Ultimately, the lack of sense in Nazi ideology has led some historians to see the concept of 'struggle' as a useful summary of what Hitler believed. His autobiography was called 'My Struggle', and the struggle of will was central to his vision of the world.

■ **Activity**

Revision exercise

Review this section to remind yourself of the key themes of Nazi ideology. Copy and complete the table below to summarise the key themes.

Key theme	Meaning in Nazi ideology
Nationalism	
Socialism	
Race and anti-Semitism	
Volksgemeinschaft	

■ The rise to power of Hitler from 1928 to January 1933

It is important to recognise that despite an ideology that was meant to appeal to a wide range of German voters, the Nazi Party had little success in winning popular support before 1928. Hitler had some initial success in raising the profile of the party after he took control from Drexler in 1921. By 1923, Hitler had increased party membership to about 2,000, including two particularly influential figures, the ex-First World War General Erich von Ludendorff and the ace fighter pilot Hermann Goering. The party had adopted the swastika symbol. The flag, with a black swastika inside a white circle on a red background, deliberately made use of the three colours of Imperial Germany, in contrast to the red, black and yellow of the Weimar Republic – colours that nationalists said represented Communism, Jews and the Church. Hitler was inspired by Mussolini's example to try to seize power by a show of strength and on 9 November 1923 he led the party in the Munich Putsch. However, the March on Rome was not the fascist seizure of power; negotiation with those who were in a position to grant power was the key to Mussolini being made prime minister.

The Munich Putsch

Hitler and the Nazi Party's ill thought-out attempt to seize power was foiled on the morning of 9 November 1923. The Bavarian governor von Kahr was making a speech in a Munich beer cellar on the evening of 8 November when Hitler and Goering led a group of armed *Sturm-Abteilung* (SA) members into the hall. Hitler announced the beginning of a national revolution and that 600 armed men were surrounding the cellar. Von Kahr was arrested by the SA, although he was released after agreeing to co-operate, enabling him to warn the Munich police. Hitler was persuaded to continue the Putsch by General Ludendorff and the next morning 3,000 Nazis marched towards the centre of Munich. Hitler thought he had secured agreement with the Munich police chief and the Putsch would not therefore be resisted. However, 100 police met the march and opened fire. Sixteen party members and three police were killed. Hitler was arrested and stood trial for his treachery in 1924. His closing speech was a propaganda triumph, in which he won nationalist support by stating his intention in trying to seize power was to be a destroyer of Marxism rather than just a minister. He received a lenient sentence of five years, of which he served only nine months, at Landsberg prison. Goering was shot in the thigh and was smuggled out of the country to Austria. To control the pain he was given morphine, which became a lifelong addiction. The police turned their guns away from the war hero Ludendorff and he was acquitted at the trial. He was elected to the Reichstag in May 1924 as a Nazi Party delegate.

Fig. 6 *The end of the Munich trials, 1923. General Ludendorff leaves the courthouse after his case is dismissed for lack of evidence*

The Munich Putsch gave the Nazi Party exposure, but while Hitler was imprisoned the movement split between north and south, nationalists and socialists, and revolutionaries and democrats. Although Hitler was able to unite the party at the February 1926 Bamberg Conference, it was of little consequence. The Nazi message was not particularly relevant to most Germans who were enjoying economic prosperity. The Nazis won only 14 seats in the December 1924 Reichstag election and just 12 seats in the May 1928 elections. It seemed that the party would fade into history.

The economic crisis in agriculture and industry

Nazi support in 1924 came from the south of Germany, particularly Bavaria. However, from 1927 the Nazis started to win support from an unlikely quarter. Small farmers in the north German plain began to turn to the party as successive Weimar governments seemed to be ignoring their interests. In 1924, the coalition government, dominated by the Social Democratic Party (SPD), abandoned the policy of protection that had prevented cheap imports of foreign food. Cheap food was popular with the working class whom the SPD represented, but meant German farmers lost out. Grain prices collapsed, with the price of wheat, rye and feedstuffs falling from 250 marks a tonne in 1927 to 160 marks by 1930. Pig farmers in north Germany suffered as a result of cheap bacon imports from Denmark. A double blow occurred in 1927, with a poor harvest and an outbreak of foot-and-mouth disease. Some 13 million farmers were affected and there were no State benefits to help them out – national insurance did not cover the self-employed.

Many small farmers found themselves having to borrow against the value of their land and then found they could not meet repayments. A demonstration of 30,000 farmers in Oldenburg in 1928 was followed by a demonstration of 140,000 in Schleswig-Holstein later that year. By the late-1920s, the average agricultural income was 44 per cent below national average. The Nazis forged a link with the rural community by attacking the high levels of interest charged by banks and promised a people's community in which tariffs would be restored, interest payments would be reduced and foreclosures would stop. The Nazi view of Germany was that the banks were Jewish and German farmers were being victimised. Many German farmers were attracted by the promises of support and thought little of anti-Semitism, whereas other rural communities happily accepted Nazi racial views. There was a clear correlation from 1930 onwards between how rural an area was and the number of Nazi voters; in the September 1930 Reichstag election the Nazis won 27 per cent of the vote in rural Schleswig-Holstein on the Danish border, compared to only 12.8 per cent in Berlin.

What finally destroyed the German economy was the Wall Street Crash of October 1929. Share prices on the American stock market collapsed, with devastating effects for Germany. Payment of reparations had proved to be crippling and the German government had unwisely printed money in an attempt to meet domestic bills. The result was hyperinflation and the collapse of the German currency. In 1918, a pound was worth about 20 marks, but at the peak of inflation in 1923 a pound was worth about 20,000 million marks.

Fig. 7 *Hyperinflation of German currency, 1923. The depreciation in value of money made paper notes almost worthless and caused poverty. The cartoon shows a mother, half-buried in bank notes, holding up her starving child and crying out for bread*

At the same time, Germany failed to make reparations payments to France and Belgium, who responded by occupying the Ruhr region in November 1923. The crisis was solved by the introduction of a new currency and by rescheduling the debt under the Dawes Plan of 1924, which also encouraged foreign loans and investment into Germany. Most of these loans came from the USA. Between 1924 and 1930, long-term American loans to Germany accounted for $1,293 million out of a total of $1,430 million. In addition, $1,560 million was owed in short-term loans and $217 million in direct investments from American companies like General Motors, which had opened factories in Germany.

Fig. 8 *A 100,000 mark note from February 1923. The continued use of marks and the use of the Imperial symbol, the double-headed eagle, are evidence of the continued support for the empire and lack of support for the Weimar democracy from key institutions like the banks*

Unfortunately, rather than being used to increase the productivity of the German economy, many of these loans were wasted on reparations payments and on social and welfare provision, like swimming pools. The German economy was dependent on the well being of the American economy. When the Wall Street Crash hit the USA, American banks recalled their loans and American companies closed their factories to cut costs. The result was that German banks and businesses collapsed. In 1931, five major banks collapsed, including the State Bank, together with 20,000 businesses.

> There was great competition for jobs. Northeim's sugar-beet refinery needed an additional two hundred men each autumn after the crop was in. In September 1930 over nine hundred applied for these jobs. Wages were lower but the jobs were still desired because they re-established the worker's right to regular unemployment benefits. The maximum period a worker could receive regular unemployment payments was one year – less depending on how long he had previously been employed. After that the unemployed worker came under the care of the city Welfare Office, which ordinarily supported orphans, cripples and the aged. There was no limit to the length of time a worker could stay on the Welfare Office rolls, as long as he had no other income.
>
> Normal wages of a semiskilled worker were about 30 marks per week; regular unemployment pay was 15 marks per week, and 'emergency' benefits were only slightly less. But the welfare dole was only 8.75 marks per week for a married man and half as much for a single man. The process of moving downwards through the different grades of benefit was speeded up when it was decided in November 1930 that 'emergency payments' would be made only to those who could 'prove need'. This was the first of a series of measures designed to ease the strains caused by unemployment on the State and local budgets.

3   *The impact of unemployment in a small German town. Adapted from W. S. Allen,* **The Nazi Seizure of Power,** *1984*

Exploring the detail

Table 1 *Official unemployment in Germany, 1928–32*

Sept 1928	650,000
Sept 1929	1,300,000
Sept 1930	3,000,000
Sept 1931	4,350,000
Sept 1932	5,102,500
Jan 1933	6,100,000

It has been estimated that the total unemployed was as high as 8.5 million when those who were not covered by insurance are included.

The collapse of the economy led to mass unemployment. More than 5.5 million Germans were unemployed by the end of 1932. This level of unemployment meant that the government did not have enough money to pay meaningful benefits as not enough workers were paying national insurance. Typical weekly payments of 5 Reichsmark were not enough to buy food. The unemployed lived rough in cities, and a spoon and bowl became a prized possession as it meant you could get a meal from the mobile soup vans provided by charitable organisations. The Nazis also set up soup kitchens in many small towns. The suicide rate increased. Many members of professional middle classes were told they would have to work for less pay or face becoming unemployed. Their children faced up to the prospect of not being able to go to university as planned, but there was no work to go to as an alternative. Fear of becoming unemployed gripped the German middle classes, alongside the growing fear that the mass of unemployed workers would rise up in a communist revolution.

The attraction and strengths of the Nazis and Nazism

The Nazi Party's message had not fundamentally changed but in the Germany of 1930 people were now listening. In the September 1930 Reichstag election, the Nazis made a breakthrough, winning 18.3 per cent of the vote and 107 seats. The peasant farmers of north Germany and the small traders and artisans of the small towns of southern Germany were particularly strong in their support for Nazism, as were the under-35s. The working class mainly supported left-wing parties, with the Social Democratic Party (SPD) being the largest party and the Communist Party of Germany (KPD) also growing in support.

The middle-class fear of the working class meant they frequently turned to the Nazi Party as the only reliable protection from the extreme left. The paramilitary wing of the party, the *Sturm-Abteilung* (SA, or 'Stormtroopers'), took to the streets to fight the left, disrupted meetings of the SPD and KPD, and beat up members of the *Reichsbanner*, the SPD's paramilitary force. Such actions won support from industrialists; for example, Kierdorf, the director of Germany's largest mining company, gave the Nazis 100,000 marks. Alfred Hugenberg was the chairman of the rival German National People's Party (DNVP) but he turned to Hitler to lead his campaign against the Young Plan. Hugenberg lacked a powerful speaker and therefore placed his media empire of 500 newspapers and the Universal Film Corporation at Hitler's disposal. Such exposure ensured the Nazi message was heard at a time when unemployment had reached 23 per cent and only 63 per cent of the total population were in full-time work.

Between 1930 and 1932, there were three Reichstag elections and a presidential election. Until the second Reichstag election of November 1932, support for the Nazi Party grew. The Nazis became the largest party in the Reichstag in July 1932, winning 37.3 per cent of the vote, the highest level of support for a single party. The Nazis did not, however, win a majority of the vote and therefore of seats in the Reichstag. This meant that it was the responsibility of the president, Paul von Hindenburg, to choose the chancellor. Between 1930 and 1932, he chose three other chancellors before he turned to Hitler. It is important to understand both why the Nazis became the largest party, meaning that Hitler could pressure the president into appointing him chancellor, and why Hindenburg resisted appointing Hitler until January 1933.

Fig. 9 *'Hitler, our last hope.' This Nazi propaganda targets the working-class unemployed, although it was often the middle classes, who held jobs but feared unemployment, that were won over to Hitler*

■ **Exploring the detail**

The Young Plan

This plan was introduced in 1929 to reduce Germany's reparations and to reschedule the debt over 59 years. It therefore accepted the Treaty of Versailles and condemned Germany to pay '80 gold marks every second for 60 years', as one campaign poster stated.

■ **Key profile**

Hindenburg

Paul von Beneckendorff und von Hindenburg (1847–1934) was president of Germany from 1925 to 1934. He had come out of retirement to lead the German army in the First World War. His election as president in 1925, at the age of 78, was seen as evidence of a desire for a strong, traditional style of leadership. Hindenburg found himself having to select successive German chancellors during the political crisis of 1930–32. His appointment of Hitler in 1933 marked the end of any form of democracy in Germany.

The failures of democracy and the role of the elite

The growth in Nazi support is only half of the story of German politics between 1928 and 1933. The period also saw the collapse of democracy. The democratic parties of the Weimar Republic failed to solve the problems facing Germany, support grew for extremist parties on the left and the right, and democratic solutions seemed to be impossible to find, leaving Hindenburg with little choice but to turn to Hitler. When the agricultural and industrial depression hit, Germany was being governed by the grand coalition. From 1924 to 1928, the left-wing SPD worked alongside the German Democratic Party (DDP), the German People's Party (DVP), the Centre Party and the German National People's Party (DNVP).

Chancellors of Germany, 1928–33

1928 June	Hermann Müller, SPD
1930 March	Heinrich Brüning, Centre Party
1932 May	Franz von Papen, non-party
1932 December	Kurt von Schleicher, non-party
1930 January	Adolf Hitler, NSDAP

A closer look

Table 2 *German political parties and their key supporters*

Party	Religion of supporters	Class and age of supporters
National Socialist German Workers' Party (Nazi Party, NSDAP)	Protestant	Lower middle class, farmers and the young
German National People's Party (Nationalist Party, DNVP)	Protestant	Aristocracy and middle class
German People's Party (DVP)	Protestant	Industrialists and middle class
Centre Party (*Zentrum* or simply 'Z')	Catholic	Catholics of all classes
German Democratic Party (Democrats, DDP)	Protestant	Liberals and State-employed middle class
Social Democratic Party (SPD)	–	Workers in trades unions
Communist Party of Germany (KPD)	–	Revolutionary working class and the young

These first four parties all generally tried to make the Weimar Republic work and sought to resist extremism. The Nationalist Party was generally opposed to the SPD and the Weimar Republic, but it joined the grand coalition, providing Germany with great political stability. However, in 1928 the party lost 2 million votes as a result of joining the coalition. Alfred Hugenberg was elected chairman and the party once more opposed the Weimar Republic. The chancellor from June 1928 to March 1930 was the Socialist Hermann Müller. His coalition collapsed under the pressure of finding a solution to the Wall Street Crash, as the need to cut public expenditure exposed the great difference between the parties. The SPD favoured cutting expenditure on armaments, which was resisted by the DVP; in turn, their suggestion to cut welfare spending was rejected by the SPD. Heinrich Brüning from the Centre Party replaced Müller, but he did not have the support of most of the Reichstag so he relied on the support of Hindenburg and **presidential decrees** to govern. He held an election in September 1930 to try to increase support for a democratic coalition, but the result was a huge increase in support for the NSDAP and the KPD.

Brüning struggled to find any solution to the problem of unemployment, optimistically hoping it would blow over. Once this failed to happen, he looked for other solutions. His proposed customs union with Austria would have broken the terms of the Treaty of Versailles and his plan to create jobs by getting the unemployed to work on the bankrupt East Prussian estates was rejected by Hindenburg. Brüning had also led Hindenburg to believe that his victory in the April 1932 presidential election would be a foregone conclusion. Hindenburg felt humiliated that the combined votes for the extremist candidates, Hitler and the KPD leader Ernst Thälmann, almost equalled his share of the vote. He

Key term

Presidential decrees: the Weimar Constitution established a democratic republic with an elected Head of State, the president. Although the intention was for parliamentary government, in the event of national crisis, Article 48 gave the president the power to rule by decree. Between 1929 and 1932, over 100 decrees were passed, compared with only 29 laws enacted by the Reichstag. The president also had the power to choose the chancellor.

thought the election had highlighted the divisions in the country as well as providing the extremist parties with valuable propaganda.

The role of the elite

The new chancellor, Franz von Papen, was an aristocrat. Although he was a leading member of the Catholic Centre Party, he was not a member of the Reichstag. His appointment was meant to reassure the people that those who were born to rule were in power rather than those with narrow party political interests. Instead, von Papen lacked credibility at a time of depression and crippling unemployment. He lifted the ban on the SA, plunging the country into even greater violence between the Stormtroopers and the *Reichsbanner*. Within five weeks, 99 people had been killed in street fighting, mainly in Prussia. The socialist government of Prussia was now dismissed by the chancellor and the Prussian State was placed under martial law. Elections were held in July 1932, but these only confirmed that democracy was dead. The Nazis won 37.3 per cent of the vote and 230 seats, becoming the largest party, whereas the KPD won 14.3 per cent of the vote and 89 seats. Hitler's demand for the chancellorship and the power to rule by decree was rejected, so he refused to join any coalition.

Key profile

Franz von Papen

Franz von Papen (1879–1969) was German chancellor between July and November 1932. He was a member of the highly conservative Herrenklub, which believed that its members' wealth and position gave them the right to govern Germany. As chancellor, he appointed a Cabinet that contained four barons and a count. After his dismissal as chancellor, he was intrigued to regain power for the traditional rulers of Germany and saw Hitler as a puppet chancellor who could be controlled by Germany's traditional elite.

In September 1932 a vote of no confidence was passed against von Papen's government. New elections had to be called and Hitler thought the final Nazi victory was at hand. Instead, the Nazis lost 2 million votes and 34 seats, polling 33.1 per cent of the vote. This decline in performance in the second election of the year was mainly caused by voters' discontent with the Nazi Party, as Hitler's refusal to join any coalition government despite being leader of the largest party smacked of self-interest. The party was also increasingly short of money and so relied more on strong-arm tactics. Violence and radicalism put off many Germans who had voted Nazi only four months earlier. Von Papen argued that the only way out of the electoral deadlock was the use of emergency powers and he asked Hindenburg for dictatorial powers, but this only led to Hindenburg dismissing him. The new chancellor was General Kurt von Schleicher. He tried to create a coalition with broad-based support, including the trades unions and the left-wing of the Nazi Party, which he thought could be persuaded to split from Hitler. The plan failed and Hindenburg was left in an uncomfortable position. He did not want to appoint a lower middle-class Austrian lance corporal to the position of chancellor, particularly as he feared Hitler would dismantle democracy. As the former leader of the Imperial German army, Hindenburg intensely disliked the idea of the SA, which he saw as a private army of untrained thugs.

Activity

Source analysis

Read the sources on the attraction and strengths of Hitler and the Nazi Party.

1. Identify the strengths of Hitler and the Nazis.

2. Organise your notes under subheadings. If you find this difficult, use the headings in Hint 1. If you need further help, use the questions in Hint 2 to guide your note-making.

Source 4

Many businessmen remained unconvinced by Hitler's (often deliberate) vagueness on economic policies and continued to greet Nazism with a degree of scepticism. Nevertheless, in 1932, in the context of the growing political crisis, attitudes were shifting. A small number of businessmen and bankers handed a petition to Hindenburg on 19 November 1932, which falsely gave the president the impression of a far wider basis of support amongst the business community for Hitler.

The Programme the German Workers' Party, 1920,
Adapted from Mary Fulbrook, Hitler, 2004

Source 5

Ages of leading Nazis and other politicians, 1930

President Hindenburg	83 years old
Alfred Hugenberg	65 years old
Franz von Papen	51 years old
Adolf Hitler	41 years old
Hermann Goering	37 years old
Joseph Goebbels	33 years old

Hint 1

Possible subheadings:

- Support of business
- Support of the army
- Propaganda: modern images
- Propaganda: the Nazi message
- Hitler's abilities and image
- The Nazi Party

Source 6

The 1932 presidential election campaign

While his opponents travelled by train and struggled to cover the country, Hitler travelled by plane in a campaign named the 'Führer Over Germany'. The image of Hitler descending from the skies was common in newsreel films. Hitler visited 20 cities in 7 days.

Source 7

Also working to the advantage of the Nazis was the increasingly favourable attitude of the army, which from 1929 progressively lost faith in the ability of Weimar democracy to provide the stable economic framework under which a programme of rearmament could take place. In 1931 Hitler made clear his intention of producing such a programme.

Adapted from R. Gordon, 'Hitler's rise to power', Modern History
Review, September 2002

Fig. 10 *The attraction and strengths of Hitler and the Nazi Party*

Source 8

In the 1930 election the Nazis won 107 seats. The Nazis were able to exploit this extraordinary success through a combination of dynamic leadership, Hitler's gifts as an orator and their skill at propaganda (especially the tremendous impression created by the open-air rallies such as the 1930 Nazi Party Congress which was attended by nearly 200,000 people. They also paid careful attention to their clearly identifiable areas of electoral support. The Nazis were strong in the rural areas of Protestant north Germany, such as Schleswig-Holstein, and in the east, around Posen, Pomerania and East prussia. They were also strong in rural towns all across Germany. They were popular with the lower middle classes, the elderly and students, but their most devoted followers were farmers and farm workers.

Adapted from R. Gordon, 'Hitler's rise to power', *Modern History Review*, September 2002

Source 9

Just as the Nazis were winning support from both the upper and lower middle classes, they also won significant support from the working class. Usually ignored or dismissed as unimportant, the NSDAP's success in gaining a working-class following made it unique in Germany. It was the only party that could genuinely claim to be a party of all the people.

Adapted from T. Childers, *The Nazi Voter*, 1985

Source 10

It is important to realise that the impact of propaganda was not simply the result of Goebbel's skill in exploiting symbols and rallies, great as this was, or Hitler's undeniable talents as a speaker. It was also the result of the fact that the Nazi message reached parts of Germany other parties did not reach and that they targeted specific interest groups with specific messages. The NSDAP got its speakers, even some of its major figures on occasions, into rural districts and small towns which had often been neglected by the older political parties. Furthermore, the propaganda section of the party trained its speakers to address local issues, such as the problem of agriculture in chleswig-Holstein, or the threat to small shopkeepers in Hanover created by the building of a new Woolworth's store.

Adapted from D. Geary, *Hitler and Nazism*, 1993

Source 11

By the end of 1931, Northheim's Nazis could look back on a busy year. The number of meetings was not greater than in the previous year, but the character had changed. In the first place, the NSDAP was able to draw on the pool of Reichstag delegates elected the previous year, for local meetings. No fewer than five Reichstag delegates appeared on Nazi platforms in Northeim in 1931, in addition to the leader of the Nazi parliamentary group in the Prussian parliament. This was a rich selection for a town of ten thousand. Furthermore, the NSDAP was beginning to play upon the militaristic yearnings of Northeim's citizens. During the year they provided three former officers as speakers and staged five paramilitary parades. Finally, 1931 saw the beginning of Nazi 'evenings of entertainment': infused with as much pageantry as politics, but with varied appeal and a distinct change of pace from the usual three to five hours of speeches. The Nazi record becomes even more astounding when one considers that Northeim had only about sixty actual members of the NSDAP.

Adapted from W. S. Allen. *The Nazi Seizure of Power*, 1984

■ Hint 2

Answer the following questions to identify the strengths of Hitler and the Nazis.

1 Read Source 4 in Figure 10.

  a Who were supporting Hitler and the Nazis by the end of 1932?

  b Why were they supporting Hitler?

2 Read Sources 5 and 6.

  a What do you notice about the age of the leading Nazis compared with the other politicians?

  b What impression did the 'Führer Over Germany' campaign give of the Nazi Party?

  c Why was the image of Hitler descending from the skies significant?

3 Read Source 7.

  a Which group was increasingly supportive of the Nazis?

  b Why were they supporting the Nazis?

4 Read Sources 8 and 9.

  a Who supported the Nazis? Think about class, region and age.

  b Why was the Party Congress a powerful piece of Nazi propaganda?

  c Out of all the German political parties, what could the Nazis alone claim?

5 Read Sources 10 and 11.

  a Why was Nazi propaganda superior to the propaganda of rival parties?

  b How had the 1930 election helped Nazi propaganda?

However, the president was old and trying to keep the republic together was beyond him. The army let it be known that they favoured the appointment of Hitler to protect the State from Communism; the former president of the Reichsbank, Hjalmar Schacht, made it known that the business and financial world saw Hitler as the lesser of two evils. Otto Hindenburg was a close ally of von Papen and he persuaded his father to go along with von Papen's plan; the former chancellor saw a way to control Hitler and restore power to himself and the aristocracy. Hitler would be chancellor, but there would only be three Nazis in total in the 12-man coalition cabinet, and von Papen himself would be vice chancellor. The elite would gain access to the mass support of the Nazi movement and either Hitler would solve the economic problems or the Nazis would lose support as they too were defeated by circumstances. Hitler was appointed chancellor on 30 January 1933. Von Papen triumphantly proclaimed 'We've boxed him in; we've hired him as our act.'

Table 3 *Election results, May 1928 to March 1933*

Party	Number of seats				
	May 1928	**Sept 1930**	**July 1932**	**Nov 1932**	**March 1933**
NSDAP (Nazis)	12	107	230	196	288
DNVP (Nationalists)	73	41	37	52	52
DVP (People's Party)	45	30	7	11	2
Centre Party	78	87	97	90	84
DDP (Democrats)	25	20	4	2	5
SPD (Social Democrats)	153	143	133	121	120
KPD (Communists)	54	77	89	100	81

Table 4 *Presidential election results, April 1932*

Candidate	Number of votes (millions)
Hindenburg	19.4
Hitler (NSDAP)	13.4
Thälmann	5.0

Activity

Talking point

There is historical debate as to whether Hitler's rise to power was the result of the economic problems Germany was facing or whether the strength of Hitler and the Nazis was responsible.

1 Look for evidence to support one of these views and evidence to challenge the alternative view.

2 As a group, debate the two different viewpoints.

Activity

Statistical analysis

Study Tables 2, 3 and 4.

1 Draw a graph showing the changing political fortunes of the political parties between May 1928 and March 1933.

2 Explain the changes to a partner in your class.

3 Which party's support was the most stable? Explain why.

4 Where did Nazi and communist support come from?

The establishment of the dictatorship from January 1933 to the army 'Oath of Loyalty'

Fig. 11 *The Führer and the army. New recruits of the Wehrmacht swearing an oath of loyalty to Hitler in Munich, 1935*

Key chronology

The establishment of the dictatorship

1933 February	Reichstag fire and the ban on the Communist Party (KPD).
1933 March	Nazis win 288 seats in the Reichstag election; Enabling Act passed.
1933 May	Destruction of the trades unions.
1933 July	One-party State confirmed.
1933 July	Concordat with the Catholic Church.
1934 July	Night of the Long Knives.
1934 August	Death of Hindenburg; Hitler appointed Führer; army 'Oath of Loyalty'.

Between January 1933 and August 1934, German democracy was finally killed. Hitler banned his political opponents and established a one-party State, crushed the trades unions who could have used their power to bring him down, ensured the SA was brought under his control, took the post of president on the death of Hindenburg and received an Oath of Loyalty from the army. The success of Hitler and the Nazis during this period was due to a combination of the use of legal power, terror, propaganda and political cunning.

Hitler's main aim was to free himself of his coalition partners as soon as possible, so he asked Hindenburg to call another election. Hitler had been forced to accept the offer of the post of chancellor on Hindenburg and von Papen's terms because after three elections in a year the party was almost bankrupt. However, as chancellor, Hitler could call on the organs of the state to spread the Nazi electoral message, and the radio was immediately put to use for party propaganda. The SA's campaign against Communists and the *Reichsbanner* intensified, and with the Nazi Wilhelm Frick as Minister of the Interior they received considerable licence. Goering had been made Minister of the Interior for Prussia, and he now drafted the SA as auxiliary police. The burning of the Reichstag on 27 February 1933, for which the Dutch Communist Marinus van der Lubbe was executed, led to a ban on the KPD. This, and SA intimidation at the polling booth, helped the Nazis to win 43.9 per cent of the vote and 288 seats, but this was not the majority Hitler craved. With the support of the DNVP the Nazis were able to govern, but Hitler had not come this far to share power. On 23 March the Enabling Act was passed, which gave Hitler the power to rule by decree for four years. With the KPD banned and the SA present in the voting chamber at the Kroll Opera House, only the SPD deputies voted against the act, which was passed by 441 votes to 94. The Centre Party had been assured of the religious liberty of German Catholics and the Nationalist Party favoured strong government.

Exploring the detail

The Reichstag fire

The arsonist arrested on the scene was Marinus van der Lubbe, who was carrying a Dutch Communist Party membership card. Nazi propaganda presented the arson attack as part of a communist plot, and the KPD Reichstag deputies were arrested and the party banned. However, journalists who visited the building that evening saw so much inflammable material that they doubted that one man could have been responsible for starting the fire. Suspicion grew that the Nazis may have started the fire themselves, as a tunnel ran from Goering's office in the Prussian Ministry of the Interior to the Reichstag.

Hitler was able to force state and social institutions to submit or coordinate with the party and National Socialism, a process known as *Gleichschaltung*. The non-Nazi State governments were now dissolved and replaced with unelected Nazi governments. The Law for the Restoration of the Professional Civil Service came into effect on 7 April 1933. Civil servants could be demoted, retired, made redundant or sacked. Retired civil servants had to declare any party affiliation and sign a declaration that they supported the Nazi government. The effect of the law was to allow the civil service and education to be purged of Jews, democrats, socialists and communists. The trades unions perhaps could have stopped Hitler – they had stopped an attempt by ex-army officers to seize power in Berlin in 1920 (known as the Kapp Putsch after their leader Dr Kapp, a senior civil servant) – but they had been weakened by the depression. Hitler first granted them 1 May as a national holiday to signify the union of the Nazis and labour. He assured the unions that 'German Socialism' could meet their needs. A day later, the SA and the *Schutzstaffel* (SS, or 'protection squad') arrested the leaders of the main unions and seized their assets. On 10 May, all unions were dissolved and the German Workers' Front (DAF) was introduced, the Nazi union that aimed to control the workers rather than represent their interests. The political parties were crushed next; the SPD was banned on 22 June, Hugenberg was forced to resign from the cabinet on 26 June and, a day later, the DNVP dissolved itself. In July, a law was passed preventing the establishment of any new parties. The Catholic Centre Party had no political ambitions beyond protecting Catholic interests and, following negotiations with the Vatican, a Concordat was signed between Hitler and the Pope guaranteeing religious freedom and protection for Church property and education. The impact of a symbol of moral authority conniving with the Nazi regime went a long way to legitimising the Nazi revolution.

Key profile

Ernst Roehm

Ernst Roehm (1887–1934) was the closest to a friend that Hitler had. He was an ex-First World War soldier who revelled in war, joining the Freikorps after the war had ended. He took part in the Munich Putsch, although he was released on probation after his trial and moved to Bolivia. Hitler asked him to return and take charge of the SA in 1930. By 1934, his power was so great that Hitler was persuaded it was necessary to execute his old friend during the Night of the Long Knives.

Hitler now needed to secure his control over the means of armed force. The SA had been at the forefront in the struggle for power. Led by one of Hitler's oldest comrades, Ernst Roehm, the organisation had grown in size to around 500,000 men. Roehm had a vision of a force of 1 million Stormtroopers forming the basis of a new German army. Hitler was not so sure. Roehm and the SA represented the socialist wing of the party and they now sought a social and economic 'second revolution'. Hitler had never intended such action, and as he negotiated with business and financiers, the SA was an embarrassment. Equally, the army detested the force, and Hitler could see that the untrained thugs of the SA would be no match for the officer corps of the Wehrmacht. The SA leadership was also rumoured to be rife with homosexuality and Roehm himself was a homosexual. Von Papen spoke out against the Nazis in a speech in June 1934 and Hitler feared a conservative revival.

Goering and Himmler persuaded Hitler that action must be taken against the SA leadership. The army would supply the weapons and Himmler's SS would carry out the strike. Between 30 June and 2 July, the Night of the Long Knives was carried out. Roehm was arrested and shot, alongside 200 others who were identified as a threat including former chancellor von Schleicher and his wife. Von Papen was placed under house arrest. A law dated 3 July justified the murders as necessary in defence of the State. Hitler secured his control of the SA, and gained the support of the army, business and most Germans who were delighted that the extremists had been defeated. All that remained was for Hindenburg to make way for Hitler; he died on 2 August and Hitler combined the positions of chancellor and president in the new office of Führer of Germany. The army swore an Oath of Loyalty to Hitler's person, in the same way that they had sworn an Oath of Loyalty to the kaisers. The dictatorship was complete.

■ Key profiles

Hermann Goering

Hermann Goering (1893–1946) was a First World War fighter pilot who commanded the famous von Richthofen Flying Circus and achieved celebrity status as a result of the adulation the German press heaped on war heroes. He joined the NSDAP in 1922 and took part in the Munich Putsch, fleeing Germany in its aftermath. He was elected to the Reichstag in 1928 and was one of three Nazi members of the cabinet following Hitler's appointment as chancellor. Goering played a leading role in the Night of the Long Knives, which allowed him to remove Roehm as a rival. He took the positions of Commissioner for the Air and Head of the Four Year Plan Office, as well as creating the political police of Prussia that was later integrated into the Gestapo (the secret police) under Himmler. Goering was a popular figure with the German people, and his public profile and commitment to Hitler made him an effective number two in Nazi Germany. He was captured by American troops in May 1945 and found guilty on all counts at the Nuremburg Trials, where he was sentenced to death. He committed suicide with poison that was smuggled into his cell a matter of hours before his intended execution.

Heinrich Himmler

Heinrich Himmler (1900–45) was a chicken farmer from Landshut in Bavaria. He was appointed deputy leader of Hitler's small personal bodyguard, the SS, in 1926. He became Reichsführer-SS in 1929, as leader of the 280-strong SS. He focused on recruiting racially pure members. He controlled all the German police outside Prussia from 1933 to 1936, and took over the Prussian police from Goering in 1936. He later absorbed the Gestapo into the SS and, by 1942, his SS empire was running concentration and extermination camps, providing front-line combat divisions and special units responsible for the execution of Jews and Bolshevik Party members in occupied territory. He was captured by the British in 1945 and committed suicide by taking poison before he could stand trial.

Fig. 12 *Hermann Goering*

■ Summary questions

Review the events that led to the establishment of the Nazi dictatorship between January 1933 and August 1934.

1 Draw a timeline identifying the key events.

2 a Consider the methods Hitler used in these 18 months. Identify examples of the use of legal powers, terror, propaganda and political cunning.

b Which of these methods do you think was the most effective? Explain why.

German totalitarianism in the 1930s

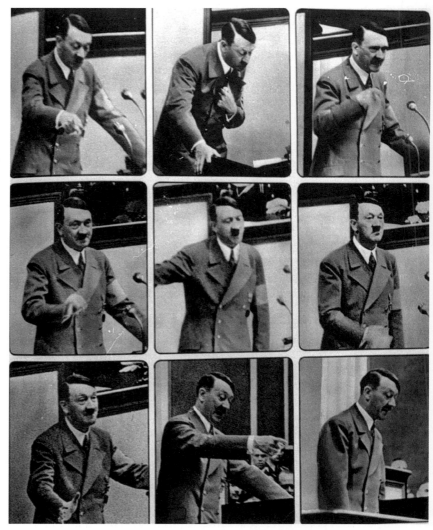

Fig. 1 *The Führer in action. A sequence from a Hitler speech, 1939*

The intolerance of diversity

Nazi Germany is clearly an example of a state that is totalitarian in terms of the intolerance of diversity. Nazi ideology was as monolithic as Soviet Communism or Italian Fascism, with a particular focus on race. The theoretical justification of intolerance was as follows:

- Like Fascism, National Socialism stressed the subordination of the individual to the state. The belief in duty and sacrifice in pursuit of a common goal was crucial and precluded any alternative, individual beliefs. The common goal was the perfect state that Hitler pursued.

- Germany had been a great power under the Kaiser before the First World War. The Kaiser's Germany had been an authoritarian state rather than a true democracy and so, although there were legal political parties, the Kaiser chose the chancellor. Bismarck was chancellor from 1871 to 1890 and he made the Social Democratic Party (SPD) illegal from 1878 to 1890. Although this was not intolerance of any other political parties, it was intolerance of those who were not pursuing common goals and whose loyalty was suspect. There was a history therefore of Germany refusing to grant liberty to those who threatened the overall security of the State.

■ **Key profile**

Otto von Bismarck

Otto von Bismarck (1815–98) was prime minister of Prussia from 1862 to 1870, during which time he led Prussia to victories over Denmark, Austria and France. These three wars were known as the Wars of Unification that created the German Empire. As German chancellor, he recognised the threat to the unity of the new German nation by enemies within who were loyal to someone other than the German Kaiser. He therefore carried out campaigns against German Catholics and the Social Democratic Party (SPD).

■ The recent history of Germany since 1919 was clear evidence that allowing political and personal freedom and diversity created a weak and chaotic State. Weimar Germany had been a liberal democracy and yet it was associated with a national humiliation, the Treaty of Versailles, a government so weak that left-wing and right-wing revolutionaries tried to seize power, civil disobedience, the invasion of the Ruhr by France and Belgium, hyperinflation, unemployment and misery. In addition, German values had been eroded by decadent and degenerate behaviour during the Weimar era. The Nazis particularly disliked female liberation, typified by working women and open lesbianism, as well as male homosexuality, prostitution, and those who accepted welfare benefits from the state rather than working for the state. People with these character traits were considered to be dangerous as they undermined the *Volksgemeinschaft* the Nazis wished to create.

■ **Cross-reference**

To revise the meaning of the *Volksgemeinschaft*, see page 96.

■ Democracy had allowed Germany to be ruled by coalition governments who tried to protect their own self-interests rather than acting in the best interests of the nation. Coalition governments had also failed to find an answer to Germany's problems. Democracy actually meant collective inaction and weakness as people hid behind others and refused to take responsibility. Nature taught that the purpose of life was struggle and only the fittest would survive. Democracy and Socialism sought to protect the weak but, as they had no use to the state due to their weakness, they should suffer as nature intended.

■ Alternative ideologies like Socialism and Communism were evil because men were not equal and the nation State, not the international movement, was what mattered.

■ Nazi ideology believed in the Führerprinzip, the idea that the leader was always right as he alone understood the needs of the German nation. The Führer would also bring the strong leadership necessary to save Germany. Hitler was the all-powerful Führer, who embodied Germany. Inevitably, individuals would have to lose their rights and freedoms as a consequence of his rule, but the liberal belief in individual rights and freedoms were not just misguided, they were actually harmful to the common good.

■ The logical conclusion of Hitler's belief that people were not equal was the racism that was crucial to National Socialism. This racism meant the intolerance of other 'inferior' ethnic groups – essentially Jews, although gypsies and Slavs (particularly Poles and Russians) also suffered greatly because of these beliefs. Hitler believed in a *Herrenvolk* (master race) that must be protected from *Untermenschen* (sub-humans). Nazism was intolerant of inferiority as much as it was of diversity. Hitler's belief in racial struggle came from his belief that either the German race would control and enslave the inferior races to the east or the German nation itself would be crushed. Racial intolerance was a life or death struggle for Hitler.

Anti-Semitism

The most notorious element of Hitler and the Nazis' intolerance of diversity was the anti-Semitic policies that were followed by the German State. The origins of Hitler's anti-Semitism are not wholly clear. Fanciful theories have suggested that Hitler took revenge on the race of the doctor who had failed to save his mother, yet he seems to have been grateful for the care Dr Bloch gave Klara Hitler before her death in December 1907. Hitler referred to his years in Vienna between 1907 and 1913 as the formative influence on his life. He was an admirer of the charismatic anti-Semitic mayor of Vienna, Karl Lueger, and collected *Ostara*, although this magazine focused more on racial theories in general than on anti-Semitism in particular. Hitler did identify in *Mein Kampf* the point at which he started to consider the question of Jews in Germany, describing a meeting with a kaftan-clad Jew with black hair locks. It seems reasonable to see Hitler's anti-Semitism as one of a confused set of general ideas formulated before the First World War.

The First World War was in so many ways the defining point in Hitler's life, and his struggle to understand the defeat of Germany saw him accept the ideas of those who blamed 'outsiders', including socialists and especially Jews. Hitler had no difficulty finding anti-Semitic literature to fuel his anger. Julius Langbehn's popular *Rembrandt as Educator* (1890) identified Jews as poison in German society, who had to be exterminated. Houston Stewart Chamberlain furthered the idea of alien races as a biological threat to German racial purity. His book, *The Foundations of the Nineteenth Century* (1899) stressed the importance of racial purity. Hitler was greatly influenced by the book and deeply moved when he met Chamberlain in 1923. Hitler's hatred of Communism was linked to his anti-Semitism by Alfred Rosenberg and this connection intensified Hitler's view that Jews were a world plague who had to be removed, first from Germany and then from the rest of the world. Whether this was the origins of the eliminationist anti-Semitism of the Nazi Final Solution is still debated by historians.

■ **Cross-reference**

To recap on **Alfred Rosenberg**, see pages 96–97.

■ A closer look

The historiography of the Holocaust

The origins of the Holocaust are still the source of intense debate between historians. Some believe that there exists a straight line between Hitler's anti-Semitism, as expressed in the programme of the NSDAP from 1920 and in *Mein Kampf*, to the decision to murder European Jews. Historians like Lucy Dawidowicz are known as 'intentionalists', in that they see a deliberate plan or intention for the Holocaust. The 'Final Solution' to the Jewish question in Europe was therefore always to eliminate all European Jews. They also see Hitler as central to the development of the Holocaust, in that he gave an order at some point in the summer of 1941. Although written evidence of this does not exist, the links between Hitler's speeches and Himmler's orders demonstrate a clear plan. The Holocaust had always been planned, beginning in 1941 because Hitler took advantage of the war against the Soviet Union to carry out murders that were easy at a time of world war.

These arguments are challenged by a group of historians known as 'functionalists', who believe that Nazi policy was not planned and there was 'a twisted road to Auschwitz'. In 1938, the 'Final Solution' was to force Jews to leave Germany and by 1940 the Final Solution included plans to relocate European Jews to the island of Madagascar. Historians like Hans Mommsen argue that instead there was a process of 'cumulative radicalisation', meaning that there was no plan but the circumstances led to increasingly extreme actions. Jews were initially shot because German leaders in eastern Europe could not manage the numbers of Jews in camps. This was then followed by the use of mobile gas vans and, after this was approved by the Nazi leadership, by the construction of gas chambers. In recent years, Ian Kershaw has tried to synthesise the two views by demonstrating the importance of Hitler and of the desire of committed Nazis to win Hitler's favour by 'working towards the Führer' – carrying out actions they knew he would approve of, but which he had not expressly ordered.

Cross-reference

Key texts that cover the different interpretations of the **Holocaust** are included in the Bibliography on pages 139–140.

Ironically, Germany was not a likely centre for extreme anti-Semitism. It did not have a particularly large Jewish population: in 1919, it was about 503,000, less than 1 per cent of the total population. Although the Jewish population had increased as a result of the Russian Revolution, which had led wealthy Jews to flee Russia, German Jews were considered to be highly assimilated. The Weimar Republic's constitution guaranteed freedom of religion and cities like Berlin were multi-racial and religiously diverse. In fact, anti-Semitism was considered to be more a feature of France, Austria, Poland, Russia and the Baltic States.

The first indication of Nazi racial ideas being put into practice came in the spring of 1933. The Nazi *Gauleiter* (district leader) of Nuremburg, Julius Streicher, organised a boycott of all Jewish shops and medical and legal practices on 1 April 1933. The action was taken partly to try to keep control over the extremists amongst the SA, who were increasingly carrying out violent attacks against Jews. The boycott was not particularly successful and the Nazi leadership decided not to repeat it. Many Germans did not connect the 'Jews' of Nazi propaganda with their local shopkeepers, and many housewives actually stocked up at Jewish shops fearing that this was just the beginning of a policy that would lead to food shortages. In addition, 1 April was a Saturday, meaning half the shops were closed already for the Jewish Sabbath. The boycott was not repeated, but the Nazi leadership found itself continuing to have to restrain local action rather than driving forward an anti-Semitic programme.

Persecution of Jewish communities in small towns was the result of actions by local Nazi groups, not as a result of state direction. This led to migration to larger towns in 1933 and 1934, and inevitably to violence in the cities in the summer of 1935. At the same time, the Nazi government was forced to limit the extent of their anti-Semitic policies to keep the support of the president and the elite, and because the need to tackle the economic problems were a far greater priority. The president of the Reichsbank, Hjalmar Schacht, defended Jewish business from extreme measures. In 1933, the government intervened with a large loan to Tietz, a Jewish business, to prevent it from collapsing and intensifying the unemployment problem. The Law for the Restoration of the Professional Civil Service of 7 April 1933 was meant to exclude Jews from public employment, but President Hindenburg insisted that Jews who had fought in the First World War, or whose fathers or sons had died in the war, were to be exempt from the law. In August 1935, Hitler was forced to ban individual actions against Jews because of the damaging impact it was having on the German economy.

The Nuremburg Laws were introduced on 15 September 1935. The Law for the Protection of German Blood and German Honour banned marriages and sexual relations between Germans and Jews and the Reich Citizenship Law defined who was a member of the German Reich.

■ **Cross-reference**

The **Law for the Restoration of the Professional Civil Service** is covered on page 108.

■ **Activity**

Revision exercise

Review Chapter 5 and the section on Nazi ideology. What evidence is there that the Nuremburg Laws were consistent with Nazi ideology?

■ **Activity**

Source analysis

Study Source 1. What do you think was meant by 'German or kindred blood'?

> I.I. A subject of the State is a person who belongs to the protective union of the German Reich, and who therefore has a particular obligation towards the Reich.
>
> II.I. A citizen of the Reich is that subject only who is of German or kindred blood and who, through his conduct, shows that he is both desirous and fit to serve the German people and Reich faithfully.

1 *The Reich Citizenship Law, 15 September 1935*

The Nuremburg Laws can be seen as an inevitable part of the Nazi ideological belief in racial differences and a desire to protect German blood. It is worth noting that Hitler announced the laws as the finale to the 1935 Nuremburg Party rally, but only as a replacement for his intended speech on foreign policy which he was persuaded was ill-timed. Furthermore, the law was not as extreme as Hitler wanted, because a law of 14 November allowed restricted German citizenship to those with only one or two non-Jewish grandparents. These Jews of 'mixed blood' were known as *Mischlinge* and were considered to be a less serious threat. This pattern of inconsistent and incomplete repression continued. Hitler made it known in 1935 that he did not want to see the removal of signs forbidding Jews from entry to public parks and cafés, but in the summer of 1936 the Berlin Olympic Games meant that anti-Semitism had to be toned down and signs removed. In 1937, 'Aryanisation' of Jewish businesses increased, which involved the forced sale of Jewish companies at reduced prices to Germans.

The *Anschluss* with Austria in 1938 led to the incorporation of a further 200,000 Jews into the Reich. All anti-Semitic decrees now applied to Austria as well, although anti-Semitism was probably

Fig. 2 *Onlookers grin while Jews are forced to perform menial tasks after the Anschluss, 1938*

stronger in Austria anyway. Austrian Nazis acted immediately, forcing Jews to clean the streets. The year 1938 saw a general increase in the pace of discrimination. All Jewish property had to be registered, emigration was encouraged by the establishment of the Office of Jewish Emigration in Vienna and Polish Jews were expelled from Germany. The policy of encouraging emigration was not as successful as might have been imagined; although 250,000 Jews left, many preferred to stay in Germany believing that the excesses would die down. Cities like Cologne and Hamburg were not especially anti-Semitic and one Jewish survivor, Karl Meyer, has testified that he lived for five years in Cologne without being attacked. In addition, Switzerland insisted on the addition of the letter 'J' to all Jewish passports so they could restrict Jewish emigration, and most countries were reluctant to take Jews as migrants because, as a result of Nazi policies, they were often poor and unemployed.

13·MÄRZ 1938
**EIN VOLK EIN REICH
EIN FÜHRER**

Fig. 3 *'One People, One Empire, One Leader.' The Nazi annexation of Austria was justified on the grounds of race as it would create a united empire of Germans who had been denied national self-determination at the Paris Peace Conference*

The *Anschluss*

The *Anschluss* was the union of Germany and Austria. The existence of two German-speaking nations dated back to the unification of Germany in 1871, when 38 German states were united as the German Empire and one German state remained outside the Reich – Austria-Hungary, which was governed by a German royal family and ruling class, but which had its own multi-ethnic empire. When Germany was unified in 1871, several million Germans were not included. To German Nationalists, the Germany of 1871 was therefore only 'Little Germany' and the union of all Germans remained the goal of German Nationalists. At the end of the First World War, the Austrian Empire collapsed and several independent nations were formed, including the German nation of Austria. However, both the Treaty of Versailles and the Treaty of St Germain explicitly banned the union of Germany and Austria.

The creation of a unified Greater Germany was a key part of Nazi ideology: it was point 1 of the 25-point programme and was mentioned on page 1 of *Mein Kampf*. Hitler first attempted a takeover of Austria in 1934 when he threatened to invade to restore order after the assassination of the Austrian chancellor Engelbert Dollfuss by Nazi SS troops dressed in Austrian army uniforms. Mussolini marched troops to the Brenner Pass in the Alps between Austria and Italy and Hitler was forced to back down. However, the *Anschluss* was merely delayed. In February 1938, Hitler demanded that the Austrian chancellor Kurt von Schuschnigg should come to Germany, where he was forced to accede to Hitler's demands for Austrian Nazis to be given key government posts and for the Austrian Nazi Party to be legalised. The president of Austria also had to agree and this bought Schuschnigg time. He returned to Austria and announced a plebiscite (referendum), giving the Austrian people the chance to resist Hitler. Hitler first gained Mussolini's agreement to direct action and then invaded Austria before the plebiscite could take place. The invasion was not resisted and Hitler therefore succeeded in uniting Germany with the country of his birth on 13 March 1938. In April, both the German and the Austrian people voted in favour of the annexation, giving some legitimacy to the German takeover.

Kristallnacht (Night of Broken Glass)

The assassination of the German diplomat Ernst vom Rath in Paris on 7 November 1938 was the spark that intensified anti-Semitic actions in Nazi Germany and took the intolerance of diversity to a new level. The assassin was Herschel Grynszpan, a Polish Jew.

Retaliation was carried out on the orders of Reinhard Heydrich. On the night of 8–9 November, *Kristallnacht*, a violent **pogrom**, took place.

Key term

Pogroms: violent attacks against minorities in a society. European Jews had been victims of these attacks for centuries. In 1190, the Jewish population of medieval York was wiped out after a massacre at Clifford's Tower. Pogroms against the Jews were a feature of 19th century Russia and Austria.

Key profile

Reinhard Heydrich

Reinhard Heydrich (1904–42) was head of the Reich Security Service (the SD) and Himmler's second-in-command as Deputy Reichsführer-SS. He joined the SS in 1932 and this tall, blond, athletic Aryan appeared to be the ideal Nazi. He was a gifted pianist and his entry in the 1916 Music Directory of Germany revealed his real family name of 'Suss', indicating Heydrich was part Jewish. Self-loathing caused by fears that he may have been part Jewish led him to ruthless persecution and, together with Himmler, he was the architect of the Holocaust, chairing the Wannsee Conference on 20 January 1942, where the Final Solution was formally organised. He was also the governor of the Czech lands of Bohemia and Moravia, and his ruthless treatment of the Czechs ended with his assassination by British-trained Czech agents on 29 May 1942. The SS's revenge was savage. The village of Lidice, where the agents had been harboured, was wiped off the map and the people killed or sent to camps.

Fig. 4 *Reinhard Heydrich*

In 15 hours, 177 synagogues had been destroyed. Around 7,500 Jewish-owned stores were looted and destroyed. Some 91 people lost their lives and 30,000 Jewish men were sent to concentration camps.

Cross-reference

Concentration camps are introduced on page 126.

The origins of the pogrom are revealing. Two leading Nazis had something to gain by promoting such a dramatic action that would win favour with Hitler. Joseph Goebbels was keen to win back his place in Hitler's favour following his affair with a racially inferior Czech actress. Hermann Goering had gained control over the economy in 1936 through the Four Year Plan Office, but his attempts to re-arm and provide high living standards were creating an economic crisis. He saw the opportunity to further exploit the Jewish community and a fine of 1 billion marks was charged, with the 6 million marks paid out by insurance companies to be given to the State.

Cross-reference

Hermann Goering is profiled on page 109.

Key profile

Joseph Goebbels

Dr Joseph Goebbels (1897–1945) joined the NSDAP in 1922 and was initially on the socialist wing of the party and a critic of Hitler. However, he was mesmerised by Hitler at the 1926 Bamburg Conference and became a dedicated supporter. He was made Minister of Propaganda and Popular Enlightenment in March 1933 and his understanding of propaganda played a key role in the Nazis' successful consolidation of power. He was married with six children and his family was considered to be the image of the perfect Nazi family. Goebbels was a personal favourite of Hitler. After Hitler had committed suicide, Goebbels and his wife killed their children and then committed suicide.

Fig. 5 *Joseph Goebbels*

Jewish businesses were also attacked. *Kristallnacht* was a widespread attack that took place in full view of the German people and the world;

it was the first act of repression that was fully reported in Britain. It is true that actions were carried out by the SA and few ordinary Germans joined in, but there was no resistance and the Catholic and Protestant churches failed to condemn the violence. Emigration increased. Within days, a decree forced all Jews to transfer retail businesses to Aryan hands and Jewish children were expelled from German schools. German Jews could no longer hope that Nazism would lose its venom and many had no way of earning a living anyway now that their businesses had been destroyed.

On 30 January 1939, Hitler celebrated the sixth anniversary of his appointment as chancellor by giving a speech to the Reichstag in which he made clear the extent of Nazi intolerance. He argued that if the international Jewish movement brought war on Europe and Germany, he would ensure that this led to the 'annihilation of the Jewish race in Europe'. Once war had begun in September 1939, a curfew was introduced for all Jews, emphasising that they were not part of the nation, and Heydrich gave orders that ghettos should be set up in German-occupied Poland. In October, the deportation of Austrian and Czech Jews to Poland began and, from November, Jews in German-occupied Poland were forced to wear an armband or yellow star. The final horrific stages of Nazi intolerance of racial diversity were to follow, from deportations to ghettos and internment camps, to mass murder in the extermination camps built across Poland.

Activity

Revision exercise

Review the text on the historiography of the Holocaust. Identify evidence from this chapter that can be used to support the intentionalist and the functionalist interpretations of racial policy in the years 1933–9.

Activity

Revision exercise

1 Use the information above to copy and complete the table below.

Year	Events
1933	
1934	
1935	
1936	
1937	
1938	
1939	

2 Explain why Nazi Germany was not immediately intolerant of its Jewish population.

Gypsies: the Sinti and Roma

Anti-Semitic policy and the Final Solution dominate studies of the Third Reich, but the fate of other outsider groups was also sealed by Hitler's accession to power. Gypsies were viewed as outsiders in most European countries and the 30,000 population of German gypsies (Sinti) had been under surveillance before 1933. Their persecution is a typical example of the Nazi refusal to tolerate those who diverted from their vision of the *Volksgemeinschaft*. Gypsies looked different, spoke a different language and adopted strange customs. In a society that saw a fixed address as the norm, their transient lifestyle was seen as abnormal. In addition, their refusal to work in fixed employment was seen to be evidence that they were useless to Germany and were a burden on the average, honest, hardworking German. They were blamed for crime and social problems and considered to be culturally inferior. German criminologists argued that there were certain groups in society who were more prone to commit crimes, including black people, Jews and gypsies. This belief in 'nature rather than nurture' found support among folk stories of gypsies who kidnapped children.

In 1933, the Research Centre for Racial Hygiene and Biological Population Studies in Berlin identified six tribes of gypsies, including Sinti (German gypsies) and Roma (Hungarian immigrant gypsies). The Nazi attitude towards gypsies was based on their desire to promote a people's community of those with German blood. Those whose blood was not 'German' were not considered to be part of the Reich and the 1935 Nuremburg Laws classified gypsies as an alien strain that could infect German blood. In particular, research was thought to be crucial to identify *Mischlinge* gypsies, as those of mixed blood (in contrast to *Mischlinge* Jews) were considered to be of greater threat to German purity. As they were frequently integrated into German society, *Mischlinge* gypsies could not be easily spotted which, according to the Nazis, allowed them to continue to spread their inferior blood that carried asocial traits.

Understanding the intolerance of diversity in Nazi Germany in relation to gypsies requires an understanding that actions of the Nazi State were often popular and forced on the government, both locally and nationally, by popular pressure. In many ways the Nazis legitimised some of the less appealing aspects of human nature. A squatters' settlement of 1,200 people including about 70 gypsies in Düsseldorf was torn down following an outbreak of typhus and an assault on government housing officers. The gypsies were moved to a new camp that was watched over at night by an armed guard. They had to pay six marks' rent, denied welfare payments and forced to enter compulsory labour schemes. Local people preferred to see those whom they considered to be 'work-shy' laying railway tracks rather than earning an irregular income from busking. Complaints from local residents led to the establishment of camps in Cologne and Frankfurt.

The Reich Central Office for the Fight Against the Gyspy Nuisance was established in 1936 to coordinate central government action. In 1938, a decree was issued, 'Combating the Gypsy Plague', which introduced systematic registration of the different sub-groups identified by Nazi racial experts. In 1939, special identification papers were issued to gypsies, differentiating between those of mixed blood and those of pure German blood. Pure gypsies received brown identification papers, *Mischlinge* gypsies light blue papers and nomadic non-gypsies grey ones. The gypsy population of Germany grew as the Reich expanded, and the German victory over Poland in September 1939 created the opportunity for deportations to Poland from Germany and Austria. During the war, gypsies suffered greater restrictions and attacks on their liberty, culminating in sterilisation, experimentation and extermination. Only 5,000 of the 30,000 gypsies living in Germany in 1939 survived the war.

Activity

Revision exercise

1. Explain why the Nazis persecuted gypsies. (Hint: you could consider ideological reasons, cultural reasons and the pressure from German citizens.)

2. Identify similarities and differences between the persecution of gypsies and Jews.

Asocials

The desire to create the *Volksgemeinschaft* required the exclusion of racial aliens from the people's community. The largest group were Jews, and the Sinti and Roma communities were also easily identifiable and viewed with discomfort where they lived side by side with the 'normal' German population. A final group were the social outsiders whose behaviour or physical appearance led the Nazis to believe that they were degenerate or biologically inferior. The 'genus' (genes) was regarded as deeply valuable and therefore those who were 'degenerate' (lacking the right genes) were dangerous to the nation. The community of 'national comrades' needed to be inoculated from the plague of these 'social outcasts' who were considered to be congenital criminals.

Activity

Challenge your thinking

1 Study the list below. Identify which groups are 'national comrades' who would fall within the *Volksgemeinschaft* and which groups are 'asocials' who fall outside this people's community.

- Jews
- Married women
- Sinti
- Work-shy people
- Homosexual men
- Married women in employment
- Ex-First World War soldiers
- Beggars
- Roma

- Members of the German Workers' Front (DAF)
- Disabled people
- Lesbians
- Homeless people
- Married women with children
- Criminals
- Alcoholics
- Prostitutes
- Members of the SPD

2 Explain why each group you placed in the 'asocials' list was seen as dangerous by the Nazis. Use this information to complete the table.

National comrades	
Asocials	**Why did the Nazis consider them to be dangerous?**

The main groups targeted by the Nazis were people who were homeless, work-shy or juvenile delinquents; those with disabilities or learning difficulties, or those who refused to use their bodies for the good of the state.

Homeless groups

The homeless were a grave concern to the Nazi regime. Large groups of homeless people were seen as a threat to public order, although it was recognised that a mobile labour force was required as part of the plan to help kick-start the economy and end the depression. As a result, a distinction was drawn between those who were fit to work and those who were deliberately homeless because they wanted to avoid employment. Mass arrests of beggars and the homeless took place in September 1933. The Law against Dangerous Habitual Criminals and concerning Measures for Security and Correction of December 1933 was also applied to the homeless (as well as gypsies on many occasions). The Preventative Detention Decree of 1937 was also used against the homeless, illustrating the view that the insistence of the liberty to roam free implied a mindset that rejected the need to put the state first. For this reason, being homeless became a matter for the police rather than for the welfare services. Many tramps were forcibly sterilised.

The 'work-shy'

Overlapping with homelessness were those whom the Nazis considered to be 'work-shy'. They were no longer tolerated after 1936 when full employment was reached and a larger labour force was required. A round-up in Berlin before the 1936 Olympic Games ensured the image of National Socialism was not undermined. Two out of the 10 work companies in Dachau concentration camp were made up of the work-shy. In the summer of 1938, approximately 11,000 beggars, tramps, pimps and gypsies were rounded up under the code name 'Work-shy Reich' and sent to Buchenwald concentration camp, where they were forced to wear a black triangle.

Single, childless or homosexual citizens

The Weimar Republic had allowed people the freedom to be single, childless or gay. Nazi Germany did not allow the private life of its citizens to remain private. The rejection of Weimar freedom and the aim of increasing population resulted in positive measures to encourage procreation, including loans of 600 Reichsmark for couples who married which were converted to a gift of 150 Reichsmark for each child born. However, there were concerns that larger families were often of racially inferior stock, so the Race Policy Office of the party kept a national eugenics register that listed reputable large families separately from antisocial ones living at public expense. Authorities granting marriage loans did so only after satisfying themselves that the applicants were racially valuable.

Being an unmarried mother or fathering a child outside marriage might be considered asocial in some societies with social norms otherwise similar to those of the Nazis. However, divorces were encouraged for childless couples and many wives were abandoned, often after 20 years of marriage, with the full support of the regime if it allowed a man to father more children. Families were also subject to close scrutiny. The local Youth Office could arrange for children to be removed to a politically reliable home. Parental offences included friendship with Jews, refusal to enrol their children in the Hitler Youth and membership of the Jehovah's Witnesses. Women lost control of their bodies; abortions were considered to be acts of sabotage against the Germans' racial future.

Fig. 6 *A Hitler Youth rally in the 1930s*

The Hitler Youth and the League of German Girls

The Hitler Youth was founded in 1926 as a branch of the SA. In 1931, Baldur von Schirach became leader. During the process of *Gleichschaltung* it absorbed other youth groups except those that were Catholic. By 1934, the Hitler Youth had over 3 million members, and in 1936 it absorbed the Catholic youth groups and membership became compulsory.

German boys aged 10–14 joined the Deutsches Jungvolk (German Youth, or DJ) before moving into the Hitler-Jugend (Hitler Youth, or HJ) between the ages of 15 and 18. The movements focused on Nazi ideology, physical activity and outdoor activities, instilling commitment to National Socialism and military discipline. Boys were given a uniform and a dagger, and told that they were the future of Germany. Loyalty to the Hitler Youth and the Nazi State was more important than loyalty to parents and family, and Hitler Youth members inevitably clashed with parents who were former Socialists or Communists. Such teenage rebellion sometimes led to members informing on their parents.

Girls joined the Jungmädel (Young Girls, or JM) at 10 and advanced to the Bund Deutscher Mädel (League of German Girls, or BDM) at 15. They learned dogma and domestic skills, as well as undertaking a year of farm or labour service. In addition, they had to demonstrate physical fitness, with the aim of preparing their bodies for childbirth, knowledge that was needed sooner rather than later in many cases; approximately 100,000 Hitler Youth and BDM members attended the 1936 Nuremburg rally, with 900 girls aged between 15 and 18 returning home pregnant.

Homosexuality was condemned and legally constrained as another act that was against the Nazi belief in procreation. The illegality of any actions that prevented the birth rate rising was confirmed in the establishment in 1936 of the Reich Office for the Combating of Homosexuality and Abortion. In fact, homosexuality was already illegal under the Reich penal code of 1871, but it had been tolerated in Weimar Germany and there had been proposals to repeal the law. The Nazis now reinforced traditional values. In 1933, homosexual bars were closed and decrees issued against public indecency. The purge of the SA was partly motivated by the perception that homosexuality was rife in the ranks of the leadership. Particularly heavy penalties were imposed on members of the SS and Hitler Youth. Mass arrests followed, and between 1936 and 1939, 30,000 homosexual men were sentenced to death in German courts. Female

■ Cross-reference

More information on the **purge of the SA** can be found on pages 108–109.

homosexuals were not subject to such harsh treatment, but women were increasingly forced from their professional jobs to take up the role of wife and mother. Lesbians who refused to accept this role were easily identifiable and many were sent to Ravensbrück, the all-female concentration camp.

> Ilse Sonja Totzke is a resident next door to us in a garden cottage. I noticed the above-named because she is of Jewish appearance. I should like to mention that Miss Totzke never responds to the German greeting [Heil Hitler]. I gathered from what she was saying that her attitude was anti-German. On the contrary she always favoured France and the Jews. Among other things, she told me that the German Army was not as well equipped as the French. Now and then a woman of about 36 years old comes and she is of Jewish appearance. To my mind, Miss Totzke is behaving suspiciously. I thought she might be engaged in some kind of activity which is harmful to the German Reich.

2   *A statement made to the Gestapo in 1940*

Activity

Source analysis

Study Source 2.

1   Why do you think Ilse Totzke was denounced?

2   Review the reasons for the intolerance of diversity. What further reason does this source suggest was responsible for the intolerance of diversity in Nazi Germany?

Juvenile delinquents

The Nazi concern with juvenile delinquents was two-fold. By definition, youths who were involved in criminal activities were not integrated into the State through party youth organisations. There was also an increase in crimes committed by youths in the years before the war. Although overall criminal convictions fell from just under 500,000 to 300,000 between 1933 and 1939, juvenile offences increased from 16,000 in 1933 to over 21,000 in 1940. Therefore, in 1939 the Reich Central Agency for the Struggle Against Juvenile Delinquency was established, followed by a youth concentration camp in Moringen near Hanover where inmates were subject to biological and racial examinations.

People with learning difficulties

The Nazi obsession with physical strength as an indicator of racial purity was accompanied by a concern that those who were 'feeble minded' should not be allowed to damage the purity of racial stock. The Nazi attitude was evident in school textbooks which reflected the values of their society and subtlely indoctrinated German school children.

> Every day, the State spends RM 6 on one cripple; RM 4 ¼ on one mentally ill person; RM 5 ½ on one deaf and dumb person; RM 5 ⅗ on one feeble-minded person; RM 3 ½ on one alcoholic; RM 4 ⅘ on one pupil in care; RM 2 ¹⁄₂₀ on one pupil at a special school; and RM ⁹⁄₂₀ on one pupil at a normal school.
>
> Using this information, what total cost do one cripple and one feeble-minded person create, if one takes a lifespan of forty-five years for each? Calculate the expenditure of the State for one pupil in a special school, and one pupil in an ordinary school over eight years, and state the amount of higher cost engendered by the special school pupil.

3   *Adapted from a contemporary maths textbook*

Activity

Source analysis

Study Source 3.

1   What do you think was the purpose of Nazi education?

2   How effective do you think this school textbook would have been in helping to achieve the Nazi goal of *Volksgemeinschaft*?

National Socialism had accepted the theory of eugenics that had become popular in the 1920s, which argued that racial stock could be improved by selective breeding. The idea that the nation's stock could be improved found favour because of concerns about declining birth rates and the loss of the best male physical specimens in the First World War. In August 1929, Hitler had argued in a speech that 'If Germany were to get a million children a year and were to remove 700,000–800,000 of the weakest people then the final result might even be an increase in our strength.' The economic depression created a huge burden on the State in terms of welfare payments and the prospect of saving money by sterilising those with hereditary defects only enhanced the appeal of eugenics to the Nazis.

In July 1933, Hitler pushed through a law permitting the compulsory sterilisation of those with hereditary defects. These included schizophrenia, which is not hereditary, and 'feeble-mindedness' and 'chronic alcoholism', which were not clearly defined. Furthermore, the hereditary courts that made the decisions often determined fitness on the basis of being 'work-shy' or a former member of the KPD. Between 1934 and 1945, between 320,000 and 350,000 people were sterilised under the law.

From 1939, the Nazis murdered those with defects and illnesses, meaning that in the eyes of the State they had nothing to contribute to the *Volksgemeinschaft*. Initially, Hitler approved a request from the parents of a baby with learning difficulties to be killed and ordered all similar cases to be treated in the same way. Approximately 5,200 disabled children were killed. In August 1939, Hitler decided to extend the programme to adults and under the T-4 Euthanasia Programme around 72,000 were killed before the programme was abandoned in 1941 following protests from the Catholic Church. The numbers involved were so great that the Nazis had experimented with the use of poison gas and, once the T-4 programme had ended, the methods used were adopted in the pursuit of the Final Solution.

Competing political ideologies

The ideological enemies of National Socialism were ruthlessly pursued. National Socialism was a monolithic ideology and therefore other beliefs and values could not be tolerated. The formal expression of alternative political and religious values came through the existence of rival political parties. The Nazi creation of a one-party state was not based on the desire for total power alone; the suppression of other parties was also the suppression of other sets of ideas that were wrong and risked undermining the national community. Therefore, other political parties were banned or decided to disband before they were banned.

The SPD split, with some members continuing to work in Germany before they were found, arrested and sent to concentration camps. Others fled Germany. Their headquarters were in Prague until the Nazi annexation of the city in March 1939. The leaders then fled to Paris, where many were captured once France fell in 1940.

The Catholic Centre Party gave up their political rights in the Concordat of 1933 in the belief that they would be able to protect their religious liberty. Their success was mixed. The Catholic youth groups were forced to integrate with the Hitler Youth in 1936 and the pressure of deputy chancellor von Papen in July 1933 was not enough to stop sterilisation for those with hereditary illness becoming law. The papacy failed to criticise the anti-Semitic measures of the 1930s and give a moral lead to any anti-Nazi movement, essentially because it was not anti-Nazi. However, it did succeed in forcing the abandonment of the euthanasia campaign, which it found morally reprehensible. However, this success

Cross-reference

More information on the **Concordat of 1933** between the Catholic Centre Party and the Nazi Party is given on page 108.

Fig. 7 *A poster advertising **Triumph of the Will**, a propaganda film from the 1934 Nazi Party rally in Nuremberg*

was rare because the Nazis set out to ensure that other ideas were crushed. This was to be achieved in two ways. Those who were too young to have fully formulated ideas or were uncommitted to any cause were to be indoctrinated through propaganda. Those who could not be influenced or won over were to be ruthlessly repressed.

Goebbels as Minister of Popular Enlightenment and Propaganda coordinated the Nazis' attempts to link people to the regime. He believed in appealing to emotion rather than reason and always sought to reinforce existing prejudice rather than trying to transform people's views. Furthermore, he tried to control all aspects of forms of mass communication as the means of reaching the population. As a result, all German broadcasting was brought under Nazi control through the Reich Radio Company. Around 13 per cent of employees were dismissed on political and racial grounds. Cheap, shortwave single-channel radios were produced by the regime, and by 1939 70 per cent of German households had access to one of these *Volksempfangers* ('people's receivers'). In August 1933, Goebbels, in a speech when opening a radio exhibition argued that 'The purpose of radio is to teach, entertain and support people.'

The press in Germany was brought under Nazi control through Eher Verlag, the Nazi publishing house, buying up two-thirds of German newspapers. The Editor's Law of October 1933 made the editor responsible to the Propaganda Ministry for all the content of their paper. The *Völkischer Beobachter*, the Nazi newspaper, reached a circulation of over 1 million as teachers, civil servants and university professors felt it prudent to buy and carry a copy, although overall circulation fell by 10 per cent during the period 1933–39 due to the sterility of the content. Film was Goebbels's particular obsession. He hated obvious propaganda films like *Hitlerjunge Quex* (1933) in which a member of the Hitler Youth was murdered by Communists. He preferred to provide entertainment through glitzy and glamorous escapist films such as *The Patriots* (1936).

Goebbels had much to celebrate in the newsreels that accompanied feature films. Nazi economic policy saw great success. By 1936, there were only 400,000 unemployed compared to 6 million at the end of 1932. Standards of living improved for most non-Jewish Germans. In the harsh winter of 1935–6, the party organised the Winter Relief charity and the government subsidised the price of food. Cheap consumer goods like *Volksempfangers* were available in the shops. The Strength Through Joy movement organised leisure activities and provided cheap holidays both abroad and at home, and May Day became a national holiday.

In addition, Hitler's foreign policy was a resounding triumph in the period 1933–9. He overturned the Treaty of Versailles, introducing conscription in 1935 and gaining agreement from Britain for Germany to build a navy. He remilitarised the Rhineland in March 1936 and, in 1938, the Reich was expanded. Austria was united with Germany in March through the *Anschluss*, a union of blood. In September 1938, the Sudetenland was added to Germany, with the 3 million Germans in the north-west of Czechoslovakia joining the Reich. All of these achievements helped to create a mass of Germans who buried their heads to the extremism of the Nazis which, after all, affected a tiny minority of the population – and a minority that were resented by many Germans anyway.

For those who resisted the allure of the propaganda machine, the Nazi State terror apparatus set out to crush independent thinking. The SS had destroyed the power of the SA in 1934, as well as removing conservative opponents to the regime. The Gestapo were the secret police, famed as omnipotent, omnipresence and omniscient. They could arrest and detain people without trial and treatment of prisoners was subject only to their own internal disciplinary proceedings. Their powers removed individuals' rights in favour of the State. The SD was the intelligence arm of the SS, which provided information on all opposition groups with sections covering Jews, Jehovah's Witnesses, the Church and different political opponents.

The first concentration camp was set up at Dachau near Munich in 1933. Theodor Eicke was commander of the camp before becoming responsible for all camps in August 1934. Enemies of the State were detained in the camps, like the Lutheran priest Martin Niemöller who was detained in Dachau or the SPD Reichstag deputy Julius Leber, imprisoned between 1933 and 1937. Other inmates included 200,000 of the 300,000 members of the KPD, members of the SPD and trade unionists who caused trouble, like the 20 Autobahn workers in Franconia who went on strike in 1934. Over 100,000 deaths took place at Sachsenhausen near Berlin. Hitler himself said, 'Terror is the best political weapon for nothing drives people harder than a fear of sudden death.'

However, the strength of the Gestapo needs to be clearly understood. The regime was not as systematic as one might think, at least not

■ **Cross-reference**

To revise the **Treaty of Versailles** and its impact on German thinking, re-read pages 91–93.

More information on the *Anschluss* is given on page 116.

before 1938. By the end of 1934, only about 3,000 prisoners remained in the camps, mainly committed Communists. The Gestapo was underfunded and struggled to do any more than respond to information received. The Düsseldorf region, with a population of 4 million, operated with only 281 agents, and Gestapo agents in Saarbrücken recorded that 87.5 per cent of their investigations were the results of information received.

Limits to intolerance

The Nazi regime was able to crush a great deal of racial, social and political intolerance in the years 1933–9 but it would be foolish to believe that the regime was entirely successful in its pursuit of uniformity. Fear of repression did not prevent 5,000 Jews surviving in Berlin alone because of the actions of 'national comrades'. In his study of Nordheim, William Sheridan Allen has shown how the head of the local Nazi Party, Ernst Girmann, drew back from arresting the head of the local SPD, Carl Querfurt, because the two men had grown up together on the same block, a personal relationship which prevented Girmann from being totally ruthless.

 Activity

Revision exercise

Using the evidence on pages 112–127, identify examples of diversity that suggest there were limits to Hitler's totalitarianism. Use these examples to copy and complete the table below.

Area of study	Evidence
Limits to racial intolerance	
Limits to the intolerance of gypsies	
Limits to the intolerance of asocials	
Limits to political intolerance	
Limits to the power of the Nazi State	

The Führer myth and Nazi ideology, including the Führerprinzip

The origins of the Führer myth

In the early 1920s, Hitler had seen himself as the drummer who would gather support for the leader who would save Germany from its suffering and restore the nation to greatness. Increasingly, however, he came to believe that he was the man of destiny who would save the nation.

Exploring the detail
Punishment in the concentration camps

Eicke's rules for the treatment of prisoners were brutal. Discussing either politics, or the punishment of fellow inmates, or trying to contact the outside world was punishable by death by hanging; any refusal to work or an act of rebellion meant shooting on the spot. Going to the toilet or smoking without permission resulted in special punishments, including tree-hanging, where prisoners had their hands tied behind their back. They would then be lifted on to a nail and suspended above the ground. The shoulders were slowly and extremely painfully pulled out of their sockets. No prisoner who suffered such punishment ever 'resisted' again.

■ Cross-reference

Hitler's resignation and **reinstatement** in 1921 is discussed on page 95.

Two events in the early years of the movement were essential in the development of the Nazis' ideas on leadership. The reinstatement of Hitler as leader of the NSDAP following his resignation from the party convinced him of his importance to the movement. His success in winning over the northern revolutionary socialists at the 1926 Bamberg Conference also seemed to be evidence that he was a man apart. It was significant that the most important Nazi Hitler won over was Joseph Goebbels, who became obsessed with Hitler, writing 'Adolf Hitler, I love you!' in his diary and comparing him to Christ. Goebbels was the key figure responsible for creating the 'Hitler myth', the idea at the centre of Nazi propaganda and Nazi belief.

Fig. 8 *The worship of the Führer. An eager crowd proclaims 'Yes! Führer we follow you!'*

At the heart of the myth was the idea that Hitler was a man apart, sent by destiny to save Germany. The economic depression, the political instability and the international status of Germany all required action and the existing Weimar system seemed to be incapable of this. Hitler was the man who restored the strength of the country. He was seen as decisive, with a youthful energy in contrast to previous chancellors who had lacked any direction or vision. Furthermore, he rapidly provided success for Germany, taming unemployment, overturning the Treaty of Versailles and taking actions against the internal enemies of the German people. He claimed to represent the will of the German people and his actions were genuinely what the masses wanted, with the exception of the ideological left wing. Hitler was hugely popular with the vast majority of the German population; although local bureaucrats of the Nazi regime, from *Gauleiters* to block wardens, were frequently detested, the popularity of Nazism soared because Nazism was actually Hitlerism. The same phenomenon was true in the Soviet Union, where Stalin's popularity soared despite the excesses of terror.

The worship of Hitler developed through everyday social rituals like the adoption of the Heil Hitler salute. His birthday became a public holiday. Important organisations swore loyalty to him. The SS were his personal bodyguard and inevitably swore an Oath of Loyalty, but the oath the army swore after the death of Hindenburg represented acceptance of Hitler as supreme leader by one of the key organisations in the state, and one that was traditionally conservative and nationalist not revolutionary and Nazi. Hitler was already Führer of the Nazi Party and German chancellor, but by combining the positions of chancellor and president in 1934 he created the new post of German Führer. As Führer, Hitler had no constitutional constraints on his power and his powers were never defined in law, making him truly all-powerful and beyond the law. His decisions, often taken during late-night conversations with favoured party members, could lead to mass murder but, as in the case of the Final Solution, no written orders were ever recorded. Individual Nazis tried to act in the way in which he would approve, 'working towards the Führer' as Ian Kershaw has argued.

Everyone who has the opportunity to observe it knows that the Führer can hardly dictate from above everything which he intends to realise sooner or later. On the contrary, up till now everyone with a post in the new Germany has worked best where he has, so to speak, worked towards the Führer. Very often and in many spheres it has been the case – in previous years as well – that individuals have simply waited for orders and instructions. Unfortunately, the same will be true in the future; but in fact it is the duty of everybody to try to work towards the Führer along the lines he would wish. Anyone who makes mistakes will notice it soon enough. But anyone who really works towards the Führer along his lines and towards his goal will certainly both now and in the future one day have the finest reward in the sudden legal confirmation of his work.

4   *From a statement made in 1934 by Werner Wilkins,*
a senior civil servant and devout Nazi

Activity

Source analysis

Study Source 4.

1 In less than 20 words, explain what is meant by 'working towards the Führer'.

2 How do you think the idea of 'working towards the Führer' developed among Nazi officials?

The myth was developed by Goebbels' Propaganda Ministry. The Nuremburg rallies were occasions of mass worship, with 500,000 acolytes listening to the words of the high priest of Nazism. Goebbels also used film to great effect. Goebbels was keen to limit Hitler's exposure in order to maintain the idea of the special man, apart from the rest of the nation. He therefore chose to portray him through allegory. *Bismarck* presented Hitler as the heir to the great German statesman (chancellor Bismarck had united Germany through three wars between 1864 and 1871) and made a profit of almost 2 million Reichsmark. Most of the history films that featured Hitler in this way stressed the importance of the leader and their role in historical change rather than impersonal forces. Goebbels did not approve of Leni Riefenstahl's *Triumph of the Will*, but the film was the overt cinematic expression of the cult. Commissioned by Hitler, the biopic featured himself descending from the skies en route to the 1934 Nuremburg rally. At the rally, as various Nazis address the faithful, the camera pans along a line of Hitler Youth members, the vast majority of whom have adopted Hitler's hairstyle.

Nazi ideology and the Führerprinzip: reasons for the concept

The Führerprinzip ('principle of the Führer') developed from the 1926 Bamburg Conference. Hitler's Nazism, like Italian Fascism, rejected both Communism and liberal democracy. In rejecting these political ideologies, Hitler rejected the belief that history was shaped by economic forces and as a result of the clash of diametrically opposed positions, as Marx had argued. There could be no spontaneous uprising of National Socialism in Germany. Equally, Hitler rejected democracy and the belief that the general will would be exercised through the ballot box for the benefit of the nation. He believed that democracy was weak and flawed, in that it allowed cowards to avoid doing the right thing by arguing that it was against the people's will.

The Führerprinzip took inspiration from the work of the 19th century philosopher Friedrich Nietzsche, who formulated the idea of the superman, a new breed of man. It was not easy to see Hitler as Nietzsche's superman given his physical appearance, yet Kershaw has argued that in some ways Hitler's slightly ridiculous image enhanced the myth, as his rapid successes appeared even more remarkable. German history was also critical in the development of the myth. When the Kaiser had ruled, the German Empire was a source of pride for the nation. Democracy had brought the disaster of the Weimar Republic. It was also true that it was easier to follow Hitler than the ideas of National Socialism, which could be confused and contradictory. Belief in a strong leader was expressed in the 25-point programme and in *Mein Kampf*. It was also a defining feature of Hitler's speeches in the period 1930–3

Cross-reference

To recap on the influence of **Nietzsche** on the development of fascist ideology in Italy, re-read page 84.

Activity

1 Explain why the cult of Hitler developed in Nazi Germany. Focus on ideological reasons as well as circumstances.

2 Consider which of the reasons you have identified is the most important.

Fig. 9 *The Führer as the heir to Germany. The cult was developed by images that linked Hitler to great Germans of the past. Left to right: Frederick the Great, Otto von Bismark, Paul von Hindenberg, Adolf Hitler*

when he offered few concrete solutions to the problems facing Germany other than strong leadership and an end to the weakness provided by democracy and coalition governments.

Learning outcomes

Through your study of this section you should be aware of the development of Nazi ideology with reference to the key themes of Nationalism, Socialism, race and anti-Semitism, and the *Volksgemeinschaft*. You should understand the importance of the economic problems facing Germany, the appeal of Nazism and the Nazi Party and the failure of other politicians in explaining why Hitler was made chancellor. You should be clear that Hitler was not elected chancellor and have an understanding of why Hindenburg would not appoint him chancellor in 1932 but did in 1933. You should understand how Hitler destroyed democracy in the period from January 1933 to August 1934 and have reached a judgement as to the relative importance of the different methods used by Hitler.

Having studied the section, you should be in a position to assess the reasons for the development of the intolerance of diversity in Nazi Germany and be able to reach a judgement on the extent of intolerance of the different groups in German society and politics. You should understand the methods used to promote the *Volksgemeinschaft*.

You should understand the nature of the Führer myth, how and why it developed and the place it held in Nazi ideology. Through your understanding of the intolerance of diversity and the Hitler myth, you should also be able to reach a judgement on how far Nazi Germany was totalitarian in the 1930s.

Practice questions

(a) Explain why Hitler did not become
chancellor in 1932. *(12 marks)*

Study tip We have already noted that it can be difficult to argue why something
did not happen as opposed to why it did happen. However, follow the
basic technique outlined on page 49 and identify a list of reasons why,
from which you can decide why one reason is more important than the
others. This question is asking you to use your knowledge of Hitler's rise
to power. You need to consider the Weimar constitution as well as the
events of the year. Remember that Hitler did not win a majority, and
therefore he could only become chancellor if he was offered the post by
Hindenburg. Think about why Hindenburg was reluctant to make Hitler
chancellor.

(b) 'How far was Hitler's consolidation of power
in the period January 1933 to August 1934 the
result of the use of terror? *(24 marks)*

Study tip This question focuses on the period when Hitler transformed Germany
from a democracy (at least on paper) to a one-party dictatorship. You
should have already thought about the different methods Hitler used. Your
answer needs to consider evidence of the use of terror, such as the actions
of the SA in the 1933 Reichstag election. To show balance, consider the use
of legal power, such as the Enabling Act, as well as the political cunning
the Nazis showed in their dealing with the Catholic Church or the trades
unions. Remember that you need to reach a judgement; was the use of
terror more important early in the period?

Conclusion

In trying to consider a common understanding of totalitarianism in the Soviet Union, Fascist Italy and Nazi Germany, this chapter considers three issues. The common roots of the development of totalitarianism will be explored, with reference to the impact of the First World War. The way in which historians and the world view the different flavours of totalitarianism will then be considered. Finally, the extent in which these states were truly totalitarian will be assessed.

The significance of the First World War and the development of totalitarianism

On 20 October 1941, the German General von Kleist's armoured corps began their assault on the Soviet city of Stalino. Attached to von Kleist's force was the Italian Expeditionary Corps in Russia (CSIR). This assault represented the inevitable consequence of the development of totalitarian ideologies within the totalitarian states of the Soviet Union, Fascist Italy and Nazi Germany. By definition, totalitarian ideologies refuse to accept the existence of alternative political ideas. More specifically, at the very heart of both Fascism and Nazism was an unrelenting hatred of communism; governing in the interest of the working class and putting one class internationally before the needs of the nation disgusted both Mussolini and Hitler. The joint action of Fascism and Nazism against a city named after the leader of the communist Soviet Union was the epitome of the struggle that Mussolini and Hitler had fought to protect their countries from the menace of communism. The successful resistance of the Soviet Union ensured the destruction of extreme right-wing ideologies and the triumph of communism, at least in the 20th century.

Activity

Revision exercise

Copy the following chart for each question, then shade each one to show which classes or races were central to the ideology of:

1. Stalin in the USSR
2. Mussolini in Italy
3. Hitler in Germany.

USSR	Italy	Germany
Upper class	Upper class	Upper class
Middle class	Middle class	Middle class
Working class	Working class	Working class

In searching for explanations of the development of 20th century totalitarianism, some form of shared explanation is required as it is unlikely that three major powers would have found their own unique roots to a similar system of government. The common cause of totalitarianism is the experience of the First World War. No other event changed the world as profoundly as the impact of four years of carnage. Without the First World War, Russia might very well have transformed its political system but it would probably not have adopted a political system in which a tiny elite, representing a minority (the working class), imposed their rule on both the traditional elite (the tsar, the aristocracy and the Church) and the majority of the population (the Russian peasants). In 1914, Lenin was deeply pessimistic about the prospect of revolution. War, and specifically defeat in the First World War, destroyed tsarism in Russia, and the failure to recognise that the only way to stabilise the regime was to end the war led to the fall of the Provisional Government.

The survival of the Bolshevik State in the years 1917 to 1921 had a profound impact on the rest of Europe. In Britain and France, the fear of a workers' revolution kept the elite awake at night, but the worst had passed for victory in the war meant that the destruction and sacrifice was never directly called to account by the people. In Italy and Germany it inspired all those who were angered by the war and its consequences to believe that they too could turn the world upside down. The certainties of the 19th century were replaced by the belief that the actions of a few men of destiny could transform the nation. It is worth remembering that a German citizen could wake up to learn with great surprise that the war was over and they had lost, as Sebastian Haffner's memoirs recall, and that (however briefly) communist regimes did govern Berlin and Bavaria in 1918. We now know that the *biennio rosso* was not the prelude to a Communist Italy but we cannot read history backwards. Post-war Europe could have developed very differently.

This led to the growth of different views of the future and competing visions of Utopia. Both Mussolini and Hitler fantasised about a world in which their nation had been glorious victors of the First World War. Italy had won the war but lost the peace. Italy's aims were for

Fig. 1 *The Thaelmann Battalion of German volunteers, made up of Socialists and Communists who took their chance to fight Fascism in Spain as they felt it was impossible to do so in totalitarian Germany. Italian anti-fascist volunteer units also fought in Spain*

■ **Exploring the detail**

The Spanish Civil War and totalitarianism

The 1930s saw a precursor to the Second World War clash between right and left. The Spanish Civil War was fought between 1936 and 1939. The Spanish Republic was opposed by rebels under General Franco. The Republic was supported by the Soviet Union and international workers' brigades and increasingly became seen as communist. The rebels were supported by Mussolini and Hitler, and Franco formed a pseudo-Fascist Party, the Falange.

Italian-speaking parts of Austria and African colonies – for Fiume and Abyssinia, the territory that Il Duce secured. The Treaty of Brest-Litovsk of March 1918 was the conclusion to the war between the Kaiser's Germany and the new Bolshevik State. Trotsky, who negotiated the treaty, found himself compelled to accept the loss of Ukraine, the Baltic States and Poland. The Treaty of Versailles stripped Germany of all its gains in the east, territory that Hitler greedily gobbled up in the first two years of the Second World War. What led them to seize power and create that world was the fear that, if they did not, a communist dystopia would instead be forced on their nation. The suffering of the Great War would be followed by an even greater suffering as a foreign disease would infect their country and destroy the nation itself. Liberal democracy was not strong enough to resist the onslaught of communism. Totalitarian dictatorship would therefore ensure that communism would be stopped and could be eradicated from the mindset of the people.

The First World War caused millions to question their traditional leaders and their faith. Part of the attraction of totalitarianism to the people of each state was the way in which the state took control of their lives and gave them something and someone to believe in, contrasting with the lack of stability experienced during the war and civil war in Russia and during the post-war period in Italy and Germany. The extent of genuine support for each regime is difficult to truly identify, but the certainty of totalitarianism must have been attractive to people who had seen everything they understood to be normal turned upside down. It does not seem unlikely that, for many, the suffering of the First World War and the turmoil of the post-war years fundamentally challenged their religious faith. The importance of ideology within totalitarian states and the worship of the leader as the high-priest of the new religion make greater sense when considered in this context.

Fascism and Nazism are therefore the bastard offsprings of communism, and the gun-shot fired by Gavrilo Princip had a significance that extended beyond the outbreak of the First World War. The First World War destroyed the empires of Russia, Germany, Austria-Hungary and the Ottomans (Turkey). It cost an estimated 20 million lives. Its impact on the world was cataclysmic. Only an event of this magnitude could account for the establishment of three regimes that collectively were responsible for an estimated 86 million lives (20 million combat deaths in the Second World War, 40 million civilian deaths, 6 million Jewish victims of the Holocaust and an estimated 20 million deaths in the Soviet Union as the result of collectivisation and terror).

■ Perceptions of totalitarian regimes

In February 2006, the British historian David Irving was found guilty by an Austrian court of denying the Holocaust and sent to prison for three years. In 1989, he had given a speech and an interview in which he had denied the existence of gas chambers at the Nazi extermination centre Auschwitz. Although he had stated before the trial began that he had changed his views and that he was not a Holocaust denier, he was found guilty because Austria is one of 11 countries that have passed laws prohibiting any written or spoken comment that denies that the Holocaust took place. In Italy, Alessandra Mussolini, the grand-daughter of Benito Mussolini, was elected as an MP in 1992. She became a member of the European Parliament in 2004 as a representative of an extreme right-wing neo-fascist party. In 2003, the prime minister of Italy, Silvio Berlusconi, was quoted as saying that 'Mussolini never killed anyone,' adding, 'Mussolini sent people on holiday to confine them [banishment to small islands such as Ponza and Maddalena which are now plush resorts]' (*Guardian*, 12 September 2003). The *Daily Mail*'s review of *Koba the Dread* by Martin Amis (see Bibliography), is quoted on the cover of the paperback copy of the book: 'A powerfully written, well-documented polemic reminding us of how 20 million humans were starved, murdered or tortured to death by Uncle Joe.' The juxtaposition of mass murder with the avuncular image of Stalin brings together these contradictions in a single regime.

These different reactions to totalitarian regimes reflect the fact that we do not instinctively equate the three regimes as being all that similar. In that sense, describing them as 'totalitarian' is not necessarily helpful. There were great differences between the states. Mussolini's Italy does not carry connotations of shame and revulsion; it is difficult to imagine anyone proudly fighting to keep the name 'Hitler' alive, but Alessandra Mussolini fought to have her children named after herself along with their father's name. Nazi Germany will always be synonymous with the war of aggression launched by Hitler in September 1939, and with the Holocaust and the systematic attempt to exterminate European Jews, a policy that so jars with the liberal view of human relations that we want to deny freedom of expression to those who, like Irving, make statements with which we disagree. Mussolini's Italy is not viewed in the same way. Mussolini is considered to be a comic figure, a master of propaganda who fought his 'battles' for Lira, Births and Land, each of which failed as Mussolini failed to bend nature to his will.

Hollywood has given us *Schindler's List* and *Captain Corelli's Mandolin*, films that seem to confirm the amoral evil of Nazism as epitomised by Amon Goethe, the sadist portrayed by Ralph Fiennes in *Schindler's List*, while Nicholas Cage's portrayal of Captain Corelli is humorous and humane. More importantly, the moral superiority of Italians is confirmed by their futile resistance to Germans. However, the Italians were guilty of atrocities in Albania and Greece, two countries that Italy invaded in pursuit of the new Roman Empire. As Mussolini's recent biographer, R. J. B. Bosworth has argued, the fact that Western historians have never calculated the cost of the Italian annexation of Abyssinia does not change the fact that Ethiopians have estimated that between 300,000 and 600,000 people died as a result of fighting or occupation.

Perceptions of Stalin are perhaps the most difficult to understand. The author Robert Harris has argued that the 'West likes its dictators red'. Stalin and Bolshevism are viewed with indulgence by many Western historians. The Second World War saw Britain and the United States united with the Soviet Union in the Grand Alliance versus Hitler and 'Uncle Joe' played a crucial role in the destruction of Nazism. Furthermore, Stalin did not systematically set out to destroy an ethnic group, as Hitler did. Soviet State terror was carried out against those who it was believed had tried to destroy the system; in other words, because of what they did, not because of who they were. The fact that the terror was in many cases indiscriminate and claimed the lives of those who were at worst guilty by association is sometimes overlooked. However, most importantly, the attempt to create an equal society in which people are treated in a 'fair' way is one that is still deeply attractive to many in the West.

It is pointless to try to reach a judgement as to the difference between the evil of the different dictators. It is important to recognise that each of the regimes did more than just crush small numbers of opponents. Life was transformed. The state may not have been everywhere, but it was powerful enough to prevent you doing what you wanted to do, with whom you wanted and when you wanted. It controlled what you could say and, ultimately, although no comprehensive evidence can exist as to what every citizen of these states thought, it must have led people to be conditioned into thinking in a particular way by the constant repetition of ideas through school, work, leisure activities, radio, news and the omnipresent symbols. One analogy will suffice. Young children in capitalist societies learn the idea of property and possessions within the first 12 month of their lives, and by the age of 16 students are conditioned to believe in private ownership; count the number of Marxists in your teaching group and then count the number of students who say that Marxism would never work. Twelve years of Nazi rule saw people make judgements that went beyond the norm; nurses who helped kill disabled people during the T-4 Euthanasia Programme, doctors who decided who could work (and therefore live) and who were too young or too weak and therefore would die in the gas chambers of Auschwitz. Twenty-three years of fascist rule in Italy must have had an impact on the way people thought and behaved and 74 years of communist rule was so transformational that, as recently as 2006, 20 per cent of Russians said they would vote for Stalin if he was to stand for president and only 40 per cent said they would definitely not. These people desire the stability and order that Stalin brought, in contrast to the free-market frontier capitalism of Russia today, where political opponents are still arrested and murdered, crime is out of control and the state cannot pay its employees. These Russians who would vote for Stalin today remind us why so many citizens of three different nations were prepared to accept all the extremes of totalitarianism.

The extent of totalitarianism

It is valid to use the concept of 'totalitarian' in relation to Stalin's Soviet Union, Mussolini's Italy and Hitler's Germany. The extent of totalitarian rule may differ, but essentially all three regimes were aiming to control all aspects of people's lives with some success.

Activity

Revision exercise

1 Review the key features of a totalitarian State in Chapter 1.
Copy and complete the table below to compare the
totalitarianism of the three regimes.

Theme	The Soviet Union	Fascist Italy	Nazi Germany
An official ideology			25-point programme and *Mein Kampf*
The one-party State	January 1918 and the abolition of the Constituent Assembly and the resignation of the last non-Bolsheviks from the government in March 1918		
The monopoly over the means of mass communication			
The monopoly over the means of terror		The MSVN, murder of Matteotti, the creation of the OVRA	
The monopoly over the control of the economy			
The cult of personality			

2 Consider the extent to which each State was totalitarian.
Copy and complete the table below for each of the three States.

Name of regime: USSR/Italy/Germany (delete as appropriate)	Evidence for totalitarian government	Limits to totalitarianism
An official ideology		
The one-party State		
The monopoly over the means of mass communication		
The monopoly over the means of terror		
The monopoly over the control of the economy		
The cult of personality		

3 When you have completed both tables, mark on the line below where you
would position each State to indicate your judgement on the extent of
their totalitarianism. Explain why you have reached your judgement.

Limited control ——————————————————————————————— Complete control

Glossary

A

acolyte: a follower who has absolute belief.

anti-Semitism: hatred of Jews.

B

bourgeoisie: according to Marx, the middle class who owned the means of production (i.e. factory owners).

C

concentration camp: prison camps for political opponents of the Nazi regime.

CGL: the Italian Socialist Trades Union.

Cheka: the Soviet secret police set up by Lenin.

D

dacha: a holiday home for leading Bolshevik Party members.

DAF: the German Workers' Front, or the Nazi trades union movement, led by Robert Ley.

DDP: the German Democratic Party, or Democrats.

DNVP: the German National People's Party, or Nationalists.

Dopolavaro: the fascist organisation that provided leisure activities.

DVP: the German People's Party.

dystopia: the opposite of utopia – an imperfect world.

G

Gestapo: the German secret police.

Gleichschaltung: the Nazi policy of coordinating organisations with the Nazi State.

Gulag: the system of labour camps in the Soviet Union where political prisoners were sent.

H

hyperinflation: a colossal rise in prices.

K

KPD: the Communist Party of Germany.

kulak: a rich peasant in the Soviet Union.

L

League of Nations: the international organisation set up after the First World War to solve disputes between countries and therefore prevent war.

M

Mischlinge: Germans who had 'mixed blood'.

MSVN: Volunteer Militia for National Security, created by Mussolini.

N

NEP: the New Economic Policy, introduced by Lenin in 1921, which restored some capitalism to the Soviet economy.

NKVD: the Soviet secret police from 1934.

NSDAP: the National Socialist German Workers' Party (Nazi Party).

O

OVRA: the Italian secret police.

P

pejorative: negative connotations of a word.

PNF: the National Fascist Party, set up by Mussolini.

proletariat: according to Marx, the working class who were exploited by the bourgeoisie.

PPI: the Italian Popular Party, the political party of the Catholic Church in Italy.

PSI: the Italian Socialist Party.

R

Ras: local fascist leaders, or 'bosses'.

Reichsbank: the State bank of Germany.

Reichsbanner: the German Socialist Party paramilitary force.

S

SA: the *Sturm-Abteilung* or Stormtroopers, the Nazi paramilitary force.

Show Trials: public trials of leading Bolsheviks in which they confessed to crimes against the State.

Socialism in One Country: Stalin's policy for the Soviet Union, which stated that the country needed to modernise to survive.

SPD: the German Social Democratic Party.

Squadre: Italian fascist paramilitary groups that attacked socialists and Communists.

SS: Hitler's personal bodyguard which ran the concentration camps and carried out the Final Solution.

T

transient: someone who travels around rather than having a fixed home.

U

United Opposition: the grouping formed by Trotsky, Zinoviev and Kamenev to oppose Stalin during the power struggle; sometimes called the New Opposition.

utopia: commonly taken to mean the perfect world.

V

Volksgemeinschaft: the Nazi people's community of Germans.

Vozhd: 'the boss' – the name given to Stalin by the party faithful.

W

World Revolution: the idea that the Soviet Union could only survive by spreading revolution abroad.

Z

Z: the German Centre Party (Zentrum), the party of the German Catholics.

Bibliography

Introduction to totalitarian regimes

Lee, S. (2000) *Europe and the Dictators*, Routledge.

Pearce, R. (1997) *Fascism and Nazism*, Hodder & Stoughton.

An excellent lecture on totalitarianism by Stephen Kreis is available at www.historyguide.org/europe/lecture10.html

Novels

Orwell, G. (1990) *1984*, Penguin.

1 The USSR and Marxism

Students

Lynch, M. (2005) *Bolshevik and Stalinist Russia 1918–1956*, Hodder & Stoughton.

Marx, K. and Engels, F. (2002) *The Communist Manifesto*, Penguin Classics.

Rappaport, H. (1999) *Joseph Stalin: A Biographical Companion*, ABC-CLIO.

Swain, G. (2003) Stalin's rise to power. *Modern History Review*, February.

Whittock, M. (1997) *Stalin's Russia*, Collins Educational.

Teachers and extension

Amis, M. (2003) *Koba the Dread*, Vintage.

Antonov-Ovseyenko, A. (1981) *The Time of Stalin: Portrait of Tyranny*, Harper & Row.

Applebaum, A. (2004) *Gulag: A History*, Penguin.

Arch Getty, J. (1985) *Origins of the Great Purges*, Cambridge University Press.

Thurston, R. (1996) *Life and Terror in Stalin's Russia 1934–1941*, Yale University Press.

Volkogonov, D. (2000) *Stalin: Triumph and Tragedy*, Orion.

For a chronology of Stalin's life, including film and pictures, go to www.stel.ru/stalin/joseph_1935-1953.htm

Novels

Orwell, G. (1998) *Animal Farm*, Penguin.

Sebag Montefiore, S. (1997) *My Affair with Stalin*, Phoenix.

2 Fascist Italy

Students

Blinkhorn, M. (1994) *Mussolini and Fascist Italy*, Routledge.

Goodlad, G. (2004) Mussolini's domestic policies 1922–40: Mussolini wanted to transform Italy into a self-sufficient nation of supermen. How close did he come to succeeding? *Modern History Review*, November.

Pollard, J. (1998) 'No matter the image created for him, Mussolini's cult of leadership involved a range of compromises'. *New Perspective*, 2, December.

Robson, M. (1992) *Liberalism and Fascism, 1870–1945*, Hodder & Stoughton.

Townley, E. (2002) *Mussolini and Italy*, Heinemann.

Young, A. (2000) Mussolini: an unprincipled politician? *Modern History Review*, April.

Teachers and extension

Bosworth, R. J. B. (2005) Coming to terms with Fascism in Italy: Mussolini casts a long shadow. *History Today*, November.

Bosworth, R. J. B. (2001) *Mussolini*, Oxford.

Bosworth, R. J. B. (2007) *Mussolini's Italy*, Penguin.

Clark, M. (1984) *Modern Italy 1871–1982*, Longman.

Mack Smith, D. (2001) *Mussolini*, Orion.

The translated text of *The Doctrine of Fascism* is available at www.worldfuturefund.org/wffmaster/Reading/Germany/mussolini.htm

DVD

Zeffirelli, F. (dir.) (1999) *Tea with Mussolini*.

3 Nazi Germany

Students

Boxer, A. (1997) *Hitler's Domestic Policy*, Collins Educational.

Haffner, S. (2002) *Defying Hitler*, Weidenfeld & Nicolson.

Pine, L. (2000) Nazi family policy. *Modern History Review*, April.

Welch, D. (2002) Hitler's history films. *History Today*, December.

Teachers and extension

Allen, W. S. (1984) *The Nazi Seizure of Power*, Franklin Watts.

Bessel, R. (ed.) (1987) *Life in the Third Reich*, Oxford.

Burleigh, M. (2000) *The Third Reich*, Macmillan.

Dawidowicz, L. (1979) *The War Against the Jews*, Penguin.

Farmer, A. (1998) *Anti-Semitism and the Holocaust*, Hodder & Stoughton.

Grunberger, R. (1971) *A Social History of the Third Reich*, Penguin.

Kershaw, I. (1999) *Hitler 1889–1936*, Penguin.

Kershaw, I. (2000) *Hitler 1936–1945*, Penguin.

Rees, L. (2005) *The Nazis: A Warning From History*, BBC Books.

A good starting point for Nazi ideology is www.schoolshistory.org.uk/ASLevel_History/sourcematerial_earlynaziideology.htm

Novels

Fry, S. (1997) *Making History*, Arrow.

Harris, R. (1992) *Fatherland*, Arrow.

Acknowledgements

Author acknowledgements:

Thank you to my wife Carly and daughter Charlotte who waited patiently for me to finish with Stalin, Hitler and Mussolini so that we could focus on Jack Bauer and Postman Pat.

The author and publisher would also like to thank the following for permission to reproduce material:

Source texts:

p15 Sarah Butler and Rajeev Syal, *£1.2bn payday for the toga tycoon*, Times Online, 21 October 2005; pp16–17 V. I. Lenin, *What is to be Done?*, 1902. From V. I. Lenin, *Collected Works*, 4th English edition, quoted on www.marx2mao.com; p20 Lenin's Political Testament, 25 December 1922. Quoted in M. Lynch, *Stalin and Khrushchev*, Hodder Arnold H&S, 1990; p26 J. V. Stalin, *Concerning Questions of Leninism*, 25 January 1926. From J. V. Stalin, *Problems of Leninism*, 1976, quoted on www.marx2mao.com; p27 N. Bukharin, 'The New Economic Policy and our Tasks', *Bolshevik*, 1 June 1925. Quoted on www.marxists.org/archive; p33 Lev Kopelev. Quoted in J. Lewis and P. Whitehead, *Stalin: A Time for Judgement*, Thames Methuen, 1990; p34 Extract from a report by M. MacKillop to the British Foreign Office, May 1936. The National Archives (PRO): FO 371/20350 ff 11, 17, 61–62; pp37–38 Extract from a report by M. MacKillop to the British Foreign Office, May 1936. The National Archives (PRO): FO 371/20350 ff 11, 17, 61–62; p41 Extract from a report by M. MacKillop to the British Foreign Office, May 1936. The National Archives (PRO): FO 371/20350 ff 11, 17, 61–62; p44 Extract from Stalin's funeral oration. Quoted in M. Lynch, *Stalin and Khrushchev*, Hodder Arnold H&S, 1990; p45 Adapted from A. Alexandrov *et al.*, *Stalin: A Short Biography*, 1947 (translation published by Foreign Languages Publishing House, Moscow, 1949); p48 Extract from a letter from Stalin to a Bolshevik Party member, 1930. Quoted in J. V. Stalin: *Works*, vol. 13, Moscow, 1955; p52 Mussolini speaking in 1920. Adapted from a London Board GCE examination paper, pre-1993; p52 Mussolini speaking in 1922. Adapted from a London Board GCE examination paper, pre-1993; p53 Adapted from B. Mussolini, *The Doctrine of Fascism*, 1932, quoted on www.fordham.edu/halsall/mod/mussolini-fascism.html, and 1938, quoted in R. W. Breach (ed.), *Documents and Descriptions: The World Since 1914*, 1966; pp60–61 Mussolini's fascist proclamation, 28 October 1922. From *The Times*, 30 October 1922, quoted in R. W. Breach (ed.), *Documents and Descriptions: The World Since 1914*, 1966; p67 Adapted from B. Mussolini, *The Doctrine of Fascism*, 1932; p70 Francesco Nitti,1929. Quoted on www.spartacus.schoolnet.co.uk; p73 Mussolini, 1926. Quoted in R. N. L. Absalom, *Mussolini and the Rise of Italian Fascism*, Methuen Educ., 1969; p77 Quoted in R. Wolfson, *Years of Change*, Hodder Arnold H&S, 1979; p84 M. Robson, *Italy: Liberalism and Fascism 1870–1945*, Hodder & Stoughton, 1992; pp91–92 Sebastian Haffner, *Defying Hitler*, Weidenfeld & Nicolson, 2002; pp94–95 Extract from the German Workers' Party 25-point programme, 1920. Adapted from J. Noakes and G. Pridham, *Nazism 1919–1945: A Documentary Reader*, vol. 1, Exeter, 1983; p100 Adapted from W. S. Allen, *The Nazi Seizure of Power*, Grolier Publishing, US, 1984; p104 The programme of the German Workers' Party, 1920. Adapted from Mary Fulbrook, *Hitler*, Collins Educational, 2004; p104 Adapted from R. Gordon, 'Hitler's rise to power', *Modern History Review*, September 2002; p105 Adapted from R. Gordon, 'Hitler's rise to power', *Modern History Review*, September 2002; p105 Adapted from T. Childers, *The Nazi Voter*, University of North Carolina Press, 1985; p105 Adapted from D. Geary, *Hitler and Nazism*, Routledge, 1993; p105 Adapted from W. S. Allen, *The Nazi Seizure of Power*, Grolier Publishing, US, 1984; p114 The Reich Citizenship Law, 15 September 1935. J. Noakes and G. Pridham (eds.), *Nazism, 1919–1945*, 1984; p123 Quoted in L. Rees, *The Nazis: A Warning From History*, BBC Books, 2005; p123 Quoted in L. Pine, 'Nazism in the Classroom', *History Today*, April 1997; p129 Werner Wilkins, 1934. Quoted in I. Kershaw, *The Nazi Dictatorship*, Hodder Arnold, 1993

Photographs courtesy of:

Edimedia Art Archive 42 (top), 52, 79 (top), 79 (bottom), 82, 86, 89, 128; Getty Images iv; Glasgow University Caledonian Collection 26; Courtesy of Stephane Magnenat 88; Nelson Thornes 99 (bottom); Photo 12 24, 62, 65, 77, 107; Photo 12/Bertelsmann 98; Photo 12/Ullstein-Bild 30; Topfoto 10, 11 (bottom), 16, 19 (bottom), 20 (bottom), 21, 46 (bottom right), (top left), 117 (top); Topfoto/Alinari 20 (top), 67; Topfoto/HIP/Jewish Chronicle Archive, Edimedia 115; Topfoto/Roger-Viollet 18, 37, 63, 85; United Archives 43, 125; World History Archive 1, 11 (top), 12, 19 (top), 19 (centre), 35, 42 (bottom), 46 (top centre), (bottom centre), (top right), (bottom left), 50, 51, 58, 81, 83, 90, 99 (top), 101, 109, 110, 116, 117 (bottom), 122, 130, 133

Cover photograph courtesy of Corbis/Peter Turnley

For further information concerning any pictures appearing in this book, please email samuel@uniquedimension.com

Photo research by Unique Dimension Limited

Special thanks to Topfoto, Photo 12, KPA (United Archives), Ann Asquith and Dora Swick

Index